INTO THE DARK WATER

INTO THE
DARK WATER

THE STORY OF
THREE OFFICERS
AND *PT-109*

JOHN J. DOMAGALSKI

CASEMATE

Philadelphia & Oxford

First published in the United States of America and Great Britain in 2014.
Reprinted as a paperback in 2019 by
CASEMATE PUBLISHERS
1950 Lawrence Road, Havertown, PA 19083, USA
and
The Old Music Hall, 106–108 Cowley Road, Oxford, OX4 1JE, UK

Copyright 2014 © John J. Domagalski

ISBN 978-1-61200-712-0
Digital Edition: ISBN 978-1-61200-235-4

Cataloging-in-publication data is available from the Library of Congress and
the British Library.

Printed and bound in the United States of America

For a complete list of Casemate titles, please contact:

CASEMATE PUBLISHERS (US)
Telephone (610) 853-9131, Fax (610) 853-9146
Email: casemate@casematepublishers.com
www.casematepublishers.com

CASEMATE PUBLISHERS (UK)
Telephone (01865) 241249
Email: casemate-uk@casematepublishers.co.uk
www.casematepublishers.co.uk

CONTENTS

To
Edward Domagalski,
U.S. Army — Korean War

ACKNOWLEDGMENTS

Writing about a story from World War II—a conflict from seventy years ago—is a tremendous undertaking. It could not have been done without the help of many individuals. The list is often too lengthy to publish, but a few are worthy of special thanks. Karen Hone and Gary Westholm provided written recollections from their late fathers. The vivid writings of the former torpedo boat sailors helped bring the story of *PT-109* to life. As with any naval history project, the excellent staffs at the National Archives and the Naval History and Heritage Command provided abundant assistance in locating documents and photos. The World War II PT Boats Museum and Archives in Germantown, TN provided photographs. The organization helps keep alive the memory of the brave sailors who sailed into harm's way on small boats. My agent, Ethan Ellenberg, provided great wisdom and support. The fine team at Casemate gave superb guidance throughout the publishing process. Lastly, I want to thank my wife Sandy. Without her enduring support and encouragement, *Into the Dark Water* would not have been written.

PART ONE

IRON BOTTOM SOUND

CHAPTER 1

MIDNIGHT IN BLACKETT STRAIT

The crew of *PT-109* was not at their battle stations as the small wooden torpedo boat idled slowly and quietly through the dark waters of Blackett Strait. The clock had struck midnight about two hours ago, ushering in the start of August 2, 1943. The mood of many crewmen was thick with the tension and anxiety that seemed to mark just about every night patrol. It was a routine part of everyday life for sailors on the front lines of the naval war, now just over a year and a half old.

Her position just west of the island of Kolombangara in the Solomon Islands was firmly in Japanese-held waters. It was a cloudy and humid South Pacific night. The inky blanket of blackness surrounding the boat offered the mutual possibility of protection and surprise—both for *PT-109* and for the as yet unseen enemy.

The 109, as she was commonly know to her crew, was one of fifteen American torpedo boats in the area searching for a fight with a powerful adversary—destroyers of the Imperial Japanese Navy. In command of the boat was Lieutenant (Junior Grade) John Kennedy. The lean young officer from Massachusetts had become the boat captain less than four months earlier. He recently brought *PT-109* to the front lines and the night offered the prospect for his first real scrap with the enemy.

Twelve sailors were scattered at various locations around the boat. Most were wearing their helmets and kapok life jackets as they had to be ready for action at a moment's notice. Although the men were not at their battle stations, some were standing watch on lookout duty searching for any sign of the enemy. The dark night pitted against the black backdrop of the large circular volcano on Kolombangara made it difficult for even the keenest eyes to find anything. Distant flashes earlier in the night were dismissed as enemy shore batteries.

A cluster of figures were around *PT-109's* conn. The small bridge area served as the boat's nerve center. Kennedy was in the center of the group manning the boat's wheel. Radioman Second Class John Maguire was standing next to him on his right side. Motor Machinist Mate Second Class Harold Marney was positioned at a nearby fifty-caliber machine gun mounted in a circular gun tub. Ensign Lenny Thom, the boat's executive officer, was just outside the conn on Kennedy's left side.

Ensign George Ross was standing on deck near the boat's bow acting as a lookout. The guest passenger was assigned to man the improvised thirty-seven millimeter cannon positioned on the forward deck. It had been hastily mounted for extra firepower just prior to *PT-109's* evening departure from base.

At about 2:30 a.m. something suddenly appeared out of the night. "Ship at two o'clock," Marney suddenly shouted out. It was about 250 yards off *PT-109's* starboard bow and closing fast. The call started a sequence of terrorizing events lasting no more than thirty to forty seconds.[1] From his position in the conn, Kennedy turned to look just as George Ross pointed to the approaching object. "At first I thought it was a PT," Kennedy later said of the moment. "I think it was going at least forty knots."[2]

The warship bearing down on *PT-109* was Japanese Captain Katsumori Yamashiro's destroyer *Amagiri*. The vessel displaced just over 2,000 tons and could obtain a top speed of thirty-eight knots.[3] Lookouts aboard the ship had sighted the torpedo boat only moments earlier. The order to fire was given, but the small target was too close for the forward guns.[4] Whether Yamashiro's subordinate, Lieutenant Commander Kohei Hanami, turned the warship intending to ram or avoid the PT has been disputed in the many decades since the event.[5] However, regardless of the Japanese officer's intentions, the destroyer was speeding directly towards *PT-109* on a collision course.

"Lenny look at this," Kennedy said to Thom after glancing off the starboard side. A phosphorescent wave was protruding from the base of the approaching warship's bow. "As soon as I decided it was a destroyer, I turned to make a torpedo run," Kennedy later recalled. He spun the wheel starting the boat in a turn towards the speeding *Amagiri*. The PT's response, however, was sluggish due to having only one engine in operation. He told Maguire to sound general quarters.

George Ross grabbed a shell for the thirty-seven millimeter cannon, but slammed it against the closed breech of the gun. Time did not give him another chance to load the weapon. In any case, a single gunshot from a small caliber gun would likely have had no effect on the speeding destroyer.

Historians who studied *PT-109's* final moments in detail generally agree Kennedy had about ten to fifteen seconds to make a critical decision.[6] Although he followed his initial instinct of turning the boat for a torpedo attack, the torpedoes would have been ineffective even if he had time to fire since the distance was too short for the weapons to properly arm. There was nothing the boat captain and his crew could do but wait for fate to happen. *Amagiri's* large steel bow crashed into the starboard side of the small torpedo boat ripping through her wooden hull.

The damage was catastrophic. The destroyer struck the PT near the forward machine gun station and sliced through the boat at a sharp angle. The sound of cracking wood suddenly pierced through the night. The starboard side of the 109 was sheared off from a point near the forward torpedo tube all the way aft, and one of the engines was knocked away.[7] Flames shot through the air in a brilliant explosion as the boat's high octane gasoline ignited from a ruptured fuel tank.

The force of the collision ripped the wheel from Kennedy's grasp forcefully throwing him against the wall of the conn area. Lying on his back he looked up to see the towering hull of the destroyer carving through the boat. "This is how it feels to be killed," he thought during the moment.[8] "I can best compare it to the onrushing trains in the old-time movies. They seemed to come right over you," he later added about the time.[9] In the light of the fire he caught a brief glimpse of the destroyer's slanted smoke stack as the soaring vessel passed.

The Japanese warship vanished into the darkness almost as soon as it arrived. The struggle for survival had only just begun for the PT crewmen who lived through the horrifying event. It was the start of an ordeal that would last nearly a week.

The sinking of *PT-109* marked the end of the boat's short but action-filled battle career. Under the command of three successive young officers—Lieutenant Rollin Westholm, Ensign Bryant Larson, and John Kennedy—the 109 prowled the waters of the South Pacific for just over eight months. During this time she fought Japanese warships in a series of furious night clashes near the embattled island of Guadalcanal, survived attacks from the air, conducted routine security patrols in between major campaigns when action was lacking, and followed the American advance through the Solomon Islands.

Although the boat would eventually become one of the most famous warships in American history, on the second day of August 1943 she was just another casualty in the Pacific War. Her story began more than a year earlier and thousands of miles away.

———————

Modern torpedo boats had been in existence for many decades before American naval officials took a serious interest in the craft during the late 1930s. Military spending was subdued at the time while the nation slowly emerged from economic stagnation. As it happened it was two influential individuals from outside of the seagoing service who helped to convince key naval leaders of the need for the small boats.

Former Army Chief of Staff General Douglas MacArthur was then serving as commander of all American military forces in the Philippines. In what can be regarded as tremendous foresight, MacArthur foresaw the difficulties of defending the island chain against an increasingly aggressive Japan. Aware that the availability of large warships were limited, he hoped to bolster his forces with small vessels.

The general thought torpedo boats were an ideal weapon for use among the many islands of the Philippines. "A relatively small fleet of such vessels," MacArthur said of the craft shortly after his arrival in the Philippines, "manned by crews thoroughly familiar with every foot of the coast line and surrounding waters, and carrying, in the torpedo, a definite threat against large ships, will have distinct effect in compelling any hostile force to approach cautiously and by small detachments."[10] He began calling friends in Washington hoping to procure a supply of ninety boats.[11]

The second champion of torpedoes boats was none other than President Franklin Delano Roosevelt. As Assistant Secretary of the Navy during World War I, he was well aware of the successful use of small boats in combat by European navies during the conflict, and was convinced of the their potential.[12] Congress approved funding of an experimental program for small vessels in 1938 with the stipulation that the money was to be spent at the discretion of the president. Roosevelt allowed the money to be used for developing new designs.

The navy quickly invited designers to submit plans for a variety of petite vessels, including a seventy-foot torpedo boat. Specifications for the latter included: an overall length of between seventy and eighty feet, top speed of forty knots, a range of 550 miles at cruising speed, and minimum armament of two torpedoes, four depth charges, and two machine guns.[13] A cash prize of $15,000 was available for the winner.

The navy eventually accepted three designs and built eight torpedo boats for testing purposes. Extensive trials proved all of the models to be unsatisfactory. A ninth boat, constructed by the Elco Division of the Electric Boat Company, based on a British torpedo boat, proved acceptable.[14] Designated patrol torpedo or PT boats, the craft soon became part of the United States Navy.

Naval leaders came to view the boats as a weapon that could be quickly produced in emergency conditions. The small craft could go into action almost immediately while larger warships took years to construct—exactly the crisis the American navy later faced in the early part of World War II.[15] Many senior officers believed it was still the role of large warships to take the fight to the enemy, but envisioned a variety of uses for the new boats, including coastal defense to free up larger vessels for seagoing activities, limited offensive operations, and anti-submarine duties.

Elco began manufacturing its first production class of PT boats in early 1940 at the company's factory in Bayonne, New Jersey, a grimy industrial town near New York City. Higgins Industries in New Orleans, of landing craft fame, later became a second builder. About a year later fate hurled the small craft into front line action after America's entry into World War II.

There were twenty-nine PT boats in service when hostilities began on December 7, 1941.[16] Eleven were at the New York Navy Yard waiting to be sent south to Panama. Twelve boats were in Pearl Harbor and opened fire on attacking Japanese planes. The remaining six PT's were stationed in the Philippines, having arrived in the Far East in late September as part of the American rush to get men and equipment to MacArthur. Thrust into the thick of the fighting in the opening months of the war, the latter half dozen boats ascended to legendary status and brought widespread notoriety to the service.

Japanese military forces struck the Philippines shortly after the attack on Pearl Harbor. MacArthur's air force was largely knocked out in the opening days of the fighting, prompting the large warships of the United States Asiatic Fleet to retreat south to safer waters. An assortment of small craft and the PT boats were left behind to help defend the Philippines. The land forces fought a heroic but ultimately doomed defense of the islands, withdrawing into the Bataan Peninsula and the adjacent fortified island of Corregidor in Manila Bay.

Thirty year old Lieutenant John D. Bulkeley was in command of the six PT boats comprising Motor Torpedo Boat Squadron Three in the Philippines. When Japanese bombers demolished the Cavite Navy Yard near Manila on December 10, 1941, he was left without a base of operations. The PTs sailors were forced to operate from improvised remote bases, with limited provisions, an inadequate fuel supply, and almost no spare parts.

Bulkeley and his men carried out a series of daring operations over the next four months as the defense of the Philippines slowly crumbled. The first official news of their actions came to the world in a Navy Communiqué released on January 20, 1942 outlining a PT attack on a 5,000-ton Japanese vessel in Subic Bay west of Manila. "This small boat carried out its difficult task while under fire of machine guns and three-inch shore batteries," the release reported. "Lt. John D. Bulkeley has been commended for executing his mission successfully."[17]

The American public suddenly knew about PT boats. The *New York Times* quickly reported that the vessels, "Have speeds up to seventy-nine miles per hour and carry enough explosives to sink a battleship."[18] Bulkeley's exploits were occurring at a time when the Allies were facing a series of staggering defeats at the hands of the Japanese. The PT actions soon became the only good news coming out of the Pacific front.

By far the greatest PT operation of the Philippines Campaign was the evacuation of Douglas MacArthur in March 1942. The general was directed to leave the front lines for Australia on orders from President Roosevelt. Bulkeley's torpedo boats took MacArthur and his party through 560 miles of Japanese-infested waters to the southern portion of the Philippines where the escape continued by plane.

One by one the PT boats began to fall. The sailors fought courageously until all boats were expended. They reported staging seven offensive operations, sinking four enemy vessels, shooting down four enemy planes, and taking two prisoners.[19] Bulkeley and a few key officers were themselves evacuated just before the end of the campaign. The last defenders surrendered to the Japanese in May 1942. He returned to the United States a national hero and was awarded the Medal of Honor for his actions in combat. His picture and story appeared in newspapers across the country. Perhaps more than any other single individual, Bulkeley was responsible for bringing fame to PT boats during World War II and for convincing a legion of young sailors seeking action and adventure to join the small boat service. Some of those sailors would eventually be assigned to *PT-109*.

––––––––

The launching of *PT-103* at Bayonne on May 16, 1942 marked the debut of a new type of Elco torpedo boat. The Elco 80-foot boats were larger, heavier, and better armed than the two proceeding production classes built by the manufacturer.

The boats were powered by three Packard 1,200 horsepower motors, same as the earlier designs. Specifically developed for PT boats, the marine propulsion system was based on the Packard 1925 Liberty aircraft engine. The supercharged motor weighed about 3,000 pounds and used piped in sea water as a cooling agent.[20] Each engine turned a thirty-inch diameter propeller. Small rudders, positioned directly behind each propeller, allowed for sharp turns and adroit maneuverability.

The engine exhaust fumes exited out of six pipes mounted flush on the back of the boat's squared off stern. Each was covered with a muffler to deaden the engine noise. However, the sound reduction came at the expense of speed. Bypass values were used when the boat needed to move fast. The exhaust exited out directly once the valves were open. The reduced back pressure increased the horsepower delivered by the engines allowing higher speeds.[21]

Three fuel tanks carried 100-octane gasoline allowing a maximum range of 550 miles. The new design eventually proved to be less maneuverable, but had better sea-keeping characteristics than the proceeding production types.[22]

The keel of *PT-109* was laid down on March 4, 1942 as the seventh member of the Elco 80-foot PT boat series. Launched less than four months later on June 20, she was delivered to the navy on July 10.[23] The boat's hull was constructed of mahogany planks, not plywood as has often been believed in popular culture.[24] Two layers of the planking on either side of a sheet of glue-impregnated aircraft fabric were fastened to laminate wood frames to make a sturdy seaworthy hull. Using an innovative construction technique to save labor hours, the hulls were built upside down and then turned over for the remainder of the work.[25]

The forward part of the deck was largely barren and contained little more than a petite anchor, cast aluminum access hatch, and a deck cleat. A small superstructure jutting up from the flush deck in the middle of the ship began with an angular chart house. The configuration was constructed of plywood over a wooden frame. A small bridge area, commonly known as the conn, was positioned directly behind the chart house. A simple two-pronged metal mast protruded amidships. The boat was painted in an overall grey scheme when delivered to the navy.[26]

The fitting out process was the final step in the completion of *PT-109*. The main armament consisted of four twenty-one inch torpedo tubes mounted two per side. Two circular gun tubs, offset on opposite sides of the superstructure, each contained a twin fifty-caliber machine gun. One tub was positioned almost even with the chart house on the starboard side. The second was further aft favoring the port side. A single barrel twenty-millimeter gun was mounted near the stern and packed more punch than the machine guns. The dual purpose cannon could be used against air, sea, or land targets.

A small smoke generator was positioned at the very end of the fantail. The boat could also mount depth charges for anti-submarine action, but the weapons were not frequently carried in combat. The number of crewmen varied by boat, but typically consisted of two officers and eight enlisted men.[27]

The newly completed *PT-109* soon moved from the Elco factory into Newark Bay. The immediate area was filled with oil tanks and factories that were producing the materials needed to fuel the American war machine. The boat navigated Kill Van Kull, a tidal strait separating New Jersey from Stanton Island and emptying into the Upper Bay. The 109 moved across the waterway passing the Statue of Liberty and Ellis Island before entering the East River. She cruised along a southeastern Manhattan coastline cluttered with an assortment of piers, boats, and cranes. The boat eventually passed under the iconic Brooklyn Bridge and into the Brooklyn Navy Yard. Ensign John Kempner boarded the boat on July 10 to become her first commanding officer. Only one crewman reported for duty on his first day of command.[28]

With the boat now under navy control, *PT-109* needed to undergo a series of shakedown cruises to test the boat's performance and ensure all equipment was properly operating. Such operations, however, required a crew. Five temporary sailors came aboard to begin the process. Their stay, though, would be short because new sailors were on the way. A young officer en route to Brooklyn would soon board the boat and eventually take her all the way to the front lines of the South Pacific.

CHAPTER **2**

TWO OFFICERS AND A NEW BOAT

R ollin Westholm and Bryant Larson both hailed from Minnesota, but followed very different paths to *PT-109*. Westholm was a graduate of the United States Naval Academy,
a professional navy officer, while Larson graduated college as a civilian and
came up through the naval reserves. Their first contact with each other occurred when both were assigned to the same PT boat squadron. The pair
eventually moved to the South Pacific and served together on the 109.

Rollin Everton Westholm was born on August 16, 1911 in Moose Lake,
MN.[29] He earned an appointment to the Naval Academy and entered the
school in June 1930 a couple months short of his nineteenth birthday. He
was commissioned an ensign on May 31, 1934 after completing four years
of studies.[30]

The navy of the mid-1930s was dominated by battleships. The initial assignment for most newly graduated ensigns was to spend time aboard the
big-gunned ships. Westholm's first set of orders sent him to the battleship
Texas. The splendid warship was of World War I vintage, having entered
service in 1914. His duty began on June 30, 1934 and lasted almost three
years.[31]

Westholm's classroom studies from the Naval Academy transferred into
real world experience during his time aboard the battleship. The crew aboard
a warship the size of *Texas* operated in departments, each with its own specialty. Westholm first spent nine months attached to the construction and
repair division followed by an equal amount of time in the gunnery department. His last seventeen months were in the engineering department. The

critical area operated the power and propulsion systems needed to keep the ship moving.

The young officer met his future wife while *Texas* was based at Long Beach, CA. He happened to attend a party in honor of Admiral William Halsey. Also at the event was Benjamin Tilley, a friend of Halsey's from his Naval Academy days, along with his daughter Elizabeth. Westholm was known to often tell the story of their introduction in the decades that followed his naval service. After telling her he was from Minnesota, she replied "I didn't know that we were taking Canadians into our navy."[32] The two were later married and Elizabeth became a navy wife, following her husband around various parts of the country.

Westholm generally made a good impression on his superiors during his time aboard *Texas*. The warship's commanding officer, Captain Fred Rogers, gave him high marks. "Ensign Westholm is a most valuable officer," Rogers wrote in a routine performance review. "His division runs smoothly and with a maximum of cooperation and efficiency. He is outstanding, and fully qualified for promotion."[33] Westholm was subsequently promoted to lieutenant (junior grade). When given the opportunity to request a preference for his next assignment, he listed sea duty aboard a destroyer as his top choice, followed by a shore post at the submarine school.

Superiors granted Westholm his first choice for transfer allowing the young officer to spend the next three years serving aboard destroyers. The duty allowed him to experience the small ship side of the navy. He reported to the USS *Barry* on June 13, 1937. The warship was an older 1920s era four-stack destroyer. Westholm was sent ashore to torpedo school shortly after arriving on his new ship. The torpedo knowledge would serve him well many years later aboard PT boats in the South Pacific. He later spent time as a torpedo officer, communications officer, and assistant engineering officer as the destroyer operated out of San Diego.

Orders arrived in June 1938 sending Westholm to the new destroyer *McCall*. She was nearing completion at the Bethlehem Shipbuilding Corporation yard in San Francisco, CA. He stayed aboard *McCall* for almost two years after putting the ship into commission. Westholm made a positive impression on the destroyer's commanding officer during the time, who later recommended him for future promotion.

The next three and a half years of Westholm's navy career were associated with torpedo boats. "I skippered the first successful U.S. motor torpedo boat," he later wrote of the time. "It was the *PT-9* built by the British Power Boat

Company. It was powered by three Rolls Royce Merlin engines."[34] Elco purchased the craft for testing and to use as a prototype for future designs.

Westholm was assigned to the Elco factory in New Jersey to oversee construction when the company began work on the first series of production boats in 1940. On hand for the launching and commissioning of *PT-10*, he became the boat's first commanding officer. The duty made him part of Motor Torpedo Boat Squadron Two and a subordinate of unit commander Lieutenant Earl Caldwell. Based at the Brooklyn Navy Yard, the squadron eventually took delivery of ten new boats.

On November 7, 1940 Westholm joined Caldwell in giving newspaper reporters in New York the first public demonstration of a PT boat. The two officers were at the helm of *PT-9* as she pulled out of the Brooklyn Navy Yard into the East River with *PT-10* cruising right behind. "Passing tugboat captains gaped in astonishment as one of the boats hit a fifty-knot clip for a brief stretch—without disturbance to the tranquility of the East River Piers ...," a news reporter wrote in the *New York Times*.[35] The American public was now aware of the navy's new small boat weapon.

Westholm later returned to the Elco factory to oversee the construction of *PT-20*, a larger boat of updated design. The plant's Supervisor of Shipbuilding, Lieutenant F.W. Rowe, liked what he saw in the young officer. "His ability to handle small high-speed motor boats is of the highest caliber," he wrote of Westholm. "He is keen, enthusiastic, and experienced in all phases of motor torpedo boat operations."[36]

The six month stretch beginning in June 1941 found Westholm in London serving as an assistant naval attaché. His role was to be an observer. "There I spent most of my time riding their [torpedo boats] and other small craft in the English Channel and North Sea," he later modestly wrote of the duty.

Westholm gained tremendous operational knowledge and familiarity with small boats during his stay in England. Serving as the London Naval Attaché during the same period, Captain Charles Lockwood took note: "Lieutenant Westholm has devoted his entire time to observing and studying small boat operations, policy, and technical features of their construction. He has made frequent operational trips with both MTB's [torpedo boats] and MGB's [gunboats] in waters of the war zone and has become very familiar with all phases of these craft."[37] The seagoing experience gave him an early taste of what it was like to be in a war. Westholm returned to the United States just as the nation was thrust into the conflict by the Japanese attack on Pearl Harbor.

Promoted to full lieutenant in late December 1941, Westholm was given command of newly formed Motor Torpedo Boat Squadron Four. Commissioned into service on January 13, 1942, the unit was created as a training squadron. Westholm's command, however, was of short duration and limited to the initial start-up operations, including the delivery of some new boats. The brief duty was likely the result of his past experience at the Elco factory. The facility was now constructing PT boats on a mass scale. Although Westholm was replaced by Lieutenant Commander Alan Montgomery on February 2, he continued to serve as the squadron's executive officer for almost seven months. Montgomery remembered him as having a pleasant personality and completing thorough work.

The unit operated in Rhode Island after taking delivery of ten new boats in January and February 1942. During the stay in New England Westholm received an admonition for telephoning a civilian with advanced notification of his taking several boats to Martha's Vineyard Island in July. Such actions were strictly against wartime navy regulations. A report on the incident by the base commandant noted, "... you did not exercise the good judgment expected of an officer of your rank and experience."[38] The minor infraction resulted in nothing more than a letter in Westholm's personnel file.

In early September Westholm was back in the New York area to take command of a new squadron. Motor Torpedo Boat Squadron Seven was commissioned on September 4, 1942 and took delivery of twelve new Elco boats during the same month.[39] However, Westholm's days in New York were numbered and he soon received orders that would put him one step closer to the front lines of the South Pacific.

As Rollin Westholm entered the Naval Academy to begin his journey of becoming a commissioned officer, another young man from Minnesota was almost a decade away from joining the service. Bryant Leroy Larson was born on January 24, 1920 in Minneapolis, and he experienced both good and bad economic times during his childhood years. Working for the Federal Reserve Bank, his father was able to stay employed during the 1930s when the country was ravaged by the Great Depression.[40]

Larson entered the University of Minnesota in September 1937. After completing the required preliminary courses during his first two years of schooling, he transferred into business and graduated with a bachelor's degree in business accounting on June 14, 1941.[41] Growing war clouds changed any plans he may have had to work in his chosen field. "I enlisted in the navy in the summer of 1941 and was called to duty in the V-7 School in January 1942," he wrote.

Larson was formally accepted into the United States Naval Reserve on August 13, 1941 with a rank of apprentice seaman pending future entry into the V-7 program. The V-7 Naval Reserve Midshipmen's School was initiated in 1940 to turn qualified college graduates into naval officers. Once the war started the program became a much needed pipeline to help meet the tremendous personnel demands of the burgeoning navy. Participants attained the rank of ensign upon graduation.

Administered through three universities, the program used accelerated courses on navigation, seamanship, and ordnance to ready students for navy life.[42] Larson was assigned to Northwestern University in downtown Chicago. The session began two days before his twenty-second birthday on January 22, 1942. He scored a perfect vision rating of twenty-twenty while passing the required physical exam. The keen eyesight would be of good use in the South Pacific less than a year later. His rank was changed to midshipman shortly after the start of classes. He agreed not to marry until all the coursework was completed as an additional prerequisite for acceptance into the school.

There was a special nickname for the men in the reserve program. "The V-7 trainees were known as the ninety-day wonders as the navy attempted to turn largely landlocked young men into sea-going naval officers in just ninety days," Larson explained. "By April 1942 we were nearing the end of the ninety days and were receiving orders for our first duty. My orders assigned me to a local defense school in San Francisco, probably preparing for harbor security somewhere on the east or west coast."[43] It had all the makings of a monotonous and unexciting assignment.

During the same week orders were distributed to the midshipmen, an announcement was made at a morning muster seeking volunteers for PT boat duty. Larson was well aware of the recent press reports about a squadron of torpedo boats fighting in the Philippines under the command of Lieutenant John Bulkeley. PT duty offered the likelihood of a boat command and a short road to combat. It was an inviting possibility for a young officer in search of action and adventure. Larson quickly seized the opportunity to volunteer: "Several of us stepped forward," he recalled. "It was a snap decision I have never regretted."

Larson's revised orders sent him to the newly established Motor Torpedo Boat Squadron Training Center in Rhode Island. The orders were delayed several weeks to allow for a period of leave. However, formal graduation came first. Larson was appointed an ensign on May 5, 1942.[44]

The center was located just north of Newport near the small seaside town of Melville. "There we met the new PTer's—officers and enlisted men—all volunteers from several navy schools and bases," Larson wrote. "The navy had three months to get us ready for action via a combination of classroom study and hands-on training on the Melville-based boats." He reported to the school on June 1.

Although the base would eventually grow in size and personnel, in the late spring of 1942 it was still new and developing. The facilities on land were limited to an assortment of Quonset huts. A collection of Squadron Four PT's served as training boats. Since the new center initially lacked adequate equipment, training also took place at several nearby locations, including the Naval Antiaircraft Training Center and Naval Torpedo Station.

By April there were fifty-one officers and 177 enlisted men at Melville enrolled in the intensive training program.[45] Instructors included a few officers who saw action with the boats in the Philippines. "The enlisted men concentrated on their specialties—guns, torpedoes, navigational gear [and] engines," Larson remembered. "In addition to all of the above specialties, the officer-trainees added boat operation, patrol procedures, mission strategy and tactics, and command responsibility. It was a busy time between daytime study and night patrol exercises out at sea off Rhode Island."

As Larson was completing his training at Melville, new torpedo boats were rolling out of the Elco factory in New Jersey. PT boats were not individually commissioned like larger warships. Only squadrons were commissioned to provide simplified record keeping and administration. New boats were turned over to the navy and placed into service as a member of a squadron.[46]

Motor Torpedo Boat Squadron Five was formally commissioned on June 16, 1942 under the leadership of Commander Henry Farrow. The unit was created for twelve new Elco boats—PT's 103 to 114. All of the boats were placed in service between June 12 and July 25.

The crews for the new PT's came mostly from the newly minted Melville graduates. Larson officially completed the training program on July 30, 1942. Orders issued about a week earlier sent him and seventeen others to New York. Constituting about half of the graduating class, the group set out for the Brooklyn Navy Yard and Squadron Five, while the remainder stayed behind to wait for the commissioning of Squadron Six.

———

The sailors were divided among the various new boats upon their arrival in

New York, with Larson going to *PT-109*. The duty was a tremendous opportunity for the new officer. He knew it was time to put the theory and practice learned at the PT school to good use. "Now it was time to get to work," Larson later wrote.

The young man from Minnesota boarded his new boat for the first time on July 18. "I was assigned to *PT-109* as the executive officer. The boat skipper (commander) was an officer from the prior Melville class," he later recalled referring to John Kempner.

The boat Kempner and Larson took to sea was among the navy's smallest fighting vessels. *PT-109* measured eighty feet in length with a beam (width) of twenty-three feet. She displaced fifty-one tons and could obtain a maximum speed of about forty knots under ideal operating conditions.[47]

Eight permanent crewmen came aboard the same day as Larson. He later recalled the makeup of the initial group of sailors. "The crew was largely new recruits plus two men with prior navy service, but not on the PT's." Some of the newer sailors attended specialty schools as part of their training. "We had eleven men aboard the 109—two officers, quartermaster, radioman, torpedoman, gunner's mate, three motor machinist mates, a non-rated seaman, and a navy-rated cook who, we believed had never cooked a meal before coming aboard!"

The navy veterans were the quartermaster and one of the motor machinist mates. The latter had completed classroom training on the Packard engine. "Ages ranged from eighteen to thirty," Larson continued. "The old man of the crew was [quartermaster James] Manning and thus referred to as Pappy."

The Brooklyn Navy Yard was a busy place in the summer of 1942, with new ships under construction and older vessels visiting for repairs and maintenance. The yard served as the initial base of operations for the new Squadron Five boats. Fuel was obtained from a depot located up a narrow river named Newtown Creek.[48] *PT-109* tied up to a supply barge shortly after arriving at the yard. The damaged *Marblehead* was nearby covered with a swarm of yard workers. The battle-scarred light cruiser had sailed halfway around the world to New York for repairs after an encounter with the Japanese near Java.

The men aboard the 109 used the time in Brooklyn to become acquainted with the layout of their new boat. Somewhat familiar with the older Elco models used as the Melville training boats, Bryant Larson made a quick study of *PT-109*. "Below decks and starting from the bow, there was a head [toilet] and anchor line locker, then an eight-bunk crew's quarter's, then a mid-ships area with two officer cabins on the port side and a galley and compact table to starboard," Larson remembered.

The quarters for the enlisted men provided nothing more than the basics for living. The compartment contained bunk beds, a panel of wall-mounted lockers, and a small table. The two officer cabins were assigned to Kempner and Larson. As was typical of navy accommodations, both staterooms were small, cramped, and far from lavish. The features of the forward officer cabin included a dresser, wall mirror, bunk, and a small desk. Removable panel flooring allowed access to the bilges. The after state room, typically used by the commanding officer, contained the same amenities with the addition of a locker.

The galley included cabinets, a small refrigerator, sink, and a two-burner electric stove. An assortment of pots, pans, basic kitchen gadgets, and a coffee pot made the area functional. A tank near the galley on the starboard side of the boat held 200 gallons of fresh water for the crew's use. "A ladder led up from the galley area to the chart house where the navigation gear, radio, and later the radar screen was located," Larson wrote.

The fuel tanks were positioned amidships. "We carried 3,000 gallons of high test aviation gasoline in three tanks—a flat tank in the bilge and two vertical wing tanks mounted within the bulkheads on each side of the boat," Larson described. "All tanks were located just ahead of the engine compartment."

A dayroom was located directly on top of the fuel tanks. This general purpose area contained additional bunks, a medicine cabinet, lockers, and some small shelves. The compartment straddled the main deck with a portion protruding topside. The arrangement necessitated a series of rectangular windows that closed tight to seal out the elements and interior light.

Two compartments were positioned aft of the fuel tanks. "Behind the day room was the engine compartment, and behind that was the lazarette with access to the rudders and storage space," Larson continued. The engine room contained the three Packard motors mounted in a triangle pattern. The compartment was packed with a variety of dials, gauges, and levers.

The last interior compartment at the very back of the boat, the lazarette served a variety of purposes. It contained a small work bench and storage space for spare parts and ammunition. "Topside it was all the bridge, torpedoes, and guns—and no life boats," Larson added.

The confined waters of Long Island Sound became the training ground for the new squadron. A wide variety of exercises were conducted covering boat handling, battle station drills, target tracking, and communications. Simulated torpedo runs prepared the sailors for the real action expected once they reached the front lines. The actual firing of torpedoes, though, was limited. For test purposes the normal warhead had to be replaced with a training head to allow the torpedo to surface and be recovered at the end of its run. However, the device proved unreliable and finding a spent torpedo was difficult.[49] Live-fire target practice against air targets was frequently conducted.

"While at the Navy Yard, most of us lived on board," Larson remembered. "The days were a combination of getting to know every possible detail of the boat, as well as the special equipment that each man was responsible for." An occasional voyage was even made up to the Melville training base.

The sailors knew their stay in New York was only temporary and limited to the squadron start-up. After about a month of shakedown work, it was time for the PT boats to leave the Brooklyn yard. Orders arrived sending the squadron south to Panama.

The journey to Central America was made in stages. "We first ran from New York Harbor to Norfolk, Virginia under our own power—our longest sea run to date," Larson recalled. The boats were then loaded by a large dockside crane onto either a tanker or Liberty ship for the remainder of the trip. "While on the ship's deck, the boats were secured in such a way that they could float free in the event the ship was sunk by enemy torpedoes," Larson added. On August 20 a navy photographer snapped a series of pictures showing *PT-109* sitting on the deck of the Liberty ship *Joseph Stanton*.

The second leg of the journey was the longest. "We sailed in convoy to Panama, through the canal, and unloaded on the Pacific side at the Balboa City Naval Base." The voyage ended with the boats making a short trip under their own power from Balboa to the PT base. The time in Panama was the last opportunity for training before *PT-109* and her crew went to the front lines. In taking the small boat to war, Westholm and Larson were simply continuing a naval practice that began centuries ago.

CHAPTER 3

SMALL BOATS

The concept of using small boats to attack larger enemy vessels has been around since the invention of the warship. In what many historians consider to be one of the first recorded sea battles in history, the ancient Egyptians used small craft to repel invaders at the mouth of the Nile River around 1,200 BC.[50] The aggressors, known as the Sea People, had sailed across the Mediterranean in large vessels intent on landing an army, not waging a sea battle. Built for close quarters fighting, the small Egyptian boats were powered by oar, equipped with ramming bows, and loaded with warriors armed with bows and arrows. The Egyptians prevailed in what became known as the Battle of the Delta setting a clear precedent that small boats were capable of defeating larger vessels. The idea eventually became akin to the biblical story of David and Goliath—an underdog overcoming a much stronger adversary in battle.

Many centuries later the Byzantine Empire, a predominantly Greek-speaking remnant of the Roman Empire, relied on small boats to employ a terrible weapon known as Greek fire. A mixture of naphtha, sulfur, and unknown additional ingredients—the exact formula is lost to history—combined to make a highly ignitable substance. Once set aflame the liquid material burned extremely hot and could not be extinguished with water.[51]

When Arab invaders besieged the capitol Constantinople in 677 AD with an armada of large warships known as galleys, the Byzantine defenders took to using small boats. Brave sailors manning the craft charged out to meet the attackers, unleashing Greek fire in a variety of ways, including shooting it through copper tubes and firing flaming arrows. The galleys were soon transformed into burning derelicts and the siege was lifted. The Battle of Syllaeum ushered in a peace that lasted for decades and it continued the storied history of small boats in battle.

As fighting ships progressed from oars to sail, and cannons became the naval weapon of choice, the trend across the world was to build larger vessels. The use of small attack boats was somewhat diminished, but never eliminated. The concept continued to evolve, and progressed through centuries of warship development. Many technological advances incorporated into larger ships were actually first used on smaller ones.[52] The craft eventually became known as small combatants.

Two groups of individuals were persistently attracted to small boats as time advanced—young naval officers looking for adventure and glory, and frugal government leaders seeking to find a cheap alternative to larger warships for naval security.[53] Although neither group consistently found what it was looking for, the small combatant achieved a continuous, but varied, role in naval history.

American colonists experimented will small combatants during the Revolutionary War in the late 1700s. Inventor David Bushnell developed a one-man hand-propelled submarine dubbed the *Turtle* to attack large British warships operating along the colonial coast. The idea was for the submersible to approach an enemy vessel undetected and then screw a detachable 150 pound explosive mine to the bottom of the unsuspecting prey's hull. A clock served as a rudimentary timing device to allow the detonation to take place after the submersible escaped the immediate area.

The concept was daring and innovative, but failed in practice. An attack in 1776 by Bushnell's *Turtle* against the British warship *Eagle* in New York Harbor failed when the screw could not penetrate the vessels copper bottom. Bushnell later experimented with floating mines managing to sink a small schooner off Connecticut later in the war. Interest in small boats continued to flourish as a result of the conflict.

American President Thomas Jefferson sought to use small combatants during the first years of the 1800s to provide a cost-effective way to protect America's coast from British sea power. He envisioned a navy consisting of mostly small gunboats for homeland defense. Jefferson ordered cutbacks in large warships to allow funds to be spent on the new vessels. Typical design characteristics for what were soon dubbed "Jefferson's gunboats" were for a shallow draft craft of about fifty feet in length manned by a crew of twenty and armed with two or three small cannons. Propulsion was provided by a combination of oars and sails.[54] Critics argued that the diminutive gunboats were nearly useless against large British warships and the program was eventually curtailed by future administrations.

Across the Atlantic the British were building small combatants during the middle decades of the nineteenth century. The Royal Navy used a variety of small steam powered gunboats during the Crimean War. Fought in the 1850s, the conflict pitted Russia against an alliance of European powers, including Britain and France. Most of the fighting took place on the Crimean Peninsula along the Black Sea in modern day Ukraine.

The Russians used small craft of their own in the form of sea mines. Two British warships were damaged by the floating objects. Although most of the naval fighting involved larger warships, the Crimean War allowed the development of small combatants to continue.

———

The launch of the French warship *Gloire* in 1859 ushered in a series of substantial advances in naval technology. She represented the first ocean-going ironclad warship. Powered by steam, and with her wooden hull protected by armored steel plates, *Gloire* is often considered the first true battleship.[55] Her unveiling started a quest for additional naval advancements by engineers around the world. The result was the eventual introduction of the steel hull warship.

Coinciding with the development of ironclads was an important innovation in naval weaponry. The explosive shell soon replaced the centuries-old cannon ball. Fired through muzzle-loaded guns, the weapon vastly increased the destructive power of warships.

While these advances primarily took place in Europe, it was a new type of weapon and a conflict on the opposite side of the Atlantic that again had naval planners thinking small. The American Civil War divided the United States and brought small combatants to the forefront of naval warfare. The struggle gave birth to the motor torpedo boat. The small attack boats were utilized by both sides.

Building on Bushnell's early work on explosive mines, American engineer and inventor Robert Fulton (of steamboat fame) developed a variation of a mine for use by the British Navy in the early 1800s. He called the weapon a torpedo. It was never successfully used in combat at the time by the British. However, the technology continued to evolve long after Fulton's passing, and a variant of the weapon was ready to employ during the Civil War.

Most of the U.S. Navy's warships were in the hands of Union forces when the conflict began in 1861. The breakaway southern states, more commonly known as the Confederacy, had a large coastline with many ports, but few warships of any type. Union warships blockaded many southern ports and intercepted ships delivering supplies. Desperate to remedy the situation, the Confederate Navy turned to developing torpedo boats. Naval combat during the Civil War was mostly fought near the coast or in harbors and rivers—ideal conditions for the use of small combatants and torpedoes.

The torpedoes employed in the Civil War were not the self-propelled weapon made famous by the wars of the twentieth century, but an explosive charge attached to the end of a long pole protruding from the bow of a small ship. The attacker needed to ram the torpedo into its victim's hull before igniting the charge by pulling an attached rope.

By late 1863 the new Confederate torpedo boat *David* was ready for action. The craft was fifty-feet long and powered by steam. Her cigar-shaped hull was made of wood and metal with the torpedo rod—its only weapon—protruding forward. With a very low profile and much of the hull submerged, the vessel can be considered a cross between a torpedo boat and submarine.

On the night of October 5, 1863, *David* moved out of the harbor in Charleston, South Carolina to assail Union warships on blockade duty. It was a daring attack led by young Lieutenant William T. Glassell. She approached the ironclad *New Ironsides* and punched the torpedo into her side below the waterline. The powerful explosion that followed not only damaged the ironclad, but swamped *David* as well, temporarily knocking out her power plant. Although Glassell was captured, his small combatant survived and returned to Charleston. The Union warship was damaged but able to remain on station. After extensive repairs, *David* returned to action near the end of the war. She staged two additional attacks on Union ships, but did not manage to sink an enemy vessel.[56]

The Confederate Navy made a large number of attacks with small craft against larger Union warships throughout the course of the war. Most, however, failed due to the slow speed and poor seaworthiness of the attacking boats. The force did eventually find success with a small submersible named *H.L. Hunley*. Her hull was a steel cylinder with propulsion provided by the hand power of eight men turning a propeller shaft. Like *David*, her weapon was a torpedo mounted to the end of spar jutting forward of the boat.

Hunley staged a bold attack in Charleston Harbor late on the night of February 17, 1864. Lieutenant George E. Dixon commanded the vessel with a volunteer crew. The target was the sixteen-gun Union sloop-of-war *Housatonic*. Dixon rammed the torpedo into the 1,240-ton warship and began to back away. The resulting explosion sank both vessels. The entire crew aboard *Hunley* perished in the attack. The encounter marked a partial success for a small combatant and was the first time in history a submersible sank a ship in wartime.[57]

The Union Navy also found success with small boats. Lieutenant William B. Cushing was already well known for his heroic acts in battle, when he proposed an audacious plan to attack the Confederate ironclad *Albemarle* with a motor torpedo boat. He modified a small steam launch with a spar torpedo and attacked his prey on the Plymouth River in North Carolina during the night of October 27–28, 1864. Both vessels sank in the torpedo's blast. Cushing survived the assault to become a full-fledged naval hero.

The sinking of *Albemarle* is considered one of the most daring naval actions of the Civil War. While the courageous exploits of sailors on both sides did not change the course of the conflict, they nevertheless encouraged the continued practice of small boats attacking larger vessels.

———

The development of the self-propelled torpedo changed the course of history for small combatants. It was the much sought-after delivery vehicle to send an underwater weapon to the enemy while allowing the firing warship to stay safely behind. The spar torpedo, proven during the Civil War to be deadly for both the victim and aggressor alike, was quickly rendered obsolete.

Collaborating with Austrian naval officials, Scottish engineer Robert Whitehead created the first modern torpedo in 1866.[58] Using compressed air for propulsion, the crude underwater missile was able to travel under its own power to a target. Eleven years later a refined version of the weapon was fired off the British warship *Shah* without success. The intended target, the rebel Peruvian ironclad *Huascar*, was able to turn and avoid the weapon.

The use of torpedoes gradually began to spread across the world. The first real success in battle occurred in 1878—only a year after the debut aboard *Shah*—when a Russian warship sank a Turkish vessel in the Black Sea.[59]

The development of torpedoes and small combatants quickly became intertwined. Inexpensive diminutive vessels now had the power to damage or even sink the largest of warships. Nations of all size began constructing motor torpedo boats as the nineteenth century drew to a close.

The United States Navy purchased a version of the Whitehead torpedo after failing to create a satisfactory model of its own.[60] America commissioned its first torpedo boat in 1890, appropriately named *Cushing* in honor of the Civil War sailor. She saw brief action in the Caribbean, capturing a few small boats during the Spanish-American War in 1898. Plans for additional torpedo boats were curtailed when naval leaders felt the funds could be better spent on seagoing vessels.[61]

The Japanese deployed small torpedo boats with moderate success during the Battle of Tsushima in 1905. It was primarily the big guns of their battleships, though, that destroyed the Russian fleet in that climatic naval encounter in the Far East. World leaders took note of the action.

Naval history now entered the golden age of the dreadnought. The era began with the launching of the namesake British battleship *Dreadnought* in 1906. The term soon came to symbolize a generation of warships featuring such advanced features as heavy caliber guns and steam turbine propulsion systems. Battleships quickly came to signify national power, causing countries to design larger and more powerful versions.

Other types of new warships rapidly began to emerge, such as cruisers and destroyers—all to support the role of the battleship. The value of torpedo boats began to diminish in favor of the larger destroyers with their speed, rapid fire guns, torpedo tubes, and good sea keeping characteristics. As Europe stood on the eve of World War I in 1914, the majority of torpedo boats built in the late nineteenth century were retired or relegated to coastal patrol duty.[62]

Originally known as the Great War, World War I (1914–18) found all of the world's grand powers in a conflict centered on Europe. Great Britain and France led a long list of Allied nations pitted against an alliance largely comprised of Germany, Austria-Hungary, and the Ottoman Empire (based in modern day Turkey). It also brought about the resurgence of small combatants due to four primary reasons: submarines, mines, fast production, and gridlock among the big fleets.[63]

Battleships were the primary naval weapon and the most powerful surface ships employed during World War I. All of the major European powers had the large warships—including France, Italy, and Austria-Hungary—but it was Great Britain and Germany who amassed large sea-going battle fleets. The big-gunned ships, however, mostly avoided major confrontations throughout the war. The exception was the large but inconclusive Battle of Jutland, fought in the North Sea in 1916 between the British and German fleets. The lack of clashes between the behemoths paved the way for operations with smaller ships.

With submarines, the surprise naval weapon of the war, and mines in widespread use, navies on both sides turned to small boats for patrol, escort, mine-laying and minesweeping duties. Unlike larger warships that often took years to design and build, the production of small craft was ramped up quickly. The work was far from glorious, but it filled a needed role throughout the conflict.

The Italian navy was the most effective in using small combatants to attack larger warships during the war. The country joined the Allied cause late in the conflict. The Italians developed motor torpedo boats as an offensive weapon at a time when most other large navies, including the United States, were focusing on using destroyers for combat duties and relegating small craft to other functions. Armed with two eighteen-inch torpedoes and machine guns, Italian torpedo boats were about forty feet in length and could attain speeds of almost thirty knots.[64] Their nimbleness and low profile were ideal for stealthy attacks.

The Italians were facing a powerful Austrian-Hungarian battle fleet across the Adriatic Sea. The long and narrow body of water separated Italy's east coast from mainland Europe. Operating from the city of Pola, in what is now Croatia, the Austrian-Hungarian battleships mostly stayed in the safety of port behind anti-torpedo nets. The force only occasionally ventured out for action.

Italian sailors used torpedo boats to stage a series of bold attacks on Austrian-Hungarian battleships late in the war. The craft eluded harbor defenses at Trieste to torpedo the coastal defense ship *Wien* on December 10, 1917 sending the old vessel to the bottom of the harbor. The boats struck again on June 10, 1918 using two torpedoes to sink the modern battleship *Szent István*.[65] The sinking served stark notice to admirals around the world: small torpedo boats were powerful weapons.[66] The Italian craft can be considered the true forerunners of the American PT boats that would play a crucial role in the next world conflict almost twenty-five years later.

––––––––––––

The contraction of military forces after World War I saw the number of small combatants decline during the period between the wars. Many of the boats put into service during the conflict were sold off or retired. By 1920 the British Royal Navy was down to only two small combatants from an estimated 675, and the United States returned to the notion of the boats being nothing more than "poor man's warships."[67]

The two exceptions were Germany and Russia. Restricted by armistice treaty from constructing large warships, the Germans launched a secret program to build small vessels. The work eventually led to the development of the Schnellboot or E-Boat, later used effectively as gun and torpedo boats in World War II. The Russians built small combatants primarily for economic reasons.

The lone noteworthy action involving small combatants during the inter-war period took place near the fortified Russian city of Kronshtadt off the Baltic coast during 1919. The island city guarded the approaches to present day St. Petersburg, and the area had long been the seat of Russian naval power in the region. Russia was in the midst of a civil war after withdrawing early from participation in World War I on the Allied side. The action was part of a British naval campaign in the Baltic representing the limited Allied intervention in the Russian Civil War.

The Royal Navy twice used improvised torpedo boats to attack large Russian warships near Kronshtadt. Known as coastal motor boats, the craft were fifty-five-foot-long speedboats capable of making forty knots. Manned by a crew of five, each carried two torpedoes and some light machine guns.[68] In a courageous action Lieutenant Augustus Agar led a small group of boats in sinking the Russian cruiser *Oleg* and a depot ship. A subsequent attack damaged two battleships with the loss of three of the small attackers. Agar was awarded the Victoria Cross, the British equivalent of the American Medal of Honor.

The 1930s again saw the world drifting towards war, with interest in small combatants quickly rekindled by many of the large naval powers. The British began launching the first of twelve torpedo boats in 1936—their first since World War I. Naval leaders in the United States soon became cautiously interested in the idea of torpedo boats, with one report noting design advances of the craft have been "continuous and marked in most European Navies."[69] The mild interest eventually blossomed into a full construction program creating the PT boats of World War II.

CHAPTER **4**

VOYAGE TO WAR

The PT base in Panama was officially known as the United States Naval Station Taboga. Established in August 1942, it was located on a small island in the Pacific Ocean overlooking the entrance to the Panama Canal, and was about ten miles from larger naval facilities at the city of Balboa. The base served the dual purposes of defending the approaches to the critical Canal Zone and as a training area for units waiting to be transferred to the front lines. The open ocean and many small tropical islands of the region served as an excellent training ground for PT boats en route to the Pacific.

The island featured a clean sandy beach that gently crept up from the ocean before turning into a stretch of level land. A series of high mounds rose above the sea level further away from the shoreline. The centerpiece of the base was a former casino building converted into a recreation hall. An assortment of wood frame buildings on concrete foundations rounded out the facilities.[70]

The Squadron Five boats were only the second group of PT's to arrive at the Panama base. Crewman found the tropical environment inviting after escaping the prospect of spending the winter months further north in the cold waters of the Atlantic. Although the base expanded as the war progressed, and an extensive training curriculum was later developed, the newly arrived sailors were largely responsible for conducting their own exercises.

"The purpose of the stop in Panama was to give us a chance for more intensive training," Bryant Larson recalled. He and Jack Kempner made sure the time was utilized to the fullest. They tested the crew under a variety of conditions ranging from routine operations to simulated combat. Some of the enlisted men aboard *PT-109* had an area of specialty, but most were cross-trained due to the small size of the crew. "For about three weeks, we ran patrol, firing, and navigation exercises," Larson added.

During routine time at sea when combat was not expected, the crew typically divided into two watches with either the boat captain or executive officer remaining at the conn to lead a shift. Those off duty were free to move about or rest. The arrangement was known as condition of readiness two.

The entire crew deployed to battle stations and both officers stayed together at the conn when combat was expected. One of the officers, usually Larson, manned the boat's wheel. Battle station for most of the enlisted men was determined by their specialty. Two machinist's mates manned the fifty caliber machine guns, while the third was stationed below deck in the engine room. The quartermaster served as the ammunition handler for the guns. A gunner's mate manned the twenty-millimeter cannon with the assistance of a seaman. The radioman stayed at the communication equipment inside the small chart house and the torpedoman hovered near the tubes.[71] Other crewmen served as lookouts.

————

While *PT-109* was conducting training exercises in Panama, American forces were battling the Japanese thousands of miles away on the island of Guadalcanal in the South Pacific. Part of the Solomon Island chain, the small land mass was the site of the first American island invasion of the Pacific War in early August. A desperate struggle for control of the island was ongoing and included fighting on land, at sea, and in the air.

After a month of heavy naval combat around Guadalcanal it was clear to American commanders that more sea power was needed in the region. The island environment was deemed to have ideal operating conditions for PT's. The torpedo boats stationed in Panama were the only ones available to move to the front.

Shortly after *PT-109* and Squadron Five arrived at Panama, another group of PT's was preparing to depart for the South Pacific. Eight boats from Squadron Two were ordered to form a new unit and travel to Guadalcanal in early September. The force was designated Squadron Three, taking over the name of a PT group that had been decimated in the Philippines earlier in the year.

The boats made the long journey across the Pacific in two separate groups, with the first four arriving in the war zone during mid–October and second group about two weeks later. The PT's saw action almost immediately and fought a series of frenzied night battles with Japanese surface ships. American authorities immediately saw the value of the small boats and requested more.

Preparation for further deployments led to the reshuffling of boats and people at the Panama base. Six boats from Squadron Five, PT's 109 through 114, were transferred to Squadron Two.[72] Eight boats from the newly reconstituted unit were then ordered to make ready for departure to the South Pacific. The group consisted of six older Elco 77-foot models along with PT's 109 and 110. The remaining 80-foot boats were to stay in Panama for continued training and deploy to the South Pacific at a later date. The changes were effective on September 22, 1942.[73]

Jack Kempner's command of *PT-109* ended as part of the boat's preparation for deployment. "The transfer included all boat personnel. However, the 109 skipper worked some deal to stay in Panama," Bryant Larson recalled. "I never knew why. I never asked."[74] Kempner transferred off the boat and later received orders back to the Elco plant to oversee the construction of a group of new boats. His departure brought orders for a replacement boat captain. Ensign John D. Chester soon reported for duty.

Larson knew Chester from his days at Northwestern and explains what happened next: "By navy regulations, navy serial numbers determine seniority—mine was 120763, John's was 120764. I became skipper, John was the executive officer." It was now Larson's boat to take to the war zone. Several of *PT-109's* enlisted men were rotated out as part of the changes in advance of the move.

The movement of sailors was not limited to enlisted men and boat captains, but also reached into the ranks of squadron leadership. Rollin Westholm was appointed commanding officer of Squadron Two on September 24.[75] He traveled to Panama from New York to assume control of the boats just prior to the squadron's departure. The unit had seen four commanding officers during the first nine months of 1942 as the burgeoning PT service constantly shifted resources to accommodate the rapidly increasing number of new boats.

Much like the voyage to Panama, the trek to the South Pacific would be a journey accomplished in several stages. The eight boats were divided into two equal sections for the initial segment, a long voyage across the Pacific aboard transport ships. The first section, along with Rollin Westholm, was put aboard the *Robin Wently*. The second four boats, PT's 43, 59, 109 and

110, were loaded onto the deck of the Liberty ship *Roger Williams*.[76] The boats were put on cradles to be able to float free if the ship was sunk.

The transports departed Panama as part of a five ship convoy bound for the South Pacific. The group included one warship for escort duty. "It was a long crossing with maximum speed about eight knots," Larson recalled. He soon found something to help pass the monotony. "Each boat was equipped with celestial navigation gear even though we were never expected to use it. However, I decided to take the opportunity to learn to navigate by the stars— so I practiced and took star sights every evening from the bridge of the ship, with the ship's captain or navigator as an instructor." Keeping a careful record of his work, Larson completed a map of the Pacific Ocean plotted with the convoy's daily position.

The ships reached Noumea, New Caledonia after a lengthy, but uneventful, voyage lasting thirty days. The French island was located directly south of Guadalcanal and east of Australia. It served as a forward operating base for the American naval forces battling the Japanese in the Solomon Islands. Larson quickly realized he was now very close to the fighting. "As far as the eye could see, the anchorage was filled with warships and supply vessels," he noted. "Many of the warships showed the gaping scars of a recent battle further north." It was a stark realization for the young officer. "Suddenly the war was here—not way over there!"

The arrival at Noumea marked the end of the first and longest portion of the journey for the PT boats. *PT-109* was off loaded by a large crane and made ready for sea duty. Her dull gray paint was replaced with a dark green color thought to be better suited for the tropical environment of the South Pacific.[77]

The boats were put into the sea for the next leg of the trip. "Since Guadalcanal, our destination, was too far to run on our own, and since there was no crane in the Solomons large enough to lift us off a ship, the solution was to hook us on a tow line behind a destroyer and pull us up and into the battle zone," Larson explained. The duty was given to four old World War I era four stack destroyers, all now modified to either fast transports or minesweepers.

Rollin Westholm and the first section of boats departed Noumea on November 15. Five days later the remaining four boats moved out attached to the destroyers *McKean* and *Manley*. *PT-43* and *PT-109* were tethered by tow lines to *McKean* for the voyage. The 109 was positioned off the destroyer's port quarter, while the 43 occupied the same location on the starboard side. The destroyer provided the power for movement, but the PT sailors had to stay alert because an air attack was increasingly possible as the small armada slowly moved north into range of Japanese aircraft.

Although under tow, the PT boats were not exempt from one important seagoing duty. "We had to steer our boats to keep them from hitting each other," recalled Ensign David Levy, the boat captain of *PT-59* who made the same voyage behind *Manley*. He remembered it to be a difficult undertaking. "You couldn't really control it. The boat would start going from side to side, and sometimes we'd almost get sideways."[78]

The arrangement resulted in a rough ride for the small boats. "For several days and nights we rode that tow line," Larson remembered of the trip. "It was a vomit voyage for all but the skipper—I was just too busy, tensed up, excited, to bother with vomiting!"

The journey included a brief stop at Espiritu Santo in the New Hebrides before the longer stretch to Tulagi.[79] The morning of November 25 found *McKean*, *Manley*, and their PT boat companions approaching the Guadalcanal area. The island loomed dominantly off the port side as the small flotilla approached Sealark Channel, the eastern entrance to the area.

The vessels were soon in Iron Bottom Sound. The once unnamed body of water separating Guadalcanal and Tulagi had been the scene of numerous clashes between American and Japanese naval forces in recent months. The area was familiar territory for both navies and was named in honor of the many warships now resting on its bottom. Florida Island was to the right. The land mass surrounded the much smaller Tulagi Island on three sides.

"As we entered the area our radio came alive," Larson remembered. Over the air waves came an urgent message from the American airfield on Guadalcanal. "This is Cactus Control—the condition is red, repeat red."[80] It was a warning, in coded words, that a Japanese air attack was imminent. "We were to hear from them many times in the coming months," Larson added of the control station. "Welcome to the war!"

A rookie with respect to combat of any type, Larson correctly assumed the alert was a serious matter. He ordered the boat engines started and the crew to battle stations. At 1:15 p.m. the tow line to *McKean* was cast off and *PT-109* veered away from the destroyer's side, operating under her own power.[81] She sped away towards Tulagi with Larson at the conn and all guns manned.

The boat did not see any action as a result of the air attack. "Fortunately the raid over Henderson [Field] was brief so we could then concentrate on the tricky entrance to the harbor and locate the base at Sesapi village," Larson recalled. "Entering Tulagi Harbor, we passed the entrance reef off the port side then swung left with the small island of Tulagi to port and the much larger Florida Island to starboard." At 5:15 p.m. *PT-109* moored alongside Levy's *PT-59* at the small native village of Sesapi, both boats having spent a long day at sea.

Shortly after arriving in Tulagi, Larson joined other new officers in reporting for duty to Rollin Westholm. The squadron commander, known to the boat captains simply as "Westy," welcomed the new additions in spite of having just arrived himself. "It was late afternoon and we had just finished five days underway on that tow line with little sleep and less digestible food," Larson remembered. "Westy sent the two new boats and crews up the river to moor under the jungle coverage, sent an evening meal up to them, and suggested a good night's sleep." Following those orders, *PT 109* carefully slid into a position alongside the tender *Jamestown* just after 6:00 p.m. and moored for the night.

Bryant Larson soon discovered he would not be partaking in a night of rest next to the tender. "But not for everyone," he noted of Westholm's decree for the 109. Instead, he and the other new officers were directed to sit in on a briefing at base headquarters. The nightly meeting provided boat captains with the latest information in advance of the evening patrol. "Then Westy came up with his idea of on the job training," Larson wrote. The prospects for sleep were not looking good.

Larson and Lieutenant (Junior Grade) Charles Tilden were selected to ride along on the nightly patrol. Tilden had also just arrived as the boat captain of *PT-110*. Each was assigned to venture out in a different boat. "And so we did," Larson recalled with the understanding he would probably not be getting much sleep. "We left at dusk bound for the Doma Reef patrol area." The reef was situated in Iron Bottom Sound off the northern coast of Guadalcanal near the western end of the island. It was an area well known for Japanese activity and thought to be a regular drop off point for many of the recent enemy supply runs. Since the land ashore was held by the Japanese, it truly was going into enemy territory.

Larson took note of a peculiar billboard as the boat slowly left the port area. Conspicuously located near the edge of the harbor, the large sign read, "Admiral Halsey says: Kill Japs, Kill Japs, Kill More Japs!" An additional passage below the headline extolled every sailor to do their job well.[82] Although shocking in today's context, it clearly showed the hatred towards the enemy felt by many Americans after the attack on Pearl Harbor.

The outbound voyage was not lengthy as Doma Reef was only about twenty miles from the PT base. "The skipper of the boat briefed me on the patrol procedures and then, probably to keep me awake, said we would come under fire from Japanese guns as we neared the Guadalcanal shore," Larson recalled of the start of the voyage.

As if like clockwork the boat captain's prediction came true as the PT moved across Iron Bottom Sound. "As we neared the Doma Reef area, out of the darkness came what looked like a 'Roman Candle' red ball that dropped in the ocean far short of our boat," Larson remembered. "It was a shore battery opening up on us. But it was so far off and seemed so harmless that when the skipper suggested I bag some ZZ's on the off watch, I not only did so but slept through the rest of the patrol!" Larson's first combat patrol ended peaceful and uneventfully.

––––––––

The American disposition on Guadalcanal was beginning to improve by late November 1942. Naval combat frequently took place in Iron Bottom Sound since shortly after the initial invasion in early August. Control of the sea often changed between day and night, with the Japanese holding sway over the nocturnal hours. The focal point of the land battle on Guadalcanal was Henderson Field, the partially completed Japanese air strip seized by American Marines on the first day of the campaign. It was now operating as a major American airbase. After a series of vicious infantry battles, the Marines retained control of the vital airfield and began to slowly push the Japanese to the western side of the island.

After several clashes at sea in the first three months of the campaign, the United States won a crucial victory in the Naval Battle of Guadalcanal on November 13–15. In a series of brutal and bloody encounters in Iron Bottom Sound, American naval and air forces thwarted a Japanese attempt to land a large number of reinforcements. During the same time, a sizeable contingent of American Army troops arrived unmolested. Historians later identified these events as the turning point of the deadlocked campaign.

The struggle for Guadalcanal, however, was far from over. By late November over 18,000 Japanese soldiers were thought to still be on the island.[83] Although malnourished and poorly supplied, the number represented a dangerous fighting force. The Japanese needed to provide the garrison a continuous flow of supplies if there was any hope of improving their situation on the island. The delivery of supplies was the responsibility of the Imperial

Japanese Navy. It continued to make regular voyages to the island, but on a much smaller scale since the November defeat.

Since the earliest days of the campaign, the Japanese had brought most of their troops and supplies to Guadalcanal at night from bases further north. The voyage required ships to transverse a deep water passage lined on each side with islands of various sizes. The waterway ran through the central portion of the Solomon Islands and was known simply as the Slot. It terminated at the northwest entrance to Iron Bottom Sound.

SOLOMON ISLANDS

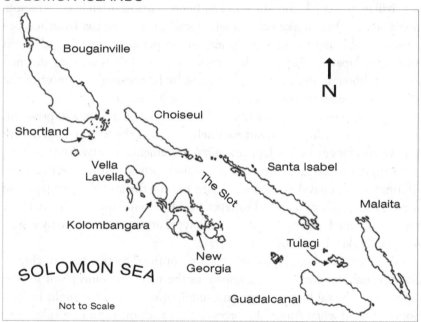

Departing bases late in the afternoon allowed the enemy vessels to arrive off Guadalcanal at night, allowing just enough time to offload their cargo before starting the return trip north. To be away from the threat of American warplanes, the ships had to be out of the immediate area by daybreak. The Americans dubbed these nocturnal runs the Tokyo Express.

A group of Japanese destroyers known as the Reinforcement Unit was charged with carrying out the supply operations. Comprised of various destroyer squadrons, the ships operated from Rabaul on the island of New

Britain. The large naval and air base was almost 600 miles northwest of Guadalcanal. A forward operating base was soon established at Shortland Island on the south side of Bougainville in the Northern Solomons to reduce the travel time.

The movements of the Japanese naval units, however, were under careful watch. An Allied spy network of coastwatchers lay hidden from view among the many islands of the Solomon chain. The unique service amounted to a secret weapon. It placed intelligence officers on islands, some occupied by the Japanese, to gather and report information about the enemy.

The island spies were typically Australian or New Zealand military officers. Many were individuals who had previously spent time in the Solomons in a civilian capacity before the war. The brave warriors often lived in remote jungle outposts and worked closely with local natives. The coastwatchers bestowed valuable assistance to the American command by providing advanced warning of Japanese ship and plane movements as well as assisting downed airmen. Although often vigorously hunted by Japanese troops, most of the undercover operatives escaped capture during the war.

Coastwatchers often gave the first warning when a Tokyo Express run was on the move. Allied aircraft routinely patrolled the Slot and alternative routes south for any hint of Japanese naval movements. The two sources, coupled with American radio intelligence, regularly provided reasonably accurate information that naval commanders used to time the arrival of the Japanese ships in the Guadalcanal area. However, the intelligence sources also had limitations. Detailed information such as the types and number of enemy vessels was usually sketchy and often inaccurate.

With much of the Japanese garrison confined to the western side of Guadalcanal, the area was well known as the main terminus point for the supply runs. Naval battles, large and small, often erupted at night in Iron Bottom Sound when American forces clashed with the incoming Tokyo Express.

PT boats joined the fight when the first elements of Squadron Three arrived at Tulagi in October. Heavy action followed for the next month as the boats made almost nightly patrols. In the short span of a few weeks the PT's participated in six battles with the Tokyo Express.[84] The action took a heavy toll on the boats with battle damage, accidents, shortages of spare parts, and breakdowns combining to make it a constant struggle to keep the PT's ready for duty. The number of operational boats slowly dwindled. When all available torpedo boats were ordered out to intercept a group of Japanese destroyers in mid-November, only three were able to answer the call.[85]

Keeping enough sailors fit to man the boats also proved to be challenging. Men were pushed to their limits of endurance and many succumbed to tropical diseases. The determined PT warriors dealt with meager base facilities, casualties, fatigue, and anxiety, but kept on fighting.

Bright moon conditions in late November were less advantageous for Tokyo Express runs, resulting in a short respite from enemy action. The break gave the weary PT men time for much needed rest and long overdue boat maintenance. The arrival of Westholm's boats in late November could not have come at a better time. Fifteen PT boats were based at Tulagi by the end of the month.[86]

GUADALCANAL & TULAGI: 1942

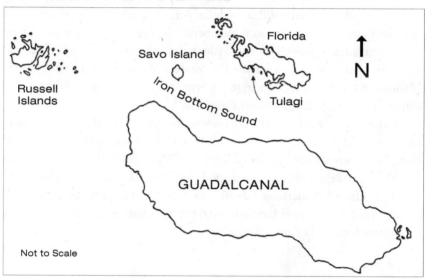

With a circumference of about three miles, the island of Tulagi was one of the smallest islands in the Southern Solomons, though it was the seat of government when the British Empire controlled the region in the years prior to World War II. It steadily grew in importance as a naval base since wrestled away from the Japanese in early August, since the area offered a well protected harbor suitable for large ships. Although the main American naval bases continued to be further south in Noumea and Espiritu Santo, Tulagi became an important forward operating station.

A detachment of Seabee's arrived with the first torpedo boats in October, and the navy construction workers built a small PT base near the village of Sesapi. Facilities included a small camp area and two floating dry docks fashioned from pontoons. An emergency channel was dredged out to allow the boats a path to the sea should the main channel become blocked.[87]

The PT tender *Jamestown* was a good addition to the base facilities. Acquired by the navy about a year before the American entry into the war, the former luxury yacht spent time at Melville before making her way to the South Pacific.[88] After arriving at Tulagi in late October, she moved up the nearby narrow Maliali River and dropped anchor in an area where overhanging trees obscured visibility from the air. The tender assisted the PT boats by providing fuel, support, and repairs.[89]

Although improvements were made to the base since the initial construction, the conditions were still considered primitive when *PT-109* arrived in late November. Bryant Larson remembered the meager facilities as nothing more than "a few Quonset huts, a drydock for boat repair, and little else." He was delighted, however, to see the PT tender. "We had last seen the Jimmy [*Jamestown*] in Melville; now here she was, buried under jungle foliage and camouflage nets, halfway around the world."

Larson swiftly learned the area landscape. "A short but quite deep river flowed into the harbor just across from Sesapi. Dense jungle foliage over hung both river shores . . ." In addition to hiding *Jamestown*, boat captains quickly learned the river was also a good place to park off duty torpedo boats.

The tranquility marking *PT-109's* first days at Tulagi would soon come to an abrupt end. Larson later summarized the change in simple terms. "A few nights later all hell broke loose!"

CHAPTER 5

THRUST INTO THE FIRE

The first week in Tulagi was a time of information gathering for Rollin Westholm and Bryant Larson. No matter how much training was done back in the United States, or during the visit to Panama, the pair was new to the South Pacific and had never faced the Japanese in combat. They were now at the front lines. Not understanding and appreciating the local situation was an easy way for a newly arrived sailor to get killed.

There was plenty to learn, but only a short amount of time for them to absorb it. The new officers studied the geography of the area, learned about recent battles through firsthand accounts, started to gain an understanding of the enemy, and began to appreciate the desperate struggle taking place on Guadalcanal and in Iron Bottom Sound.

It was clear that the torpedo boats were playing an important role in the campaign to control the sea lanes around Guadalcanal. The boats were in fact ideally suited for the situation facing the U.S. Navy in the Solomon Islands in late 1942. Although the number of cruisers and destroyers in the area was steadily increasing, the larger warships still operated from bases to the south and could not maintain a constant presence around Guadalcanal. The small torpedo boats were based locally in Tulagi and could dart out into Iron Bottom Sound on short notice. The arrangement allowed the boats to fill the void when larger ships were not available by making nightly patrols—voyages that often resulted in an encounter with the enemy. "Our navy could not maintain a constant force to repel these frequent forays by fast and powerful Japanese destroyers," Larson said, "and so it became the mission of the torpedo boats to harass and derail the Tokyo Express as best we could."

Packing the punch of four twenty-one inch torpedo tubes, a PT was capable of seriously damaging or sinking a much larger warship. A key factor to the success of a torpedo attack was the ability of the PT to make an undetected approach to the target vessel. "Surprise is one of its potential offensive weapons," a 1942 navy training manual noted.[90] After an attack, though, a boat had to make a quick escape. With no armor, the PT's and crewmen were vulnerable to gunfire of any caliber. Although the PT's took on a variety of missions as the war progressed, they largely fought in their originally intended role during the battle for Guadalcanal.

A map of the immediate area plainly showed Westholm and Larson the situation the PT men faced. Savo Island symbolically stands guard over the northwest entrance to Iron Bottom Sound. The small circular volcanic cone is directly north of the western end of Guadalcanal. It marked the final and most critical portion of a Tokyo Express run as Japanese warships completed their dash through the Slot and began the final push to Guadalcanal.

American naval officers at Tulagi had devised a good system to counter the Tokyo Express runs by the time *PT-109* arrived in the area. The general plan relied on dividing up the available PT's into several groups. A small number of boats were usually stationed near the various entrances to Iron Bottom Sound to act as scouts, often focusing on the gap between Savo Island and Cape Esperance. A larger group of PT's were then positioned nearby to act as a strike force. The latter group often lurked south of Savo to be visually out of sight of the approaching Japanese.

"The Tokyo Express had been running off and on for a fairly long time," Westholm later recalled. "It usually consisted of destroyers, with three or four acting as troop carriers and supply ships. The remainder of the [destroyers] screened them and formed a half circle around them when they arrived at their offloading position. We had engaged them on many occasions, but had been unable to stop their delivery of troops and supplies."[91]

The two officers also quickly learned that some of the training methods used back in the United States were not always practiced in the war zone. A number of the basic tactics taught at Melville had already been modified by the sailors at Tulagi based on battle conditions and experience. Among the first to be changed were the daylight torpedo runs that had been practiced over and over in Long Island Sound. "All of our torpedo attacks were at night. The Express only ran on dark (moonless) nights in order to avoid our air attacks," Larson noted. "That also meant we could use the darkness to get into firing position without being detected."[92]

"We worked out tactics as we went along," Larson recalled of the fluid situation at the front lines. The experienced boat captains learned what worked best and passed it along when new officers arrived. "All PT torpedo attacks followed the same pattern—a slow, muffled approach, the torpedo launch from 500 to 1,500 yards out, and a high speed retreat usually behind a smoke screen and under heavy fire from the destroyers," Larson recalled. It would not be long before he experienced such action firsthand.

Larson had thus far made a favorable impression on his squadron commander during the initial time the two spent together. "For a young officer he is an extremely fine leader," Westholm wrote at the time in a routine review. "He is well liked, yet industrious and efficient."[93] Westholm rated him 3.8 on a 4.0 scale for his current assignment and recommended Larson for future promotion.

––––––

The morning of November 26 began with a routine 8:00 a.m. muster call for *PT-109's* crew. The day brought some changes to the boat. Rollin Westholm decided to make the 109 the squadron's flagship. He reported aboard as commanding officer, resulting in Larson reverting back to be the PT's executive officer. John Chester then left the boat to become the executive officer of *PT-44*.

The 109 moved from alongside *Jamestown* to Macambo Island late in the day. The small isle was located in Tulagi Harbor and used as a torpedo facility. The old concrete pier of pre-war vintage was in need of repairs, but was pressed into service by the PT base force. The boat moored at the dock for the slow and laborious process of exchanging a torpedo.[94]

PT-109 made a routine mail run across Iron Bottom Sound to Guadalcanal the next afternoon. That evening she pulled out of Tulagi Harbor just after 8:30 p.m. for her first night patrol. The boat plied the waters of the Guadalcanal area with Westholm at the conn and Larson stationed nearby in what proved to be an uneventful patrol.

The last day of November brought news to the PT sailors of a possible sea battle taking place during the night in Iron Bottom Sound. Scuttlebutt had the Tokyo Express running and a group of large American warships en route to stop it. The usual PT patrols were cancelled for the night as it was too risky for the small boats to operate close to the big vessels. With no

TULAGI HARBOR: 1942–43

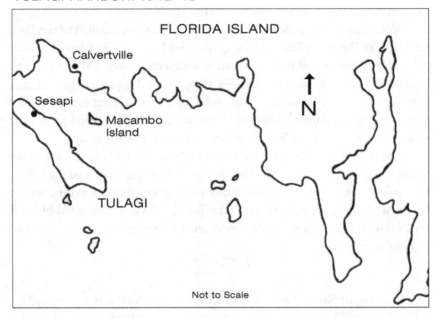

planned evening voyages, all the PT sailors could do was wait. Most used the found time to catch up on much-needed sleep.

The fierce struggle to save the badly damaged *Northampton* lasted little more than four hours. The port side of the heavy cruiser had been ripped open by two Japanese torpedoes during the last hour of November 30, 1942. Damage control crews worked desperately to contain fires raging above the waterline. It was a losing battle as the flames eventually turned into a consuming conflagration. The real damage, however, lay underwater where the warship's ruptured hull spewed fuel oil into the surrounding sea.

An orderly abandonment of the ship began at 1:15 a.m. on December 1 after the vessel took a twenty-three degree list to port. Less than two hours later the proud warship began to slowly slip beneath the ocean surface stern first. The area was home to a growing collection of sunken warships and *Northampton* was the newest addition. A pair of destroyers groped through the dark night looking for survivors.

The sound of gunfire rolling across the waters of Iron Bottom Sound told the PT sailors that the scuttlebutt about a sea battle had been correct.

Initial reports of the clash reached the PT base sometime after 1:00 a.m. A subsequent call for assistance caused a rush of activity.[95] The majority of boats were nested together in groups for the night and not able to get underway on short notice. Two boats moored on the outboard side of a nest, *PT-37* and *PT-109*, were the exceptions.

Word soon reached each boat captain to get ready to move out. Their crews worked feverishly to make each PT ready for a hasty departure. "Some nights we ran mercy missions," Larson later wrote of the evening. "We were called to get underway to search for survivors."[96]

At 2:15 a.m. the 109 pulled away from her nest and headed for the harbor entrance with *PT-37* following moments later.[97] The sailors aboard the two torpedo boats likely did not know the details of what transpired in the battle, but the situation at sea was serious. The rescue operation encompassed more than just the sunken *Northampton*. Three other badly damaged heavy cruisers were limping towards Tulagi.

A third officer joined Westholm and Larson aboard *PT-109* for the voyage into Iron Bottom Sound. An individual known only by the last name of Harper jumped on board just prior to the boat's departure. The Royal Australian Navy officer was serving as a harbor pilot for Tulagi and was to be delivered to one of the damaged ships.

The destroyer *Shaw* was patrolling outside the harbor entrance as the 109 raced out into the dark night. Crewmen sighted a distant vessel shortly after clearing land. The hazy outline slowly began to form into the shape of a warship. "Just off the Tulagi Harbor entrance, the cruiser *Minneapolis*, who lost her bow to a torpedo, was burning and in danger of sinking," Larson later remembered. His boat could not stop, but another PT later ventured out to aid the damaged warship.[98]

The 109 came upon a second ship not long after she dashed past *Minneapolis*. The dark object blinked a challenge on her signal lamp. The PT quickly replied. It was the damaged *Pensacola* slowly moving along at seven knots. A torpedo had struck the cruiser's port side, flooding an engine room and rupturing fuel tanks. Damage control parties were struggling to stop the deluge of incoming water and extinguish blazing fires.

PT-109 carefully maneuvered alongside the stricken vessel, and harbor pilot Harper climbed aboard at 2:52 a.m.[99] The departure of the Australian officer undoubtedly included some type of good luck wish from the small boat sailors who provided his transportation. "Then we went after the men of the *Northampton*," Larson wrote of the moment. The torpedo boat veered away from *Pensacola* to continue her journey into Iron Bottom Sound.

The 109 headed for Savo Island as *Northampton* was reported to have gone down a few miles south of the island. Two destroyers had already rescued a large number of survivors, but many were still in the water and in need of help.

The PT boat combed the area for the next four hours with crewmen perched topside ready to pull aboard anyone who could be found in the shadowy night. *PT-37* arrived in the area a short time later. Morning light revealed scores of sailors bobbing in the water. Some were floating upright in life vests, while others were grasping on to bits of wreckage or clinging to rafts. At 7:15 a.m. the first waterlogged *Northampton* survivors were hauled aboard *PT-109*.

The PT's worked as rescue boats for almost an hour plucking sailors out of the water as fast as possible. Some of the survivors were covered with horrible burns and a few may have been dead. Sharks were seen milling around the immediate area, prompting two sailors on the 37 to break out submachine guns. Some well placed bullets seemed to dissuade the underwater creatures from further intervention.[100]

The boats quickly became crowded as survivors filled up every available open area. The PT's were well equipped for water rescues, but not for providing medical help. The first aid kits were miniature and basic, but usually included a small amount of alcohol. The liquid medicine was used to treat the weary survivors.

John Fitch was exhausted after spending hours in the water. The young sailor escaped death by jumping off the fantail of the sinking *Northampton* just before she disappeared into the sea. His eyes were stinging from salt water when a PT boat found his raft well after sunrise. He milled among fellow survivors before finding a place to sit cross-legged near the very bow of the boat. "The PT started its big Packard engines with a roar, gained speed and bounced into a fast turn heading across the channel," he later wrote of his rescue. Fitch soon drifted off to sleep. "The next thing I knew we were docking at the little island of Tulagi."[101] He was one of the many lucky sailors rescued by the PT men.

PT-109 arrived at an area on Tulagi known as Government Landing shortly after 8:00 a.m. She moored alongside a small pier to allow the *Northampton* men to disembark. PT sailors helped the weary passengers off the boat and back onto solid ground. Glad to be safe, the survivors moved inland walking in a single file up a hill towards the jungle. The cruiser sailors undoubtedly bid their rescuers a hearty thank you before disappearing out of sight. A total of 94 survivors were saved by *PT-109*.[102] Another 86 sailors, two of whom were dead, returned aboard *PT-37*.[103]

Daylight gave the men of *PT-109* a chance to see the other damaged warships from the night before. "Upon returning to the [PT] base, there was the *Minneapolis* hard aground next to our base where they ran her to prevent sinking," Larson recalled. The 109 then passed close to the *New Orleans*, allowing the PT sailors to get a close up view of the mangled and twisted metal that was once the warship's bow. The damaged *Pensacola* also made port safely with her crewmen finally able to put out the stubborn fires. "It was a bad night," Larson added in summary after seeing the effects of war up close for the first time. The rescue operation was the first taste of action for Westholm, Larson, and their new PT boat.

————

Once beyond the rescue of *Northampton* survivors, the next week was mostly quiet and passed without any major actions for *PT-109*. The PT sailors received welcome assistance during the first days of December from an unanticipated source when about half a dozen seaplanes became available. The single-engine Curtis SOC Seagull served as the standard observation plane for large warships. The badly damaged cruisers departed the area for repairs shortly after the Tassafaronga battle, but their aircraft remained behind and were assigned to assist the PT boats. It was not long before one or two of the seaplanes typically searched for Japanese ships whenever the torpedo boats left port.[104] As the first week of December drew to a close, Westholm was about to put the seaplanes, and the proven strategy to counter the Tokyo Express, to good use.

CHAPTER 6

FIRST BATTLE

No longer willing to risk large transport ships on voyages to Guadalcanal after their disastrous November 1942 defeat in the Naval Battle of Guadalcanal, Japanese naval commanders instead devised an innovative plan using destroyers and drums to transport supplies. Heavy metal drums, normally used for oil or gasoline, were cleaned and sterilized before partially loaded with food and medical supplies. An internal air pocket was left in place to ensure buoyancy. Tied together in clusters of up to ten, the containers were placed on the decks of destroyers for the voyage south. Each warship could hold between 200 and 240 drums.

The plan relied on the speed of destroyers to make the run to Guadalcanal undetected. The drum clusters were tossed over the side in the direction of land once at a designated drop point. Personnel ashore then used ropes to pull the drums to the beach.[105] The method was advantageous because it minimized the amount of time the destroyers had to linger close to shore, allowing for a quick departure.

Rear Admiral Raizo Tanaka, an experienced and respected destroyer leader, was charged with commanding a Tokyo Express run to deliver the first batch of drums to Guadalcanal. His first mission was thwarted by the Battle of Tassafaronga, in which he lost one destroyer but sank or heavily damaged four American cruisers. That clash was the last large naval encounter involving American cruisers and destroyers in Iron Bottom Sound. PT boats would soon take center stage in future battles to stop the Tokyo Express.

The failed supply operation ensured the Japanese situation on Guadalcanal remained desperate during the first week of December. Tanaka was determined to try again. He led the second supply run to use the drum method on December 3. A coastwatcher and aerial reconnaissance reported the movements of the ten-ship force. A twilight air attack damaged one destroyer, but failed to slow the mission. No American warships were in Iron Bottom Sound to interfere with the operation. The destroyers discharged a total of 1,500 drums off Tassafaronga and promptly headed for home.

Although Tanaka accomplished his portion of the operation, the delivery was not a complete success. Many of the drums were unable to be pulled ashore under the cover of darkness due to logistical problems on land. Daylight allowed American fighter planes to machine gun many of the floating containers and only a paltry 310 drums made it safely into Japanese hands ashore.[106]

Tanaka was firm in his determination to keep trying, but not before operational changes were enacted to better ensure the majority of drums would make it to shore. A reduction was made to the number of drums tied together, the strength of the rope increased, and the distance from shore the destroyers were to release their cargo was shortened.[107] To increase the number of screening vessels, three additional destroyers were assigned to Tanaka's force.[108]

The rear admiral, though, would not personally command the third supply run. Operational control of the mission was relegated to Captain Torajiro Sato, who had capably led a destroyer division in the Tassafaronga battle. The voyage was scheduled for December 6, but was delayed one day to allow for the arrival of the new warships.

Eleven destroyers under Captain Sato's command departed Shortland at 11:00 a.m. on December 7, 1942 for the voyage south. Three warships served as escorts for the night carrying no drums. Twelve land-based Zero fighter planes and eight seaplanes provided an air escort part way down the Slot. A coastwatcher again spotted the movement and radioed a warning to the Allied command on Guadalcanal.

The air escort turned back at 4:25 p.m. The force was attacked by thirteen American dive bombers a mere fifteen minutes later. The strike was largely beaten back with the loss of several attackers, but not before one Japanese warship sustained damage. A near miss bomb killed seventeen sailors aboard *Nowaki*. It left the destroyer with a flooded engine room and dead in the water without power.[109] She left the formation under tow by *Naganami* with *Ariake* and *Arashi* acting as escorts for the return trip to Shortland. Sato pressed on towards Guadalcanal with his remaining ships.

ORDER OF BATTLE
AMERICAN PT BOATS VS. JAPANESE DESTROYERS
DECEMBER 7–8, 1942

JAPANESE (Captain Torajiro Sato)

DESTROYER FORCE: Oyashio, Kuroshio, Kagero, Naganami,* Kawakaze, Suzukaze, Arashi,* Nowaki,* Urakaze, Tanikaze, and Ariake.*

*Returned to Shortland after air attack.

AMERICAN (Lieutenant Rollin Westholm)

PATROL GROUP—GUADALCANAL COAST
FROM KOKUMBONA TO CAPE ESPERANCE

PT-43   Charles Tilden

PT-109   Rollin Westholm

PATROL GROUP—NORTHWEST OF GUADALCANAL

PT-40   Henry "Stilly" Taylor

PT-48   Robert Searles

STRIKE GROUP—SOUTH OF SAVO ISLAND

PT-36   Marvin Pettit

PT-37   Lester Gamble

PT-44   Frank Freeland

PT-59   John Searles

———

As the Japanese were preparing for their next supply run, *PT-109* spent the entire day of December 6 in the Tulagi Harbor area. The boat moored alongside the tender *Jamestown* during the morning and began the slow process of taking aboard 1,200 gallons of high octane fuel. Just before 1:00 p.m. she moved back to the base area near Sesapi, but would have to wait another night before going out on patrol. The 109 pulled away from Government Landing just before 8:00 p.m. on the evening of December 7 in the company of the other boats. She soon disappeared into the fading daylight on her way towards Iron Bottom Sound with Rollin Westholm at the conn.

The one year anniversary of the attack on Pearl Harbor would be the first sea battle for Westholm, Bryant Larson, and the rest of the boat's crewmen, who had sailed half way around the world to get to the war zone. The action also marked the first time a new Elco 80-foot boat participated in a sea battle. There was great interest among the veteran boat captains as to how the new design would perform in combat conditions.[110]

The PT boats moved across Iron Bottom Sound towards the west end of Guadalcanal as complete darkness overtook the area. At the same time Captain Sato was approaching the area from the north at a high rate of speed. With the Japanese destroyers and American PT boats on a collision course, the set-up for the evening battle was complete.

Officers at the Tulagi PT base had worked quickly to devise an operations plan after receiving the first report of Japanese ships on the move. No large American warships were available for the night, so the torpedo boats were charged with thwarting the Tokyo Express run. The coastwatcher's warning, coupled with the air attack, and additional aerial reconnaissance reports, helped to narrow the Japanese estimated time of arrival. The situation on land dictated the supply drop point would likely be somewhere between Cape Esperance on the northwestern tip of Guadalcanal and Tassafaronga to the east.

Eight PT boats were available at Tulagi for the night's mission. Westholm commanded the operation from *PT-109* and he knew to follow the advice of the veteran officers in planning for battle. It was no time to develop new ideas, but rather to stick with what seemed to be working. The squadron commander intended to use the small group tactics already proven successful by the Tulagi veterans to prevent the enemy from slipping through undetected. Westholm's battle plan divided the boats into three groups: two patrols and one strike force. Each group would be in a position to provide mutual support to the others once the enemy was located.

The boats were to use radios to stay in contact and report Japanese movements. However, the communication had to be clear and effective if Westholm's plan was to work. Each PT was equipped with a radio unit mounted in the chart house. The equipment operated at a very high frequency setting. Using a twenty-foot whip antenna mounted near the conn, the set could transmit voice or Morse code the distance of the horizon, or about 70 miles.[111]

The equipment, however, was originally designed for planes and was plagued with problems when used by PT's. Atmospheric conditions, the Japanese use of the same frequencies, and the constant pounding endured by the sets when the boats ran at high speed all combined to make radio communication unreliable.[112] Lacking radar and more advanced radio instruments, the PT boat captains had no choice but to make it work.

The first patrol group, comprised of *PT-109* and *PT-43*, would idle along a line paralleling the Guadalcanal coast from Kokumbona (located just east of Tassafaronga) to Cape Esperance. Lieutenant Charles Tilden was in command of the 43 boat. The second patrol group of two PT's was assigned to the area off the northwest tip of Guadalcanal. The force consisted of Lieutenant Robert Searles in *PT-48* and Lieutenant Henry "Stilly" Taylor in *PT-40*. Both were veteran PT skippers who arrived at Tulagi with the first boats back in October and had since seen plenty of action. The two units were positioned to be able to locate the Japanese either during their initial approach to the area or during their final run to the suspected drop-off point.

The remaining four boats comprised the strike group. Positioned to the south of Savo Island and out of sight of the approaching Japanese, the force was to move forth and attack at the appropriate time. The strike group contained Lieutenant John Searles in *PT-59*, Lieutenant Frank Freeland in *PT-44*, Lieutenant (Junior Grade) Marvin Pettit in *PT-36*, and Lieutenant (Junior Grade) Lester Gamble in *PT-37*.

Westholm was comfortable the plan offered a good chance of success. "The disposition of the boats at the time was considered the best possible to meet all possible approaches of the enemy," he added.[113] The squadron commander felt none of the groups could be outflanked by the Japanese destroyers. The PT boats also had help from above. "One SOC was in air from 11:00 p.m. to 2:45 a.m. to drop flares as requested."

The blanket of darkness shrouded the final movements of the Japanese ships. With no additional information available on the approaching enemy, Westholm's plan remained unchanged in the final hours before the encounter.

The second patrol group and strike force proceeded directly to their assigned positions. Westholm carefully planned the route of his group to maximize their chances of contacting the enemy. "The two boats on the Kokumbona to Esperance patrol had deliberately timed their run to be just east of Tassafaronga headed west at midnight in order that nothing would outflank the boats and to be able to go up the coast and intercept any ships which had slipped by Esperance and were proceeding east along the Guadalcanal coast," he later wrote.

Westholm and Bryant Larson were together in the conn as the 109 waited for the enemy to arrive. They looked out into the pitch black night searching for any movement in Iron Bottom Sound. Tension was thick as the pair faced the real possibility of encountering the enemy for the first time. The pair hoped the enemy would not slip through the various patrol groups. "The night actions meant limited visibility with patrol sections scattered over a wide area," Larson recalled. "Anything we could do to get a better track on the Express and so bring maximum boats to the attack was worth trying."[114] The months of training and preparation now seemed to be a distant memory.

The bridge area was small and cramped with a wheel centrally located. An angled instrument panel just above the wheel contained a variety of gauges, including three sets of tachometers and a compass. The area to the right of the control station was dominated by the forward fifty-caliber machine gun tub, and a small open hatch leading to the chart room below marked the end of the conn area.

By 11:00 p.m. Captain Sato was making his final approach to Guadalcanal. His destroyers were pointed towards the passageway between Savo Island and the tip of Cape Esperance. He unknowingly was on a collision course with at least one group of PT boats.

The action started off the northwest end of Guadalcanal at 11:20 p.m. when lookouts aboard *PT-40* and *PT-48* spotted a group of ships coming directly towards their position. "These boats at that time were about three miles north-northwest of Cape Esperance and the enemy ships were on a line of bearing, distance one and a half to two miles on a course about 130 degrees true," Westholm wrote of the initial contact. The course put the enemy ships on a southeasterly heading.

The confrontation that followed developed quickly and then moved at a fast pace. As with many PT boat battles, events often happened simultaneously in rapid succession. It was fought in the dark night with occasional flashes of gunfire appearing as speckles against the black backdrop.

Veteran boats captains Robert Searles and Stilly Taylor knew exactly what to do after sighting the enemy. Both immediately turned and added speed in an attempt to gain a firing position ahead of the Japanese ships. One of the engines on *PT-48* then abruptly failed. The malfunction could not have happened at a worst time. The PT was quickly spotted by alert Japanese lookouts just as the boat started to slow. The lead destroyers immediately opened fire as Searles struggled to get his boat out of harm's way. He barely cleared the bow of one enemy warship when a second engine failed, slowing *PT-48* down to a mere idle. With his main advantage of speed gone, Searles became an easy and inviting target for Japanese gunners.

Seeing the precarious predicament of his comrade, Stilly Taylor swung

BATTLE OF DECEMBER 7–8, 1942: PART I

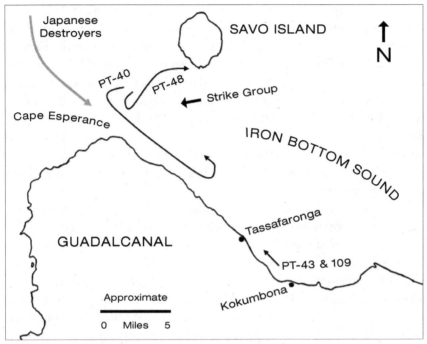

PT-40 around in a tight circle to reverse course. He then ran his boat between the idling *PT-48* and the approaching destroyers in a daring maneuver to take the attention away from his ailing companion. Taylor ordered smoke as he opened the throttles to gain speed. The 40 boat was headed back into Iron Bottom Sound.

The ruse worked as the two leading Japanese destroyers turned to follow *PT-40*. Occasional inaccurate gunfire fell in the vicinity of the boat, but she was not hit. Taylor poured on speed and soon lost his pursuers as the two destroyers reversed course to rejoin the main group.[115] Searles took advantage of the situation to slowly move to the opposite side of Savo Island where he dropped anchor close to shore.[116]

The boat captains of the first patrol group successfully radioed out a contact report enabling others to join the action. "The striking force after hearing of the contact deployed and themselves made contact at 11:35 p.m.," Westholm reported. "The enemy force which had originally been coming in fast slowed down at about that time."

All four boats of the strike force moved towards the enemy for a torpedo attack. Lester Gamble pulled *PT-37* into the lead, and after closing on the Japanese formation unleashed two torpedoes towards the first destroyer. He was unable to observe any results after turning for cover.

Right behind Gamble was *PT-59* which closed and fired two torpedoes. The target ship turned sharply to avoid the fish, but in the process exposed other vessels behind her. Boat captain John Searles believed his torpedoes may have hit one of the distant warships.

The 59 boat passed within 100 yards of the destroyer *Kuroshio* as Searles turned to begin his getaway.[117] It was extremely dangerous for a wooden boat to be so close to a powerful warship. Searles told his crew to get ready to fire every available weapon. Both the PT and destroyer opened fire simultaneously. It was anything but a fair fight as *Kuroshio* was well over 300 feet in length and displaced more than 2,000 tons.[118] Her five-inch main battery guns could easily blast the PT into pieces with a single hit.

The little torpedo boat could only muster a meager amount of gun power. Bullets from the PT's machine guns and twenty millimeter cannon raked the destroyer's deck, gun enclosures, and bridge area. A motor machinist's mate helped the cause when he leaned out of the engine room hatch to take a few shots with a rifle at the destroyer's bridge.[119] The barrage of gunfire caused ten Japanese casualties, but no substantial damage.[120]

Gunners aboard the destroyer returned fire at a range so close they could not miss. The PT boat was hit at least ten times by heavy caliber machine gun fire. Two bullets pierced one of the gun tubs setting fire to a belt of fifty caliber ammunition. Gunners Mate Second Class Cletus Osborne stayed in the tub and calmly detached the flaming belt of bullets. He tossed it on deck where the fire was extinguished. The encounter was short and furious, but Searles was able to clear the area. *PT-59* miraculously survived the frightening encounter with no crew casualties, although *Kuroshio* reported to have sunk her.[121]

A short three minutes after the first boat of the strike force attacked, the last two PT's of the group moved in for their torpedo runs. Marvin Pettit conned *PT-36* close enough to fire a four torpedo spread at one of the leading destroyers. He sped away untouched believing he scored at least one hit. *PT-44* then took aim at one of the last destroyers in formation and fired four torpedoes. As Frank Freeland turned his boat away, he was certain that two torpedoes scored direct hits. A destroyer was thought to have been sunk as a result of the encounter after a series of tremendous explosions were observed.[122]

Rollin Westholm and *PT 109* were far from the action when the battle started, but it did not take long for them to speed to the area. "When contact was reported by the boats off Northwest [Guadalcanal] they increased speed to about sixteen knots and proceeded westward up the Guadalcanal coast close in to shore," Westholm reported of his patrol group. He monitored radio reports from the various PT boats as he moved northwest towards the action.

After tangling with torpedo boats for almost twenty-five minutes, Captain Sato attempted to reassemble his destroyers for the final run to the Guadalcanal coast in order to drop off the supply drums. The two approaching PT boats of Westholm's group coupled with the sighting of an SOC scout plane patrolling above was enough to force him to abort the supply mission.[123] Sato ordered his force to withdraw and immediately set a course for the Slot.

Westholm had no way of knowing the Japanese force was already withdrawing as his pair of PT boats continued to move towards the reported action. "The PT's 109 and 43 continued up the coast and arrived off Esperance about 12:15 a.m. having sighted no enemy ships," he reported. "At this time

BATTLE OF DECEMBER 7–8, 1942: PART II

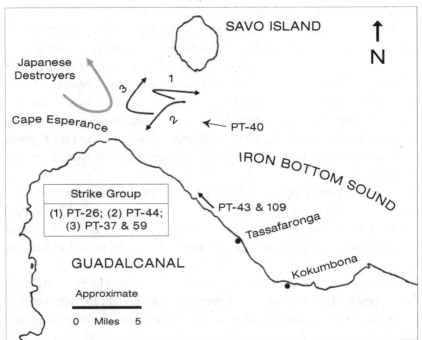

the SOC reported a group of enemy ships about seven miles northwest of Esperance." Westholm gave the order to increase speed and give chase hoping to get a shot off at the fleeing enemy.

One of *PT-109's* three machinist's mates was stationed in the small engine room near the stern as the boat sped towards the departing enemy. The cramped quarters was loaded with all of the machinery needed to keep the boat moving. Westholm's order to increase speed kept the sailor busy shifting gears to make sure each of the three engines poured on continuous power.

The extra speed did not help. "At about 12:25 a.m. the SOC reported the enemy ships were about 15 miles northwest of Esperance and headed away at high speed," Westholm reported. It was clear to him the escaping enemy was beyond reach and the two boats returned to their original patrol route.

At about the same time Westholm was giving up the chase, *PT-37* was retiring southeast when lookouts spotted a light on land about five miles southeast of Cape Esperance. Lester Gamble requested illumination from above. "The flare showed a large ship, bow on the beach and the *PT-37* fired her two remaining torpedoes at it," Westholm explained. "The ship was hit, but it is almost certain that this ship was one which was previously aground." The squadron commander's conclusion was probably correct as four Japanese transports were run aground several weeks earlier in the general area in a futile attempt to deliver reinforcements during the Naval Battle of Guadalcanal.[124]

After returning to the Kokumbona–Cape Esperance patrol line, crewmen on *PT-109* and *PT-43* also saw something on land. "At about 1:15 a.m. a light was observed on the beach one mile southeast of Esperance. Another flare was requested," a cautious Westholm recalled. It was worthy of further investigation because American sailors had no way of knowing if a supply drop had actually been made during the confusion of the night battle. "It revealed nothing except some tents or grass huts," he said of the flare. Westholm decided to leave it for an aircraft to further investigate later. "The plane strafed these but no activity was noted."

Iron Bottom Sound reverted back to silence after the Japanese force escaped to the north. "Nothing more was sighted during the night," Westholm reported. The PT boats were scattered among various positions across the area in the immediate aftermath of the action. As commanding officer of the operation, Westholm tried to keep track of each boat as best possible. PT's 36, 44, and 59 returned to Tulagi after making their torpedo runs. "The *PT-40* reported having trouble with gasoline suction and requested permission to take station southeast of Savo," he noted. "This was granted." The boat eventually made her way back to base without assistance.

There was one boat whose position was unknown. "At 4:00 a.m. the *PT-48* revealed her position and requested assistance," Westholm recalled. He was by now certain the Japanese were gone for the night. "The *PT-109* and *PT-43* proceeded to her position." The 48 had suffered engine trouble and fled to the far side of Savo Island early in the skirmish where she subsequently became stuck on a beach. At about 4:15 a.m. the 109 arrived on the scene and pulled the stranded boat out of her predicament. The three boats proceeded together back to Tulagi.

PT-109 moored at Sesapi at 5:20 a.m.[125] The long night was over for the exhausted boat crew. Rollin Westholm and Bryant Larson were now combat veterans after experiencing a full-fledged sea battle.

Westholm began work on a report of the battle in keeping with navy regulations. He gathered information from his boat captains in order to determine the sequence of events and the probable damage inflicted on the enemy. Sorting out the facts was a difficult undertaking because the confusing battle took place at a fast pace in the black night. He concluded one Japanese destroyer was probably sunk and some torpedoes may have hit other ships.[126]

The sinking claim was based on reports and observations from various boats. Of particular note was the two explosions reported by *PT-44* in the aftermath of her torpedo run. The timing seemed to be supported by two other observations, including one from Westholm's own boat. At about 11:50 p.m. crewmen aboard *PT-109* heard "a terrific explosion" to the north, which they attributed to a torpedo hit on a Japanese destroyer. At about the same time *PT-40* was returning to the battle area after slipping away from two chasing destroyers. Her crewmen reported seeing three flashes thought to be torpedo hits in the area between Cape Esperance and Savo Island.[127]

In his action report Westholm praised the efforts of three crewmen on *PT-59* for their exploits during the close brush with the enemy destroyer. For Cletus Osborne, whose actions with a burning ammunition belt were nothing short of heroic, he called for high commendation. Osborne was later awarded the Silver Star.[128] Westholm also highlighted the actions of two additional sailors who were manning guns during the encounter. "They maintained a high rate of fire on [a destroyer] at close range for a period of several minutes," he wrote. Westholm thought the pair, "should be commended for their skill and valor."

Contrary to what was reported by the individual boat captains and concluded by Westholm in his official report, none of the twelve torpedoes fired by the PT's that night hit Japanese ships. A variety of circumstances could explain the explosions reported by various torpedo boats. Some of the weapons may have exploded prematurely, while others could have detonated at the end of their runs. Flashes from enemy guns may also have been mistaken for torpedo hits. An examination of postwar records reveals no Japanese destroyers were seriously damaged or sunk as a result of the encounter.[129]

The December 7, 1942 battle in which Rollin Westholm led *PT-109* and seven other boats against a group of Japanese destroyers did not change the course of the Guadalcanal campaign. The encounter was, however, clearly an American victory. Facing great odds, the brave PT sailors turned back a Japanese supply run that otherwise would most likely have succeeded. It was accomplished without suffering the loss of a single man. Decades later an American historian wrote that the battle had "cast a different light over the date of December 7 in American naval annals ..."[130] As a result of the heroic effort on the part of the PT men, the Japanese supply situation on Guadalcanal remained serious.

The work of Westholm as the skipper of *PT-109* and as squadron commander leading the boats in battle did not go unnoticed by his superiors. Captain Thomas Shock was serving as Commander Naval Bases, Solomon Islands. "In this period he was the senior motor torpedo boat commander in the field during an anxious and hazardous time," Shock wrote of Westholm. "He has ably handled grave responsibilities far beyond [his] rank and age."[131]

Admiral William Halsey later reviewed Westholm's action report and sent a short note to the Commander-in-Chief of the Pacific Fleet. "They are performing heroic services and it is confidently expected that they will set a high record of valor and achievement in the service of their country," he said of the PT sailors.[132] For Rollin Westholm, Bryant Larson, and the crew of *PT-109*, the heavy fighting had only just begun.

CHAPTER 7

DECEMBER BLOOD

By late 1942 it became necessary to add an additional layer to the PT command apparatus due to multiple boat squadrons operating in the Guadalcanal area. Motor Torpedo Boat Flotilla One was established on December 15, 1942 under the leadership of Commander Allen P. Calvert with headquarters at Sesapi.[133] All PT squadrons operating from the base were now under a single leader. Although it took time for the new command to get organized and fill staff positions, the flotilla provided centralized control over planning, reporting and intelligence matters.

The new command also brought improvements to the primitive living conditions for the sailors at Tulagi. Little had changed since the arrival of the PT men in October. The enlisted men often ate and slept aboard their boats. The food varied little and included a regular diet of Spam. The officers tended to have their meals either at the mess hall ashore or aboard the *Jamestown*.[134] Attire in the tropic heat usually consisted of an undershirt and khaki pants torn above the knee to be converted into shorts.[135]

Base conditions began to expand by the end of the year. "Sometime in December we moved to a new home," Bryant Larson remembered. "A native village at the mouth of the river was converted to living quarters for all hands." Located on Florida Island, the village was christened Calvertville in honor of the flotilla's leader. A sign posted near the base entrance proclaimed, "Thru these portals pass the best M.T.B. Flotilla in the world."[136] Officers went from living aboard their boats to sharing small huts ashore.

The new home was welcomed by officers and enlisted men alike. "By now all of the boats were infested with cockroaches and rats—picked up while moored in and under the jungle foliage," Larson added. "Calvertville was a fancy resort by comparison—with fresh air sleeping and unlimited fresh water showers from a nearby stream." The shower facility was nothing more than a shack built by the base force. A system of pipes brought a continuous supply of cool water from a stream up in the hills. The base provided only a temporary sanctuary from the war. "But the Express still ran, and on Guadalcanal our troops were in daily bloody combat with the enemy," he noted.

As Japanese destroyers struggled to deliver supplies to Guadalcanal using the drum method, submarines enjoyed some moderate success performing the same mission. In a typical operation a submarine loaded with supplies loitered submerged in the Guadalcanal area during daylight hours to avoid detection. She then surfaced at night near a friendly shore where the cargo was offloaded into waiting motor boats.[137] Three submarines made successful night deliveries during the first eight days of December with each boat dropping off twenty or more tons of supplies.[138] The large downside to the operation was the limited amount of cargo a submarine could carry. Japanese naval leaders were eager to continue the successful string of submarine deliveries. American radio intelligence, however, was able to discern the date and approximate time of the next underwater supply run. The information was quickly passed to the PT base on Tulagi.

Rollin Westholm called John Searles to his office around noon on December 8 and showed him two top secret memos. A Japanese submarine was scheduled to surface close to the enemy-held shore at about 2:00 a.m. the next morning. One memo indicated a person of high importance might be aboard—information that was never confirmed. Westholm wanted to set up an ambush and asked Searles if he would be up for the job. The boat captain readily agreed.[139] Frank Freeland was also assigned to the mission.

The two boats, Searles in *PT-59* and Freeland in *PT-44*, left Tulagi during the evening hours. The PT's initially traveled north to throw off any watching Japanese eyes. Only after the arrival of complete darkness did the boats turn south to head for Kamimbo Bay near the west end of Guadalcanal.

The torpedo boats were waiting in ambush about 500 yards apart when the submarine suddenly surfaced right between them. *PT-44* was not positioned for an immediate torpedo shot, but Searles in *PT-59* quickly fired two torpedoes at very close range. One hit the submarine dead amidships causing a tall geyser of water to shoot high into the air, immediately followed by a tremendous explosion. The submarine sank to the bottom of Iron Bottom Sound leaving only an oil slick in her place. The second torpedo somehow missed the target and passed underneath Freeland's boat.[140] The victim was the 320-foot-long 1,970-ton submarine *I-3*.[141] The ambush marked the end of Japanese submarine supply operations.

———

PT-109 remained active in the days following her first battle with Japanese destroyers. She ventured into Iron Bottom Sound on the nights of December 8–10, but the patrols were uneventful. Although Rollin Westholm was usually at the conn, crews often rotated among various boats based on availability and needs. The second week of December found the crew of *PT-47* spending time aboard the 109.[142]

After taking aboard 1,000 gallons of fuel from *Jamestown* on the morning of December 11, *PT-109* made a routine trip across Iron Bottom Sound to Guadalcanal, and by early afternoon she was back at Tulagi. At 7:40 p.m. the boat was underway for the usual night patrol. Although Westholm led the boat on the previous night's outing, he was not aboard for this patrol. John Searles stood at the conn as the boat disappeared into the fading daylight.[143] Only a few nights earlier he was on *PT-59* when she exchanged fire at close range with an enemy destroyer.

The PT boats and Tokyo Express were set to have another violent confrontation in Iron Bottom Sound. As *PT-109* was departing Tulagi, a group of Japanese destroyers was on its way down the Slot. The supply run was to be carried out by a force of eleven destroyers that departed Shortland on the afternoon of December 11. Rear Admiral Raizo Tanaka was again in command, but he was operating aboard a new flagship, the large destroyer *Teruzuki*. Little more than a year old, she was a new type of anti-aircraft destroyer mounting eight 3.9-inch guns as her main battery armament. The weapons were rapid fire and would be deadly against PT boats.

The admiral was determined not to repeat the recent failure of Captain Sato's mission where the destroyers were unable to discharge their supply drums. To better protect his transports, five destroyers acted as escorts and carried no drums. The seriousness of the mission was underscored when Tanaka received a message from Admiral Isoroku Yamamoto, Commander-in-Chief of the Combined Japanese Fleet. "We greatly expect the success of this transport operation by the destroyers. All hands shall do their best to accomplish their missions by exerting every possible means," the admiral said in pushing his men to success.[144]

American radio intelligence sounded an early warning that the Tokyo Express was on the move shortly after the group departed Shortland on a course for the Slot. The information provided just enough time for a late-day air attack. Fourteen dive bombers operating at extreme range from Henderson Field found the enemy ships off northern New Georgia in fading daylight shortly after a flight of escorting Zeros departed. A fierce dive bombing attack followed, but Tanaka's force escaped undamaged and downed one attacker in the process.

Only five PT boats were available at Tulagi to attempt an ambush of this run of the Tokyo Express. All boats were in position by midnight after leaving base during the early evening hours.[145] Two additional boats were already lying off Kamimbo Bay near the western end of Guadalcanal, sent out by an intelligence report indicating another Japanese submarine was expected to surface in the area during the night.[146]

Using a battle plan similar to the one employed on December 7, a strike force was lying in wait off the southeast coast of Savo Island. This position kept the group out of sight of the approaching Japanese. The force numbered three boats: Lester Gamble in *PT-37*, Stilly Taylor in *PT-40*, and in *PT-48* executive officer Lieutenant (Junior Grade) Bill Kreiner was acting as boat-captain for the night. *PT-109*, with John Searles as boat captain, and a second boat acted as sentries in an attempt to locate the approaching enemy. Clear weather conditions promised good visibility on the moonless night.

Japanese lookouts with night binoculars spotted the PT boats to the south shortly after the destroyers slipped past Savo Island. Tanaka ordered two of his escorts positioned on the formation's flank to engage. Destroyers *Kawakaze* and *Suzukaze* immediately moved to take the small boats under fire. At about the same time the admiral directed the transport destroyers to proceed directly to the drop-off point near Cape Esperance.[147]

At 12:35 a.m. *PT-109* was the first PT boat to spot the approaching destroyers. Searles quickly dispatched a radio message to alert the other boats.[148] His initial contact report placed the enemy ships five miles north on a point midway between Cape Esperance and Savo Island. In a second transmission Searles reported, "Caesar passing through Rye." It was a coded message indicating the enemy ships were passing through the Esperance-Savo passage.[149] Searles then maneuvered for a torpedo run, but was stopped short of the target when *PT-109* was fired on by an unseen vessel. He abandoned the attack and gave the order for smoke.

Smoke was produced from a canister mounted to the PT's deck at the very back of the fantail. The quick unleashing of a thick cloud could mean the difference between life and death for a torpedo boat under fire by an angry Japanese destroyer. The pressurized steel bottle with a valve on one end contained thirty-two gallons of titanium tetrachloride.[150] A crewman gave the valve three full turns on Searles' order. As the gas released into the atmosphere it developed into a thick fog that grew larger as the boat continued to speed forward.

The 109 lost the attacking destroyer under the cover of the smoke screen. Minutes later Searles tried another torpedo run, but was again unsuccessful. The boat did not attempt any additional attacks during the battle.

Hiding near Savo Island, the three boats of the strike force lost visual contact with each other as they waited for the enemy to arrive. After sighting what looked to be at least five destroyers, the force moved forward, idling at ten knots in an attempt to gain a favorable attack position. The low speed was needed to prevent phosphorescent wakes from giving away the boats' positions in the critical minutes leading up to the final attack run. The PT's increased speed once close to the targets to make independent torpedo runs. Each boat fired a full spread of torpedoes in rapid succession and then turned away to head back to their protected hiding spot off Savo.[151]

The airwaves erupted with the sounds of men in battle as the boats attacked. "Enemy destroyers . . . at least six, seven, eight, nine of them," went one sighting report. "Hurry! Hurry! William is on our tail," exclaimed one boat captain being chased by an enemy destroyer.[152]

An American torpedo was speeding directly towards the Japanese flagship as the PT's fled to safety. The underwater missiles soon crashed into the port side of *Teruzuki*. The detonation caused a geyser of water to shoot up from the side of the destroyer that seemed to the PT men to go as high as the volcano peak on Savo Island. Although Gamble, Taylor, and Kreiner all claimed hits, it is unknown which boat actually fired the scoring torpedo.[153] It is known the torpedo struck near the after part of the warship with a terrific explosion. The force of the blast knocked Admiral Tanaka to the floor of the bridge rendering him unconscious. The detonation caused extensive damage, knocking off one propeller shaft, separating the rudder from the hull, and damaging the engines.

The situation for *Teruzuki* quickly worsened. The destroyer lost power and became un-navigable. Leaking fuel oil soon caught fire, turning the sea around the stricken ship into a mass of flames.[154]

The radio reports of the battle prompted two additional torpedo boats to join the fight shortly after the explosion rocked the Japanese destroyer. *PT-44* captained by Frank Freeland and *PT-110* with Charles Tilden aboard as boat captain had been patrolling the rough waters off Kamimbo Bay waiting for an enemy submarine. With nothing happening in their assigned area the two decided to head for the action after hearing the chatter from the strike force over the airwaves.

Passing around the end of Guadalcanal into Iron Bottom Sound brought the two boats into direct contact with the Japanese force. Aboard *PT-44* Lieutenant (Junior Grade) Charles Melhorn was riding along as an observer. He saw a fleeting glimpse off the port side of a distant destroyer firing at an unknown target. Straining his eyes, he was unable to get a firm location on the enemy vessel. Just then the quartermaster yelled out, "Destroyer on starboard bow. There's your target, captain."[155]

Peering through a set of binoculars, Melhorn saw two destroyers in a column about 8,000 yards off the starboard bow. The enemy was on a south to southwest heading and moving fast. The two enemy ships did not seem to have noticed the PT boat. Freeland angled the boat to close for an attack.

As the PT passed near *Teruzuki*, Melhorn became concerned that the burning ship would perfectly silhouette the boat making her a target for other destroyers. Just then another enemy warship was sighted just as she began to open fire on the torpedo boat. Freeland turned *PT-44* hard to the right, increased speed, and began laying smoke, possibly with the intent of moving to a hiding place near Savo Island. The gunfire subsided when Japanese gunners lost track of the PT in the smoke.

Melhon's earlier concern became a reality a short time later when Freeland turned to make another run at the destroyers. As the boat came out of her turn she was taken under heavy fire by a previously unseen destroyer hidden in the darkness only a few thousand yards away. It was likely either *Kawakaze* or *Suzukaze*, both of whom many have been aided by the light of the flaming *Teruzuki*.[156] Each time one of the destroyer's five-inch guns fired, a fifty-pound projectile came screaming through the darkness towards the small boat.[157]

With the close range and intensity of fire it was only a matter of time before the Japanese gunners found the PT boat. One shell scored a direct hit crashing into the boat's engine room near the back of the ship. From his position near the cockpit, Melhorn knew the ship was done. "I looked back and saw a gaping hole in what was once the engine room canopy," he recalled. "The perimeter of the hole in the canopy was ringed by little tongues of flame. I looked down into the water and saw we had practically lost way."

Freeland gave the order to abandon ship before jumping out of the cockpit. He headed towards the back of the boat with several others to get a small raft. Melhorn stayed near the conn and jumped over the side after realizing the Japanese guns were still blazing away.

He escaped death by the narrowest of margins as more enemy shells rained down on *PT-44*. "I dove deep and was still underwater when the salvo struck," he recalled. "The concussion jarred me badly, but I kept swimming under water." Just then he felt a tremendous explosion and saw the water around him turn red. "The life jacket took control and pulled me to the surface. I came up in a sea of fire, the flaming embers of the boat cascading all about me." Melhorn was unable to slip out of the life jacket and was struggling to swim away from the burning sea. However, water from the explosion rose into the air and came collapsing down squelching out most of the fires in his immediate area.

Only a few clusters of flames remained about fifteen yards away. After taking some strokes away from the fire, Melhorn faintly saw what looked like two heads in the water close to the burning remnants of the PT boat. He was concerned about the Japanese turning machine guns on any survivors found in the water and called out to them. "I told them to get clear of the reflection of the fire as quickly as possible and proceeded to do so myself," he later said. Unable to find any other survivors, Melhorn swam away from the remains of the boat and eventually made it to Savo Island.

––––––––

Rear Admiral Tanaka regained consciousness to find *Naganami* alongside *Teruzuki*. At 1:33 a.m. the wounded admiral and his staff transferred off the doomed flagship. He was treated for shoulder and hip injuries shortly after going aboard the new ship. The medical staff then ordered him to stay in bed and rest, but not before he radioed a message notifying headquarters that his flag shifted to *Naganami*. He purposefully omitted any mention of his injuries out of concern for the morale of his sailors.[158]

While the escorts were busy battling PT boats, the transport destroyers successfully off loaded 1,200 supply drums near Cape Esperance. No sooner were the canisters in the water when motorized landing craft began to pull the ropes holding together the clusters of drums. With the main portion of the mission accomplished, the destroyers began to pull out.

In spite of heroic work by damage control crews, the attempt to save *Teruzuki* failed. At 4:40 a.m. flames reached the depth charge magazine causing a tremendous explosion that began the process of sending the warship sinking into the depths of Iron Bottom Sound.[159] One hundred and thirty-eight survivors had earlier been taken aboard *Arashi* and *Naganami*.[160] Both destroyers pulled away from the stricken vessel to deal with PT boats, but dropped life boats for the remaining survivors before their hasty departure.

The rescue operation was later abandoned due to the urgent need to get the remaining destroyers out of the area. The Japanese needed to be far north by daylight or risk a scathing attack by American aircraft. The unrescued survivors consisted of seventeen officers and 139 enlisted men and included the ship's captain. They confirmed the ship went down before departing in lifeboats, eventually making landfall on the Japanese-held area of Guadalcanal.

Nine Japanese destroyers made flank speed for the Slot and were back in Shortland by mid-morning. *Arashi* arrived later in the day after returning via an alternate route with her load of *Teruzuki* survivors. No air attacks were made on any of the fleeing warships.

———

John Searles and *PT-109* continued to patrol the waters off Guadalcanal after the action subsided. At 3:35 a.m. he came across a man in the water, and Lyle Dowling of *PT-44* was pulled aboard to safety. The fireman told his rescuers how he jumped off the stricken boat moments before a massive explosion sank her. Searles radioed word of the rescue back to Tulagi. "We have just picked up a fireman off Frank Freeland's boat," he reported. "There may be other survivors out here. Better come out and look around."[161]

The crew of the 109 learned the details of what happened to *PT-44* through Dowling's firsthand account. Bryant Larson listened intently. "The first salvo from the destroyer hit the engine compartment and stopped the boat," he later explained. "While they tried to save the boat the second salvo hit the gas tanks. There were only two survivors."[162] *PT-109* proceeded to Tulagi after finding no additional survivors. She returned to sea after dropping Dowling off at Government Landing at 5:10 a.m.

Stilly Taylor took *PT-40* around Iron Bottom Sound to see if he could locate any survivors. He sighted *PT-109* as he plied the area between Savo

Island and Guadalcanal. The water was littered with the splintered remains of Frank Freeland's boat. The 40 boat pulled aboard three dead American sailors, all from *PT-44*.

Taylor decided to search along the Savo coast as dawn was breaking, hoping other survivors might have made it to the area. His hunch proved to be a good one when movement was sighted on the shoreline followed by words in English coming from near the beach. A small rubber boat was dispatched and returned with Charles Melhorn. Dowling and Melhorn were the only survivors of *PT-44*.

The work day was not yet over for John Searles and his crew aboard *PT-109*. Earlier in the night *PT-61* had run aground on Pig Rock Reef near Kamimbo Bay. It was a precarious position only a short distance off the Japanese-held portion of the island. Searles took his boat to investigate. The stranded PT was later pulled off by patrol craft *PC-476*.[163]

The 109 came across four Japanese sailors just after 6:00 a.m., presumably *Teruzuki* survivors, bobbing in the water. Three were pulled aboard, but the fourth stubbornly refused rescue. An officer on the boat then drew a pistol and began to use carefully placed bullets fired just ahead of the swimmer to force him towards the boat. The tactic was close to succeeding when a sailor emerged from the engine room and killed the Japanese man with a single rifle shot. Hearing the noise the machinist's mate wrongly concluded the officer firing the pistol was a lousy aim and decided to finish the job.[164] The three prisoners were later turned over to a marine guard at Government Landing.

The action for *PT-109* ended when she pulled up to *Jamestown* for refueling during the early afternoon. At 6:00 p.m. the boat moored alongside the pier at Government Landing. Not scheduled for a patrol, she remained at the location overnight. It was a peaceful ending to a long day full of action.

————

Both sides reflected on the outcome of the battle over the next few days. Although all of the drums were successfully discharged by his destroyers, the supply operation was a personal defeat for Admiral Tanaka. "The loss of my flagship, our newest and best destroyer, to such inferior enemy strength was a serious responsibility," he wrote after the war. "I have often thought that it would have been easier for me to have been killed in that first explosion."[165]

The pain of the admiral's physical injuries was supplemented by anguish when he learned only 220 of the drums were recovered by army troops ashore. American gunfire from the sea and air contributed to the dismal recovery rate. Tanaka then learned the Tokyo Express runs to Guadalcanal were being temporarily suspended due to the onset of moonlit nights. The December 11 operation was the last one conducted in 1942. His destroyers were ordered to leave Shortland and move further north to Rabaul where they would be available for other operations.

Back at Tulagi the PT sailors viewed the December 11 battle as a success. They had no way of knowing only a meager amount of supplies actually made into the hands of Japanese troops ashore, but suspected their attack had frustrated the enemy's operation. The boat captains correctly concluded one destroyer had gone to the bottom. Although the demise of enemy warships was reported on two previous occasions, *Teruzuki* was actually the first heavy surface ship to be sunk by torpedo boats in the battle for Guadalcanal.

The thrill of victory was tamed by the loss of *PT-44*. It weighed heavily on the minds of the PT men. Two officers and seven enlisted men perished with the boat. The sinking underscored the fears felt by every torpedo boat sailor and served as a reminder of what could happen during any night battle.

The PT sailors knew it was not a fair fight. Although the torpedo boats were one of the most heavily armed American naval vessels of World War II when considered on a pound for pound basis, they were no match for a destroyer.[166] The majority of Japanese destroyers deployed in the Guadalcanal fighting displaced between 1,500 and 2,000 tons, measured well over 300 feet in length, and could attain top speeds of over thirty knots.[167] Aside from torpedoes, which were of no use against the shallow draft torpedo boats, five-inch guns were the warship's main armament.[168] A PT boat could be blasted to pieces with a single hit. Secondary armament included thirteen millimeter heavy machines guns and other anti-aircraft weapons easily capable of piercing holes in the torpedo boats' wooden hulls.

For Bryant Larson it was not only the sinking of a boat, but the loss of a friend as well. John Chester was *PT-44's* executive officer and did not survive the ordeal. Larson's acquaintance from Midshipman's school in Chicago made the long voyage to the South Pacific aboard the 109 and had transferred to the 44 boat only a few weeks ago.

Larson not only had to come to grips with the loss, but also to try to understand what happened in case he ever found himself in a similar situation. "For some reason, Frank [Freeland] chose a high speed attack, leaving behind the boat a tremendous phosphorescent wake that was like a searchlight pointing to the boat. He never had a chance," he later wrote. "From the 44 we learned two lessons—don't make a high speed night attack, and if you are hit, under fire, and dead in the water, get all hands off the boat before another salvo blows everyone to hell." Larson likened it to bailing out of a plane while there was still enough altitude for a parachute to work. The knowledge of what to do in such a situation would later be of great benefit to *PT-109's* crew.

The three week hiatus from Tokyo Express runs at the end of December gave the PT sailors a much needed break from the hectic pace of operations. The debriefings, refueling, and rearming that typically followed a night patrol usually resulted in limited time available for sleeping. The constant cycle brought strain, hardship, and illness.

Battles only made matters worse, causing the nerves of even the most hardened combat veterans to become frazzled. The thunderous booms and flashes of gunfire coupled with the sinister glare of Japanese searchlights was enough to shake even the steadiest of crews.[169] Death always seemed to be lurking just around the corner. Equally as worrisome as perishing in combat was the prospect of being taken prisoner. A year into the war it was well known that captives of the Japanese were treated badly, if kept alive at all.

Nightly patrols continued through the lull, but with no destroyers to battle the PT boats lurked close to the Guadalcanal shoreline looking for Japanese barges and submarines. To address the growing fatigue situation the rotation of crewmen among operational boats was increased to provide as many weary sailors as possible a night of much needed rest.[170]

More help for the PT men arrived on December 15 when the first Black Cat landed at Henderson Field on Guadalcanal. A radar-equipped version of the PBY flying boat modified for night operations, the name seemed appropriate to match the overall black paint scheme. The slow amphibians were prone to enemy fighters and anti-aircraft fire during daylight hours, but the planes proved to be ideal for night operations. Trailing Japanese ships, scouting for PT boats, and spotting for night bombardments soon became regular fare for the night operators. There were nine operational planes based at Guadalcanal by the end of the month.[171]

The first four Elco 80-foot boats of Squadron Six arrived in Tulagi on December 31.[172] The new additions bolstered the number of available PT's in time for the next series of enemy operations that would begin shortly after the start of the New Year.

The lull in action did not mean *PT-109* sat idle throughout the last half of December. The boat undertook two tests during this time in the hopes of finding a better way to locate and track enemy destroyers at night. The first experiment explored the feasibility of using Savo Island as an observation point. "One morning I went ashore on Savo with three or four others to hike to the top of the island where we set up an observation post, hoping to be able to visually spot the express on the way in order to concentrate maximum PT strength via radio instructions." Bryant Larson remembered. Unfortunately the visibility did not live up to expectations. "No luck, but an interesting try."

The second test was far more sophisticated. "The next idea was radar for the PT's. At that time radar was developing fast, but not yet ready for us," Larson wrote. On December 18 base workers began a four day process of installing radar on the 109. "So we took the antenna that hung from the wings of a radar equipped plane [and] mounted them upright on the bow of the 109 . . ." The equipment was not pilfered from a plane in working order, but was salvaged from a wrecked PBY.

Finally on the afternoon of December 22 the boat went out for a short test run with the new equipment. "Test of radar satisfactory," Larson recorded in the deck log.[173] Unlike typical radar sets used on heaver warships that rotated to scan the full horizon, the set used on *PT-109* was only able to look straight ahead. In subsequent use the radar did not perform well. Larson remembered using it to try to locate an enemy warship near Savo Island. "It was a dark and squally night. The express ran right past us undetected. Another interesting try, and again no luck." Plagued by regular power supply problems and frequent break downs, the radar was later removed.[174]

With the experiments over, the 109 resumed frequent night patrols at the end of the month. With no action taking place at sea, the boat captains often looked to land. "For quite some time I had prowled close to the Japanese-held coast at dawn," Westholm recalled. "These were mornings after uneventful nights on patrol. We were looking for piles of supplies, including ammunition, as well as barges not too well hidden in the bushes near shore. If we saw a likely target we opened fire."[175]

Near the end of a patrol during the morning hours of December 26, lookouts aboard *PT-109* sighted what appeared to be a camouflaged landing barge on a Guadalcanal beach southeast of Cape Esperance. Crewmen were already manning the guns when Westholm gave the order to open fire.

Each time the Browning fifty-caliber machine guns rattled, the twin air-cooled barrels spit out rounds at a rate of 550 per minute. The belt-fed strings of bullets often included tracer rounds at regular intervals to help the gunner's aim. The single barrel Oerlikon twenty-millimeter cannon packed a greater punch and could send a small shell up to 5,500 yards.[176] The weapon was fed by a sixty-round magazine mounted on top of the gun. A bag below the barrel collected the spent cartridges.

Minutes after opening fire more targets were found and the guns aimed at two additional barges and a pile of stores. The shooting ended ten minutes later when fires broke out on all the targets. The 109 left the area and by 8:00 a.m. she was moored alongside *Jamestown* at Tulagi.[177]

The short fight was typical of actions PT boats took to prevent the Japanese Army from getting supplies. "We set quite a few on fire," Westholm recalled of the shore targets. "Once in a while we hit an ammo stockpile which made quite an explosion." Such missions were not without risk for the PT men. "As soon as they returned the fire, we poured on the gas and got away in a hurry," Westholm continued. "While we were hit by their machine gun fire a number of times, we suffered no personnel casualties, only holes in our boat, including the upper part of our gas tank."

The barge bombardment was the last substantial action undertaken by *PT-109* in 1942. The final day of the year found the boat pulling out of Tulagi just before 7:00 p.m. for a routine night patrol. Westholm manned the conn with Bryant Larson along as second in command. The calendar silently turned to 1943 as the 109 roamed the waters of Iron Bottom Sound. The two officers may have been wondering what the New Year would bring for themselves and their boat. "Then came early January and more dark of the moon nights," Larson recalled. The conditions virtually guaranteed that more action was on the horizon.

CHAPTER 8

JANUARY SURVIVAL

E ven as the Japanese were slowly losing their grip on Guadalcanal, it was still necessary for the Imperial Navy to deliver supplies to the beleaguered island garrison in an effort to prevent the further erosion of fighting power. With moon conditions set to turn favorable in early January, the Tokyo Express was getting ready to resume operations.

Although achieving only mixed results thus far, the drum method remained the only viable supply delivery option. A host of changes were implemented during the first weeks of January to help improve the prospects for success. Kapok material normally used in lifejackets was wrapped around each drum to help keep it afloat even if strafed by machine gun fire. Army officers discharged from the destroyers into small landing boats were given the responsibility of ensuring the rope lines were properly handed over to men ashore who could then pull the drums to safety.

Japanese naval leaders assumed small boats would continue to be their main opposition at sea and added a pair of enhancements to help ward off the PT's. First, escort destroyers were fitted with extra thirteen millimeter machine guns for close defense and to bolster anti-aircraft protection. The second improvement proved to be far more successful over the long term. Float planes were made available to serve as scouts over the Guadalcanal area to provide advanced warnings as to the location and composition of the torpedo boats.[178]

Admiral Tanaka's destroyers were again moved forward to the advance base near Shortland Island as a final step in preparation for the resumption of supply operations. Tanaka, however, would not be staying in the area much longer as he received orders to transfer to the Naval General Staff. He departed for Tokyo on December 29 after welcoming his replacement, Rear Admiral Tomiji Koyanagi.[179]

The first Tokyo Express run of 1943 was set to go on January 2. Koyanagi led a force of ten destroyers down the Slot. The group was equally divided between escorts and transports, with the latter carrying drums of food and ammunition.

The force was initially sighted by accident when a small group of B-17 bombers en route to another target stumbled on Koyanagi's ships and attacked. The high altitude bombing was ineffective and the destroyers emerged unscathed, but the alarm was sounded that Japanese ships were on the move. A larger group of dive bombers and fighters attacked almost four hours later just as darkness was falling. Koyanagi's gunners shot down three planes, but not before *Suzukaze* sustained damage from a near miss. She turned back, taking one healthy destroyer with her as an escort. Three float planes moved into position to scout the area ahead as the remaining eight destroyers pressed on towards Guadalcanal.

As the Tokyo Express was bearing down the Slot, *PT-109* pulled out of Tulagi at 8:15 p.m. for night patrol with Rollin Westholm at the conn. Just before midnight a Japanese float plane suddenly appeared out of the darkness dropping two bombs. Both missed off the boat's port beam. Five minutes later the boat came under fire by Japanese destroyers off the port quarter and briefly retired under smoke.

Westholm resumed patrol a short time later. He regained contact with the enemy one minute before midnight. The sighting touched off a string of events that happened in rapid succession over the next ten minutes. "Sighted enemy ship, swung left to make torpedo run," Bryant Larson recorded in the deck log.[180]

It was an opportunity for *PT-109* to fire her main armament of four Mark Eight Model Three torpedoes. Each underwater missile was just over twenty feet in length with a twenty-one inch diameter. The warhead was packed with an explosive charge of 466 pounds of TNT. A range of up to 16,000 yards was obtainable at a normal speed of twenty-six knots.[181] Each of the four torpedo tubes on *PT-109* was moveable and had to be hand cranked outboard before firing.

When Westholm gave the order to fire a torpedo, he raised his arm each time he pressed a firing button on the dashboard in the cockpit. A black powder impulse charge located at the rear of each tube then triggered electronically to actually shoot out the torpedo. Since the system was prone to malfunctioning, Torpedoman's Mate Second Class Claude Dollar was stationed near the after port side tube (always the first to fire) with a mallet. Following Westholm's visual signal, he gave the firing pin on top of the torpedo tube a good whack. The hit set off the powder charge manually to ensure to torpedo still fired even if the electronic system failed.

Closing on the target, the boat fired two torpedoes. Both appeared to make normal runs. "Observed target turn toward boat, torpedoes passed ahead of target," Larson recorded of the action. Just then another destroyer opened fire off the port quarter. Westholm again gave the order to make smoke and retired towards Savo Island.

Minutes after the torpedoes left the boat an enemy plane swooped out of the darkness with machine guns firing. The bullets fell short of the 109, landing harmlessly in her wake. Westholm then guided his boat to a position east of Savo Island marking the end of action for the night. Finding no more targets, *PT-109* set a course for Tulagi just after 1:30 a.m.

Westholm's boat was one of eleven PT's on hand to meet Admiral Koyanagi upon his arrival in the Guadalcanal area. The boats, however, were harassed from the air and made limited contact with the destroyers, resulting in a short engagement. One boat claimed to have hit a destroyer, but post war reports revealed no Japanese ships were damaged in the encounter.

The Japanese supply mission was a success. Koyanagi's ships discharged their cargo and departed the area with few problems. PT boats managed to machine gun some of the drums on the beach the next morning, but army officials on Guadalcanal happily reported recovering 540 drums and 250 rubber bags filled with provisions. It was enough supplies to cover five days.[182]

The use of float planes proved to be a great success in helping the Japanese combat the PT boats. The overhead observers were able to easily spot the boat wakes at distances of up to four miles. The pilots could plunge down out of the darkness from behind to drop bombs and strafe the boats with machine gun fire. The planes found an increasing role in battling PT boats in future operations.

A relative calm lasting five days settled over the Tulagi PT base after the first encounter with the Tokyo Express in 1943. Returning from the battle during the early hours of January 3, *PT-109* moored near Sesapi at 3:00 a.m. After time for the crew to unwind, she shifted berths to Macambo Island to take aboard two torpedoes. A couple of hours later she was back at Sesapi.

The 109 left Tulagi for a night patrol late in the day on January 8 with Rollin Westholm in command. After an uneventful evening the boat was directed at about dawn to an area west of Savo Island to search for a missing pilot. Finding no sign of the downed aviator, she returned to her patrol station at 7:30 a.m. Forty-five minutes later she opened fire on Japanese supplies on the beach. Her guns destroyed the stores, but not before she took return fire from shore. The boat returned to Tulagi when the brief action ended.[183]

Although the next Tokyo Express run was in the planning stages, Admiral Koyanagi ordered a short pause to allow for adjustments to the composition of the Reinforcement Unit. Three battle scarred veterans of Guadalcanal operations, the destroyers *Naganami*, *Kagero*, and *Oyashio*, were deemed unfit due to various machinery problems and transferred out. Two older destroyers initially arrived as replacements, but were supplemented by two new destroyers proceeding directly to Shortland from the large Japanese fleet base at Truk.[184]

On the night of January 4–5 an American force of cruisers and destroyers moved up the Slot to conduct a surprise bombardment of the Japanese airfield at Munda on New Georgia. The operation, coupled with the sighting of a large task force further south containing battleships, cruisers, and destroyers, led Japanese naval commanders to conclude a large American naval operation was about to begin in the Solomons.[185] Although false, the scare prompted orders to quickly proceed with the next supply operation, even before some of the new destroyers arrived. The mission was scheduled for January 10.

The Japanese took extra precautions to account for the possibility of a surface battle with heavy ships. Additional air patrols were planned to sweep the waters east and west of the debarkation point looking for enemy warships. The force was equally divided between escorts and transports with the latter carrying a reduced number of drums to allow for more torpedoes.

Admiral Koyanagi briefed his destroyer captains on January 9 and departed Shortland during the early afternoon of the following day. Flying his flag in *Kuroshio*, the admiral was taking eight destroyers south. Zero fighters provided an escort through the Slot until sundown, but no enemy planes appeared. Although a coastwatcher on New Georgia sounded the Tokyo Express alarm, it was too late to get planes up the Slot in time for an air attack. It would be up to PT boats to battle the destroyers in Iron Bottom Sound.

The evening of January 10 brought poor weather conditions to the

Guadalcanal area. The night was cloudy with intermittent rains squalls. Visibility was judged fair to poor.

Four PT boats were scheduled to go out on night patrol to prowl the passageway between Cape Esperance and Savo Island. Experience had thus far shown that two boats operating in tandem were the ideal number for a routine patrol.[186] An imaginary line was drawn from Morovovo, a coastal village west of Cape Esperance, to the west side of Savo Island. Patrolling west of the line was Lester Gamble in *PT-45* and Lieutenant (Junior Grade) Ralph Amsden, Jr. in *PT-39*. East of the line was Robert Searles in *PT-48* and Ensign Bartholomew Connolly in *PT-115*. The latter Elco 80-foot boat had arrived in Tulagi just two weeks earlier. Both patrol groups were on station well before the Japanese arrived.

The situation at the PT base drastically changed when word arrived of the Tokyo Express on the way. The warning came directly to Rollin Westholm in the form of a telephone call from flotilla leader Allen Calvert. "Eight enemy DD's expected to arrive in area at 1:00 a.m., 10 January," Westholm was told.[187] He immediately ordered six additional boats to get underway.

The information on the composition of the Japanese force and its estimated arrival time was accurate enough for Westholm to quickly formulate a battle plan. The two patrol groups already out were to act as scouts. The additional boats would attack once the enemy was located.

The extra boats were evenly divided to form two separate strike groups. Westholm planned to lead one group in *PT-109*. However, the boat's engines failed to start. With no time to waste the squadron commander and crew jumped into nearby *PT-112*, which was not scheduled for a voyage that night. An identical sister boat, the 112 would serve as Westholm's temporary flagship for the evening.[188]

A little bit of extra luck was riding with Bryant Larson as the boat ventured to the patrol area. "As we headed for the hot spot, our torpedoman [Claude Dollar] came to the bridge and handed me what he said was a lucky bean given to him that day by some native," Larson recalled. "He asked me to hold on to it as we might need some special luck that night. How right he was!"

Westholm's strike group included Lieutenant Clark Faulkner in *PT-40* and Charles Tilden in *PT-43*. Faulkner was the commanding officer of the newly arrived Squadron Six. Westholm led his boats to an area off the far western end of Guadalcanal between Aruligo and Cape Esperance with a specific strategy in mind. "The plan was to creep along between shore and the reef, very close to shore and as quietly as possible, making it almost impossible for the ships to see us," he later recalled.[189] He hoped the move would allow his boats to take the Japanese by surprise.

The second strike group was comprised of all veteran boat captains—John Searles in *PT-59*, Stilly Taylor in *PT-46*, and Marvin Pettit in *PT-36*. The boats went to a patrol area off the Guadalcanal coast between Doma Reef and Tassafaronga.

Tension aboard the PT's was thick as the boats patrolled in Iron Bottom Sound. The scuttlebutt at the squadron office earlier in the evening had the Japanese trying something new against the torpedo boats.[190] The rumors only added to the normal tension of a night patrol.

Frequent cloudbursts resulted in drenching downpours causing obscured visibility. The poor weather made the sky, horizon, and ocean blend together forming a continuous wall as dark as black ink.

The experiences of crewmen aboard *PT-45* were typical of those encountered by sailors all around Iron Bottom Sound during the night. Chief Quartermaster James Meadows wiped water away from his eyes as he stood at the conn. "It don't look so good skipper," he told boat captain Gamble.[191] Waves were lapping up against the side of the boat, occasionally throwing water as high as the windshield and on deck under the torpedo tubes. Looking forward he could only see figures crouched on deck near the front of the ship. The obscure forms were lookouts straining to see though the mist searching for any sign of the enemy.

The conditions were not good for the PT men, but were more than ideal for hiding a group of destroyers. The foul weather extended up the Solomons chain grounding the extra Japanese reconnaissance planes scheduled to make the trip south. When Admiral Koyanagi made his final approach to Guadalcanal, it was without any knowledge of the enemy's disposition. The admiral had no way of knowing if he would encounter torpedo boats, heavy American warships, or both, as he tried to carry out his mission.

Embedded in the thick mist, Koyanagi's force followed the weather front down to Guadalcanal. His destroyers moved through the Guadalcanal–Savo Island gap completely undetected with neither of the two PT scout patrols making any contact. Proceeding directly towards the drop off point, however, Koyanagi ran right into Westholm's strike group.

The three boats of Westholm's force were moving slowly in an easterly direction about a quarter of a mile off the coast. The squadron commander himself sighted the approaching enemy at 12:37 a.m. In the hazy distance he could see four ships in a column heading in a southerly direction. The destroyers were about one mile off shore between Aruligo and Cape Esperance. The speed of the destroyers started to slow as Westholm carefully watched. The last ship in the column suddenly turned northeast in the direction of Savo Island while the remaining three stayed on course presenting an inviting target. The ideal surprise attack set-up Westholm had hoped for instantly became a reality with the torpedo boats hidden against the dark background of the island and the destroyers seaward. There were several small fires burning ashore, possibly set as guide markers for the supply drop, but the flames had no effect on revealing the PT boat positions.

After tracking the destroyers for ten minutes and seeing the almost perfect set-up appear before his eyes, Westholm was ready to give the order to attack. However, his transmission was disrupted when a Black Cat pilot using the same radio frequency as the PT's clogged the airwaves trying to find out what was happening below. "I quickly told him and asked him to keep off the air," Westholm remembered. "He came back again asking what I had said. I am afraid I swore at him telling him to get off his radio."

After a few minutes of verbally sparring with the pilot, Westholm was finally able to get his order out. "Deploy to the right and make them good," he cracked over the radio.[192] "Unfortunately during this interruption, the four [destroyers] had started turning towards us to get a little closer to the beach," he continued. "We had to run further west than I had intended in order to get fairly good targets. We all opened our mufflers [and] turned right at top speed." The turn put Westholm's boat last in the formation.

The first boat to attack was *PT-43* with Charles Tilden taking aim at the lead destroyer in the column. He fired two torpedoes after speeding to within 400 yards of the target. Flotilla leader Allen Calvert explained what happened next. "There was a terrific crimson flash from his after port tube. It may have been an imperfect impulse charge of too much oil in the tube." Both torpedoes either missed entirely or failed to explode.

What befell Tilden was every boat captain's nightmare: having his location unexpectedly revealed at close range to a Japanese destroyer. He turned the boat hard right and opened the throttles to gain speed in an attempt to escape, but Japanese gunners quickly opened fire with main battery guns. The first salvo landed close aboard, but the second scored a direct hit. The explosion rocked the boat knocking most crewmen off their feet.

When Tilden regained his footing he could see the boat was quickly losing speed and the destroyer was closing fast. Realizing the chances of saving the boat were slim, he gave the order to abandon ship and then jumped overboard a short time later. Once overboard Tilden saw machine gun fire splashing in the water around both himself and the doomed boat. The destroyer passed so close that survivors bobbing in the water could hear Japanese sailors talking on deck.

Next behind Tilden's boat, Clark Faulkner in *PT-40* took aim at the second Japanese destroyer in column. He fired all four torpedoes before making a hard right turn and then poured on speed to start his getaway. "He watched his after port torpedo hit solidly shooting a column of water into the air," Calvert reported. "A moment later there was a second explosion at the same target." Faulkner brought his boat close to the shoreline and followed the Guadalcanal coast southeast through reef infested waters believing no destroyers would follow. His gambit worked as no Japanese warships ventured after him and the PT boat luckily did not hit any reefs.[193]

Conning the last boat in the strike force, Rollin Westholm in *PT-112* was eyeing the third destroyer. "Westy gave the command to close and fire," Bryant Larson remembered. "I took the 112 to point blank range (perhaps too close, for a torpedo needed 300 yards to arm itself) and fired all four torpedoes." All of the weapons appeared to run straight and normal. One torpedo was seen to hit sending a geyser of water sprouting high into the air. "I observed one good-sized explosion," Westholm recalled of the detonation.

Unknown to Westholm and Larson, other enemy warships were lurking in the distance at that very moment. "I had intended that after firing we would turn and at top speed go out the channel through which we had come in," Westholm remembered. Two destroyers then suddenly appeared off the port bow. Larson later speculated how the enemy found his boat. "Up to that point we were undetected—but there was a flash from the tubes as we fired and the destroyers opened up on us."

With the boat dangerously close to several destroyers, the only hope of escape was for the PT to use its speed advantage. "I pushed the engines to full speed and tried to run between two of the destroyers, the only possible escape route." Westholm ordered the boat angled to the left in hopes of passing astern of the closest warship. He hoped to make passage to safer waters once safely beyond the vessel.

A previously unseen destroyer in the vicinity of Savo Island opened fire with main battery guns just as *PT-112* turned east. "Before we could get up to speed, a shell or shells hit the engine compartment at the waterline setting it afire and stopping all engines," Larson explained. It is believed that two large shells, possibly from different ships, hit almost simultaneously. One struck the port side amidships at the waterline and the other hit near the forward bulkhead of the engine room.

The engine compartment and fuel tanks immediately caught fire. Motor Machinist Mate First Class Clayton Craig showed great courage in subduing the fire in the engine room, but suffered severe burns in the process. "He pulled the CO2 extinguisher system and the fire went out (almost)," Larson remembered. Claude Dollar suffered shrapnel wounds in the leg and was the only other sailor to sustain injuries.

Westholm now had to make some quick decisions. "We got everyone up on the bow, including our two injured men," he remembered. "After first thinking the CO2 had put out the fire, we again saw flames." More fire meant a devastating explosion could happen at any moment. Seeing the Japanese guns were still firing, Westholm concluded the chances of saving the boat were not favorable and decided not to tempt fate any longer. "With no more CO2 I ordered the boat be abandoned."

Westholm took off his shoes and directed the small life raft be tossed over the side before leaving the boat himself. The entire crew was miraculously able to safely get off the doomed PT with Craig and Westholm the last two to depart. "In the water we put our two injured men on the raft and the rest of us swam pushing the raft away from the boat to avoid enemy shells," Westholm recalled. "We had bound up the wounds of our injured to keep blood out of the water. We also kept our black socks on so as not to attract sharks." Apparently convinced the PT boat was finished, the Japanese gunfire soon subsided.

Larson thought back to what he learned from the previous battle. "From the lesson of the 44 boat, we abandoned ship at once, hoping to get in the water before the next salvo finished the boat and us," he recalled. "As we were in the water, the Japs turned a searchlight on the boat and surrounding water, saw the boat dead in the water and down at the stern (sinking), [and] held their fire and left the scene."[194] It might have been good fortune or the intervention of the lucky bean.

The sailors, however, were not able to stay together for long. "When the searchlight came on we scattered, expecting more gunfire," Larson continued. Other than battling to survive in the water, the fighting for the night was over for the crew of *PT-112*. For the remaining PT boats, though, the sea battle continued.

Only one boat from the second strike group found the enemy. Stilly Taylor came from the east in *PT-46* and spotted a destroyer heading towards Savo Island at slow speed. He closed to 2,000 yards and fired all four torpedoes. Three ran true, but one remained stuck part way in the tube. A crewman reported two possible hits after observing flashes near the target.

Moving in from the western patrol area, Lester Gamble and Ralph Amsden encountered a destroyer midway between Cape Esperance and Savo Island. They closed to 2,000 yards and fired seven torpedoes combined, but were unable to observe any results. Amsden later took *PT-39* on a chase to find another target fifteen miles west of Savo Island. He discharged his final torpedo at a distance of 2,000 yards with no observed results. The remaining boats made no contact with the enemy.

As with most of the previous PT encounters with the Tokyo Express, the night battle was a confusing melee. Commander Calvert interviewed various participants to gather information for an after-action report. He concluded the torpedo boats damaged three destroyers.[195] However, post war reports revealed only one torpedo actually hit a Japanese hull. A torpedo struck the port side of *Hatsukaze* just below the ward room causing serious damage and killing eight sailors. "She is certainly in bad shape," her captain reported of the damage, thinking he had been attacked by eight torpedo boats.[196] The stricken warship was able to make a speed of sixteen knots and left the area without assistance.

Admiral Koyanagi reported his force was ambushed by PT's close to the drop off point. He claimed to have sunk three in battle, damaged a fourth, and shot down a flying boat.[197] The transport destroyers successfully slipped into the drop off point as the battle raged to discharge their cargo without incident. The admiral quickly moved his ships out of Iron Bottom Sound and set a course for the Slot. The force sighted American planes on various occasions, but were not attacked and returned safely to Shortland Island.

Although Koyanagi successfully completed his portion of the operation, not all of the supply drums made it to shore during the overnight hours. PT boats prowling the coast at dawn opened fire on the containers still in the water and reported sinking more than 250. Japanese army officials reported soldiers recovered 250 drums containing thirty tons of food, medicine, and ammunition. Several PT's remained in Iron Bottom Sound to comb the area for survivors.

———

Almost an hour had passed since the crew of *PT-112* abandoned ship. Rollin

Westholm, Clayton Craig, and Claude Dollar ended up together in the small raft. "It wasn't long before we realized that the current was pushing us toward the Japanese-held shore," Westholm remembered. "We pushed the raft to keep it from getting nearer."

Bryant Larson was among the solitary figures scattered about in the water. "I found myself alone in my life jacket, burdened by my helmet, poncho, binoculars, pistol, and code books," he recalled. "Others were in the same situation. I knew we would be picked up by PT patrols at dawn, if not before, so I made myself comfortable and waited." He later found the raft and slowly floated towards it eventually joining Westholm's small group.

The torpedo boat did not immediately sink after the sailors abandoned her. At 1:30 a.m. *PT-112* was down by the stern, but still afloat. "We noticed that there were no more signs of fire on our PT," Westholm recalled. He and his raft mates pushed toward the boat, closing to within a hundred feet. "I swam towards it to investigate. When I was nearly there, the boat suddenly blew up in front of me. It was lucky I wasn't closer because it was a big explosion and I would have been killed." The blast abruptly ended Larson's hoping of getting back on a dry deck. "So back to the water," he lamented.

It was exactly what Westholm and Larson feared could have happened with the crew still on the boat. The detonation shot flaming remnants of the PT high into the air only to come showering down in the immediate area. Soon only a small portion of the bow remained above water. The boat lingered during the remaining hours of darkness, finally sinking one mile east of Cape Esperance when daylight arrived.

Larson's hunch that rescue was not far off soon proved correct. "While still dark another PT found us and between then and early morning every one of the crew was picked up." The sailors on the raft were picked up by Ralph Amsden's *PT-39*.[198] "Once on board, I borrowed binoculars and looked around," Westholm recalled. "I was surprised to spot *PT-43* bow first on the beach with Japanese around it and climbing on board."

Although *PT-43* was badly damaged when abandoned, she did not sink. The boat was last seen by her survivors drifting east with a destroyer hovering close by. The Japanese either boarded her or she drifted ashore on her own. Westholm then spotted smoke on the horizon. It was a New Zealand corvette dispatched from Tulagi to destroy the beached PT boat. He watched intently through his binoculars as the warship opened fire. "His first salvo was a direct hit and Japanese bodies flew in all directions. A few more salvoes and the boat was on fire and a complete wreck."

It took a dedicated search by three torpedo boats to find and rescue all of *PT-112's* survivors.[199] Once back at Tulagi, Clayton Craig and Claude Dollar were transferred to the sick bay at Government Warf. The sailors of *PT-43* did not fare as well. Searching PT's fished Charles Tilden and his surviving men out of the water. Out of a crew of eleven on *PT-43*, three enlisted men perished.

In the aftermath of the battle Westholm and Larson could only speculate if their torpedoes struck home. "Did we hit anything? I don't know the answers," Larson later confessed. "I do know we got credit for one crippling hit on a destroyer." The torpedo that struck *Hatsukaze* likely came from either *PT-43* or *PT-112*.[200]

Rollin Westholm was glad to be back on land after the long night at sea and in the water. "Once ashore on Tulagi, I cleaned up a bit, took a short rest and went down to our headquarters office," he later wrote. "There I was greeted by my boss, Commander Calvert." The two officers talked about what happened the night before. Calvert apparently did not like the squadron commander's attack plan, thinking it was too risky moving so close to shore. "He chewed me out good for pulling such a dumb maneuver."

The meeting with Calvert was not the end of questioning for Westholm. "Later I received word from Government Landing that General Patch was there and wanted to see me," he continued. "He wanted to know what had happened the night before and in particular whether any troops had been landed. I said none to my knowledge." Patch thanked him for his efforts and said he hoped to be able to drive the Japanese off Guadalcanal in a few months.

———

The January 11–12 battle was a bitter pill for the Tulagi sailors. Two PT's were sunk, including the first Elco 80-foot boat to be lost in combat. The harrowing ordeal aboard *PT-112* was a close brush with death, but Rollin Westholm, Bryant Larson, and the other *PT-109* crewmen survived to fight another day. "Luck was again with us that night," Larson later wrote, knowing he had probably cheated death. "If the shells had struck less than ten feet further forward, they would have hit the gas tanks and blown us all to kingdom come."

Luck was also riding with one of Larson's old friends. "My V7 friend, the Duck, was among the survivors—this time," he added. Known to his squadron mates as "Duck," Ensign John C. Duckworth, Jr. was among those to survive the loss of *PT-43*. Larson remembered him as among the group of officers back in Chicago who stepped forward to volunteer for PT duty.

The sinking left Larson with plenty of personnel work. "During the week that followed, I reformed the crew," he wrote. "There was a survivor's leave policy that sent any survivor home upon request. Many took it. A few did not." Most of the changes occurred on January 18 when seven enlisted men left the boat and six replacements reported for duty.[201] The final replacement arrived on January 22, the same day the 109 went into drydock for screw replacement. No additional crew changes took place for the balance of the month, except for an enlisted man who spent time in sick bay with tropical fever. Westholm, Larson, and the new crew members likely could not have imagined that the fierce battle for Guadalcanal was about to come to a sudden end.

CHAPTER 9

PRELUDE TO EVACUATION

Daylight was usually several hours old when PT boats began pulling into Tulagi Harbor from a night patrol. Crewmen followed a well established routine once ashore beginning with breakfast. If the heat was not unbearable, and other duties were completed, enlisted sailors often caught some sleep to relieve tension and fatigue.

After conveying any relevant information from the patrol to officers ashore, the boat captain and executive officer usually spent time on routine matters such as censoring outgoing mail, attending to their personal needs, or reviewing plans for the next patrol.[202] They also tried to fit in some sleep whenever possible. It was not uncommon for workers from the base force to board a boat during the day to conduct routine maintenance. Both officers and enlisted men maintained a cautious eye to keep track of what the yard men were doing to their boats.

The boat captains congregated each evening at dusk in the squadron office near Government Warf to get the latest information on the night's operation. The briefings did not always contain a great amount of information, but typically included plans for the upcoming patrol and review of the most up to date reconnaissance information. The meetings sometimes revealed that Japanese ships were en route to the area.[203]

If the Tokyo Express was expected, the briefings often included information on the enemy's likely intentions, estimated arrival time, and an outline of the patrol positions assigned to the various PT boats. Many times, however, the information was not very detailed. As one boat captain remembered, it often "… didn't help a hell of a lot."[204]

Waiting for the latest information in the squadron office was when stress really began to mount for many boats' captains. Once the briefing ended the officers returned to their boats and anxious crews. The enlisted men often waited in silence, their strained faces showing tension as they sought any shred of information as to what the night might bring.

————

The prolonged fighting on Guadalcanal had resulted in a vast graveyard for Japanese men and material, and their heavy losses showed no signs of abating. Bitter feuding erupted in December 1942 at the highest levels of the Japanese command structure, pitting navy admirals, who favored a withdrawal from the embattled island, against army generals who wanted to dig in and continue fighting. The futility of the situation was highlighted when a series of war games failed to produce even a hypothetical outcome in which the Japanese won the battle for Guadalcanal.[205]

The Imperial Navy eventually prevailed in the dispute, with growing American airpower, the tremendous tonnage of lost naval shipping, and the inability to supply and strengthen the island's garrison as the deciding factors. On December 31 Emperor Hirohito approved the evacuation of Guadalcanal.[206] The decision was communicated to top field commanders a short time later.

Time was needed to translate the broad directive into a suitable plan to remove the soldiers still fighting on the island. The Japanese situation on Guadalcanal was grave as the calendar turned to 1943. Unable to get steady food and supplies, the Japanese garrison was literally starving to death. Troops were living a meager existence barely surviving on paltry rations of rice and soybeans supplemented by grass, roots, ferns, and on occasion, even human flesh. Dysentery, malaria, and an assortment of other jungle diseases struck nearly every soldier.[207] A growing number of front line troops were unfit for combat.

The American disposition on land was very different. Although having to work through supply chain problems and having no immunity to tropical diseases, the number of troops was steadily growing. Throughout the end of 1942, battle-weary marines were relieved by fresh troops. Newly installed Army General Alexander Patch was meantime oblivious to the Japanese decision to leave Guadalcanal. He pressed forward with plans for a January land offensive to drive the enemy from key strongpoints. He hoped to crush Japanese resistance by April.[208]

———

The Japanese decision to withdraw from Guadalcanal was initially shared only with top field commanders, while army leaders on the island were kept in the dark regarding their futures. On January 4, 1943, the key Japanese army and navy commanders in the South Pacific received the shocking orders from Imperial Headquarters in Tokyo. Guadalcanal must be evacuated within one month.[209] It was unthinkable to many hardened Japanese fighters to retreat instead of staying to fight to the end. The commanders now had to determine how to turn the general order into a workable plan.

The detailed work was completed by the second week of January when army and navy commanders agreed on a basic evacuation plan dubbed Operation KE. Carried out in stages, the mission would remove all remaining Japanese soldiers from Guadalcanal by early February. The plan required a series of initial steps to be completed by the end of January to lay the groundwork for the actual evacuation.

The preliminary phase charged the Tokyo Express with completing two key deliveries to Guadalcanal comprised of one infantry battalion and extra supplies. The fresh troops would act as a rear guard for the beleaguered soldiers already on the island. Additional resources, including more destroyers and aircraft, were moved into the Northern Solomons to help ensure the success of the operation. Air units were scheduled to begin stepped up attacks on American positions in late January, and a staging point was to be established on the Russell Islands just west of Guadalcanal. The final preparation was for ground troops to complete a phased withdrawal to the western end of the island by January 26.

The actual extraction of troops was to be accomplished by three destroyer operations with pick-up points at Cape Esperance and Kamimbo Bay. Any troops remaining after the operation could be ferried by landing craft to the Russells for later pick up. The entire operation was to be completed by February 10.[210]

Changes were again afoot for the Reinforcement Unit responsible for conducting the Tokyo Express runs. Rear Admiral Tomiji Koyanagi's short tenure in command ended when he was assigned other duties. However, his replacement, Rear Admiral Satsuma Kimura, did not arrive in time to lead the scheduled January 11 supply mission. Koyanagi departed Shortland on January 12 aboard the *Naganami* bound for Truk, leaving Kimura in charge to carry out the KE Operation. The new admiral was a well regarded combat veteran who had commanded a destroyer squadron during the Naval Battle of Guadalcanal.

Rear Admiral Kimura wasted no time in preparing his force for the first mission of Operation KE. The destroyers were charged with the safe delivery of supplies and about 750 soldiers of the rear guard battalion and their equipment. The infantry unit included a machine gun company, three rifle companies, and a battery of small mountain artillery guns. Kimura was also accountable for delivering a special guest passenger. Lieutenant Colonel Kumao Imoto was responsible for hand-delivering the evacuation order to his army comrades ashore.

Kimura departed Shortland with nine destroyers on January 14 for the voyage to Guadalcanal. Early air cover gave way to poor weather conditions that shrouded his movement through the Slot. American radio intelligence provided a general warning, but gave no details of the operation, and an Allied sighting report arrived too late for an evening air attack.[211] It was once again left to the PT sailors to tangle with the Tokyo Express.

With no detailed information on the enemy's disposition, thirteen PT boats departed Tulagi to await the Japanese arrival. Heavy weather blanketed the Guadalcanal area creating dismal conditions for the boat crews. Heavy rain squalls were occurring with regularity, and occasional flashes of lightning flickered across the dark sky. The visibility was so poor that crewmen could not see the bow of their boats from the cockpit.[212]

The conditions ensured it would be extremely difficult for the PT men to find and attack the approaching enemy. The only possibility for success was for the boats to spread out in the hopes that at least one PT could locate the Japanese and then guide the others via radio reports. John and Robert Searles took two boats to patrol off Kamimbo Bay. Clark Faulkner led a two-boat patrol to a point about two miles south of Savo Island.

The remaining nine boats made up three equal strike groups. Rollin Westholm in *PT-109* led one group stationed about two miles southwest of Savo Island. The second was led by Lieutenant Allen Harris and patrolled along a two-mile line off Doma Reef near the Guadalcanal coast. Lieutenant Hugh Robinson led the third strike group. His three boats were positioned about half way between Faulkner's force and Doma Reef.

Even with the foul weather the PT sailors still had to contend with an enemy above. Crewmen on Japanese float planes had no trouble seeing the boat's wakes through the hazy weather. Around midnight Westholm left the other two boats of his group to search northwest of Savo Island. At 12:30 a.m. a float plane suddenly swooped out of the darkness attacking *PT-109* with three small bombs. All landed harmlessly in the water about 150 yards off the port side.[213] Westholm was unable to find any Japanese destroyers and missed his chance for action.

Lester Gamble in *PT-45* and Lieutenant John Clagett in *PT-37* stayed together in Westholm's absence. Lightning flashes suddenly revealed five destroyers between Savo Island and Cape Esperance just as Gamble's boat was dodging a float plane. Both boats closed to attack. Clagett discharged three torpedoes, but the results were not observed. Gamble fired two torpedoes. The first one missed, but the second was seen to hit the lead destroyer with a large explosion. The warship opened fire just as the PT's turned to leave. Gamble and Clagett opened the throttles and veered left to move up the west side of Savo Island.

Once the boats passed north of the island *PT-37* slipped away and returned to Tulagi, but *PT-45* was not as lucky. A previously unseen Japanese destroyer appeared from the east around the northern tip of Savo Island and took the boat under heavy fire. Reversing course, Gamble went back down the west side of the island and headed east. He was clear of all enemy destroyers, but ran aground on a reef in poor visibility near Florida Island. A tug boat arrived the next afternoon to pull the PT free.

The third strike group was next to find the enemy when lightning silhouetted a single ship between Savo Island and Cape Esperance. Stilly Taylor in *PT-46* and Lieutenant (Junior Grade) Ralph Richards in *PT-123* closed to attack. Taylor fired two torpedoes and Richards one, but none found the mark. The destroyer opened fire on the fleeing torpedo boats, but did not come close to hitting either one.

Richards was not done hunting. He took the 123 in a wide circle returning to the same area to find another destroyer, again with the aid of lightning. He fired his remaining three torpedoes at a range of 500 yards and observed one to be a solid hit. He sped away believing his target never saw him. The destroyer, however, did spot the PT boat and quickly opened fire. Possibly owing to the poor weather conditions, the fire was erratic and no shells came close to hitting *PT-123* as she left the area.

Hugh Robinson was unable to fire any torpedoes during the battle. His *PT-47* stalked several Japanese ships off the Guadalcanal coast, but was repeatedly driven back by gunfire.

Allen Harris riding in *PT-40* was the only member of the remaining strike group to make contact with the Japanese. He unleashed two torpedoes at a destroyer in the vicinity of Tassafaronga only to see both pass wide of the mark.

A two-boat patrol group comprised of Clark Faulkner in *PT-39* and Bartholomew Connolly in *PT-115*, was the last of the PT's to find the enemy. As the 115 was patrolling southeast of Savo Island, Connolly observed flashes of gunfire in the vicinity of Cape Esperance. He immediately raced in the direction and spotted two Japanese destroyers through the haze. *PT-115* closed to attack, firing four torpedoes at a distance of 1,000 yards. While turning away Connolly saw a flash on the target ship quickly followed by a dull red glow. He took the signs to be a direct hit. Both destroyers unleashed strong, but inaccurate, gunfire as the PT sped away.

Patrolling in close proximity to Connolly, Clark Faulkner found a target with the help of lightning. The destroyer put up a heavy wall of fire when he took *PT-39* in for a torpedo run. One salvo hit close to the boat, knocking a crewman to the deck. Other shells flung rocks and sand into the air after exploding on a nearby beach on Savo Island. Faulkner's boat soon ran aground. The destroyer, fortunately, did not close for the kill. Through persistent effort, he was able to break free before dawn with only minor damage.

Aided by the weather and float planes, Kimura's destroyers brushed back the PT attack. Boat captains claimed three hits out of seventeen torpedoes fired.[214] No Japanese ships, however, were damaged and the cargo of men, weapons, and supplies was safely delivered.

Planes from Guadalcanal found the fleeing destroyers after daybreak, making the return trip up the Slot an uneasy ride for Kimura's force. Fifteen dive bombers swooped in to attack as their fighter escort battled Zeros. Near-miss bombs damaged the rudder of *Arashi*, killed the commanding officer of *Tanikaze*, and caused minor damage to *Urukaze*.[215] The destroyers later survived a high level attack by B-17 bombers unscathed.

Rollin Westholm used morning light to prowl along the Guadalcanal coast looking for enemy supplies. At 7:15 a.m. a shore battery opened fire putting three holes in *PT-109*, but causing no casualties among the crew. Before returning to Tulagi, the boat moved across the sound to Florida Island and helped pull Gamble's grounded boat to safety.[216]

After landing on Guadalcanal with the rear guard force, Lieutenant Colonel Imoto marched east. Along the trail he frequently came across dead bodies and starving soldiers. He was frequently stopped by emaciated countrymen pleading for food and water. Arriving at army headquarters after nightfall, he delivered the shocking orders that the island was to be evacuated. He squelched protests from those preferring to stay and fight to the death by forcefully adding that the directive was the Emperor's wishes.[217]

Secrecy was a factor critical to the success of Operation KE. The Japanese plans to evacuate Guadalcanal remained well guarded, and the clandestine effort was never unbundled by American intelligence. To keep the American information gatherers off balance, the Japanese high command devised a series of feints, including increased radio traffic in the Java area to the west, a night air raid on Darwin, Australia, and fake radio messages emanating near the Marshall Islands to the east.[218] The ruse worked all too well, and American radio intelligence was not able to discern the real reason for the increased enemy activity in the Solomons.[219] The movements, however, did not go unnoticed.

The step-up in Japanese naval and air traffic in the middle of January was worrisome to Admiral Halsey. Routine aerial reconnaissance patrols revealed increased shipping at Rabaul during the last two weeks of January. It was clear that the enemy's heavy fleet units were not sitting idle when battleships and aircraft carriers were sighted milling around Ontong Java Atoll.[220] Located directly north of the Solomon Islands, the reef area was only about 350 miles from Guadalcanal.

The ominous signs pointed to a large scale reinforcement operation, similar to what was attempted by the Japanese the previous November. Admiral Halsey concluded he was yet again on the brink of a major naval battle. The assumption led him to deploy a large array of naval forces on the last days of the month to ensure the safe arrival of army reinforcements at Guadalcanal. The troops arrived safely and no sea battle took place. However, the heavy cruiser *Chicago* was sunk south of Guadalcanal by land-based Japanese bombers in what became known as the Battle of Rennell Island.

On land General Patch moved forward with his large offensive. It was the most ambitious ground operation undertaken on Guadalcanal to date. The operation began January 10 when troops moved west under the cover of heavy artillery and air support.[221] The ground forces made good progress, tearing gaping holes in the Japanese front lines and securing some key objectives in only three days. By the end of the month Patch's men started a coastal drive along the northwest part of the island. The operation continued into February.

While American ground troops trudged through the jungle, the PT sailors at Tulagi waited tensely for their next battle. Little did they suspect that the battle for Guadalcanal was about to come to a fiery end.

CHAPTER 10

GUADALCANAL FINALE

The final piece of groundwork for Operation KE took place on January 28, 1943 when six Japanese destroyers delivered a contingent of 328 men to the Russell Islands to secure the area for use as a temporary stopping point if needed during the evacuation. An attack by Guadalcanal-based planes caused no serious damage and did not impede the operation in any way.

The first evacuation run was ready to move out on February 1 after a short delay caused by the Battle of Rennell Island. A mass of destroyers assembled at Shortland Island for what would be the largest Tokyo Express run ever. A support group of three cruisers were stationed further north at Kavieng. Although the warships would not actually take part in the voyage south, they were on ready status and would be available for immediate action if necessary. A morning attack on Shortland Harbor by B-17 bombers caused no damage and did not change the timing of the operation.

An alarming development for the Japanese occurred when a reconnaissance plane reported the presence of American cruisers in the Guadalcanal area on the same day the destroyers were scheduled to depart Shortland. A flight of dive bombers was quickly dispatched to attack the unexpected warships. The "cruisers" were actually American destroyers preparing to escort a group of landing craft transporting troops for a drop off on the southwest side of Guadalcanal. The airplanes found the small force on their return trip, sinking the destroyer *DeHaven*.

Rear Admiral Shintaro Hashimoto took command of the evacuation mission after Rear Admiral Kimura sustained injuries when his destroyer was attacked by a submarine on January 19. Highlighting the seriousness of the situation, Rear Admiral Koyanagi returned to the area to participate in the operation. He was put in charge of a transport group, while Kimura remained with the unit in a reserve capacity.[222]

Shortland anchorage was a swarm of activity during the mid-morning hours of February 1. The evacuation operation began at 11:30 a.m. when twenty destroyers cleared the area and formed two columns as they eased into the Slot and gradually increased speed to twenty-eight knots. The force was organized into two groups for separate pick-ups at Cape Esperance and Kamimbo. Within each group every destroyer was designated as either a transport or escort. The transports towed a large landing craft loaded with an assortment of smaller boats. Hashimoto's flagship *Makinami* led the entire procession.

A flight of Zero fighters arrived to serve as an escort, and seaplanes scoured the nearby waters looking for submarines as the destroyer force steamed south. The ships were initially sighted just southeast of Shortland by a coastwatcher on Vella Lavella. Japanese lookouts spotted a distant American B-24 bomber at 3:15 p.m. Radio operators then listened intently as the plane sent out a plain language contact report warning of the advancing foe.[223]

American naval units around Guadalcanal were still operating under Halsey's warning that a large Japanese reinforcement operation could be underway. However, the task forces of heavy warships had already moved south after the Battle of Rennell Island and were not in position to make a return trip on such short notice. However, this did not stop area commanders from planning a reception for the Japanese visitors.

The first surprise was already in place in the form of an offensive minefield. Three hundred mines were strung along the Guadalcanal coast starting at Doma Reef and proceeding west part way to Cape Esperance. It was the first offensive minefield laid by American ships in the Pacific War.[224] Also available to help thwart the enemy was a small destroyer force under the command of Captain Robert Briscoe. The group had been operating in the area for several weeks, but was now down to three ships after the loss of *DeHaven*. The Tulagi PT boats were called into action as usual, but as with most previous Tokyo Express runs the first weapon to strike was airplanes.

A swarm of planes rose from Henderson Field and ventured into the Slot to hit Hashimoto's force in two waves starting at 6:20 p.m. The attackers included a mix of dive bombers, torpedo planes, and an assortment of fighters. The eighteen Zeros flying combat air patrol put up a fierce fight and downed four American attackers in the ensuing air battle. The only destroyer damaged was Hashimoto's flagship *Makinami*. A near-miss bomb flooded engineering spaces leaving the ship dead in the water.

Admiral Koyanagi quickly took charge of the force, radioing "I shall assume command as of now."[225] He directed the destroyers *Fumizuki* and *Shirayuki* to stay behind with the stricken flagship and continued on with the remaining ships. Hashimoto quickly transferred to *Shirayuki* and set out after the force, eventually catching up. The motionless *Makinami* was later towed back to Shortland by *Fumizuki*.[226]

The Japanese army units on Guadalcanal designated for evacuation completed the arduous journey west on foot through muddy jungle trails. Amid confusion and lack of adequate preparation, they arrived at the debarkation points in close approximation to the estimated arrival time of the destroyer force. They found no ships waiting but soon heard noises of gunfire emanating across the sea.

Admiral Koyanagi delayed the pick-up time by half an hour as a result of the hindrance brought about by the air attack. He also reassigned two destroyers from transport to escort duties to account for the ships left behind. The screening destroyers pulled ahead to make a cautious sweep of the area as the force began its final approach to Guadalcanal. Afterwards the destroyers designated for Kamimbo turned away from the main group to operate independently. PT boats were the last obstacle standing between the starving, exhausted Japanese troops and their rescue ships.

The first sighting report of the enemy ships arrived at the Tulagi PT base during the early afternoon of February 1 from the naval commander overseeing the Guadalcanal area. "Coastwatcher reports twenty possible dog dogs [destroyers] five miles north of Vella Lavella course east southeast..."[227] The ominous report put the enemy force already in the Slot. A later message reported sixteen destroyers 210 miles from Guadalcanal. Every operable PT was called to action. "Shortly after dark, the eleven available boats of Motor Torpedo Boat Flotilla One got under way from Tulagi Harbor to take up stations in the Esperance–Savo area for an attack on the enemy force," Hugh Robinson reported. The former leader of Squadron Three was now a flotilla staff officer and wrote a summary report on the battle.

The usual pre-mission jitters of the PT sailors, already heightened by losing two boats in the mid-January battle, were bolstered even further by the large number of enemy warships reported en route. If the contact information was accurate, the torpedo boats would be facing almost twice the

ORDER OF BATTLE
AMERICAN PT BOATS VS. JAPANESE DESTROYERS
FEBRUARY 1–2, 1943

JAPANESE (Rear Admiral Shintaro Hashimoto)

CAPE ESPERANCE UNIT
SCREEN: Makinami*, Maikaze, Kawakaze, Kuroshio, Shirayuki and Fumizuki*

TRANSPORTS: Kazagumo, Makigumo, Yugumo, Akigumo, Tanikaze, Urakaze, Hamakaze, and Isokaze.
*Returned to Shortland after air attack.

KAMIMBO UNIT
SCREEN: Satsuki and Nagatsuki

TRANSPORTS: Tokitsukaze, Yukikaze, Ohshio, and Arashio

AMERICAN (Commander Allen P. Calvert at Tulagi PT Base)

TWO MILES SOUTHEAST OF SAVO ISLAND
PT-39   Henry "Stilly" Taylor
PT-47   Robert Searles

TWO MILES SOUTHWEST OF SAVO ISLAND
PT-48   Lester Gamble
PT-111   John Clagett

THREE MILES NORTHWEST OF VISALE (GUADALCANAL)
PT-37   James Kelly
PT-59   John Searles
PT-115   Bartholomew Connolly

THREE MILES SOUTH OF SAVO ISLAND
PT-123   Ralph Richards
PT-124   Clark Faulkner

TWO MILES NORTH OF DOMA REEF
PT-36   Charles Tilden
PT-109   Rollin Westholm

number of destroyers as encountered in the recent fights. The grim odds of survival seemed to get lower as the night progressed, leading some of the sailors to wonder if they would make it through the battle to see morning.[228]

It was imperative that the Japanese destroyers not slip through Iron Bottom Sound undetected. The eleven PT boats were divided into five groups and positioned at various key locations. Four boats assigned to operate south of Savo Island separated into two equal patrol groups before proceeding to their station. Robert Searles in *PT-47* was in command of one group. He went to an area two miles southeast of Savo with Stilly Taylor in *PT-39*. John Clagett in *PT-111* led the other group two miles southwest of the island. Accompanying Clagett was Lester Gamble riding in *PT-48*.

John Searles in *PT-59* patrolled with two boats three miles off the northwest tip of Guadalcanal. His group was assigned to cover the Cape Esperance area, the most likely Japanese destination given the enemy's recent activity. Clark Faulkner at the conn of *PT-124* was stationed with one other boat three miles south of Savo Island. Lastly, Rollin Westholm in *PT-109* pa-

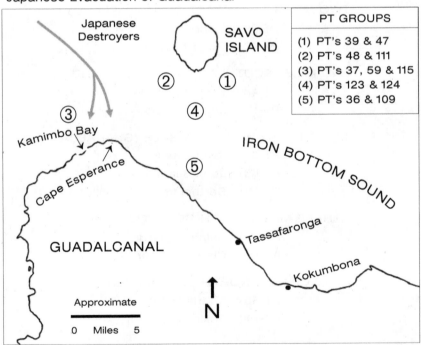

BATTLE OF FEBRUARY 1–2, 1943
Japanese Evacuation of Guadalcanal

PT GROUPS
(1) PT's 39 & 47
(2) PT's 48 & 111
(3) PT's 37, 59 & 115
(4) PT's 123 & 124
(5) PT's 36 & 109

trolled two miles north of Doma Reef in company with Charles Tilden in *PT-36*.

The weather conditions were substantially better than the last time the boats ventured out to meet the enemy. The night began with clear visibility. The conditions would help the PT men locate the enemy destroyers, but also aid Japanese planes in finding the torpedo boats. Two Zero floatplanes operating from Shortland were patrolling Iron Bottom Sound in support of the operation. Intermitted rain squalls would develop later in the night and partially obscure the visibility.

Captain Briscoe was certain the enemy was expecting PT boats, but believed the presence of American destroyers in the area would come as a complete surprise. Positioning his three warships west of Guadalcanal, he hoped to launch an attack at the opportune time. However, Japanese float planes found him first and illuminated his location with a series of aerial flares. Once his position was revealed, Briscoe was unable to close for an attack at any time during the night and his destroyers played no role in the battle. With the odds stacked heavily against him and no guarantee the PT boats would not mistake his destroyers for the enemy, the non-engagement probably served Briscoe well.

John Clagett and Lester Gamble came under attack from the air even before they could reach their assigned patrol station. At about 7:30 p.m. the pair saw the first of three flares explode over Iron Bottom Sound. The third illuminated Gamble's boat just enough for it to be strafed by a seaplane. "He returned fire with his fifty caliber machine guns, but both gunners missed astern of the plane," Hugh Robinson later reported.

The two PT's continued to their patrol area, but the heckling from the air was not over. At 9:50 p.m. a large bomb suddenly exploded in the water about 200 yards from the boats. Each PT was shaken and jarred, but did not sustain noteworthy damage.

Clagett idled the 111 boat at slow speed with *PT-48* positioned about 200 yards off his starboard quarter after arriving in position about two miles southwest of Savo Island. The pair became the first PT's to find the enemy warships at about 10:40 p.m. when Clagett sighted a destroyer about three miles east of Cape Esperance on a southeast heading. Gamble then saw two destroyers moving southwest about two miles west of Savo Island. Clagett stayed on course to attack his original sighting, while Gamble made a hard right turn to intercept the second destroyer in the column.

Hugh Robinson continued the story in his battle report starting with the attack by *PT-48*: "Gamble closed to 900 yards range on the lead destroyer in column and fired his two after torpedoes. Both missed astern," he wrote. The boat unleashed her two remaining torpedoes at the same target just as the destroyer opened fire. "It is believed that the first torpedo tracks were not observed by the enemy ships. The second torpedoes were heading well and Gamble watched them run for a few seconds."

Just then two main battery salvos from one of the destroyers splashed dangerously close to the PT boat, with one falling short and the other over. Gamble made a hard right turn, pouring on speed. Laying a smoke screen to conceal his departure, the boat captain did not see if his torpedoes hit.

PT-48 encountered another destroyer just as she successfully slipped away from her initial target. The enemy warship produced a heavy torrent of fire with light weapons. With multiple destroyers in close proximity, Gamble quickly saw the makings of a trap. With enemy fire now coming from the starboard bow, he made a sharp turn to the left and headed for Savo Island. Gamble gave the order to abandon ship after nosing *PT-48* up to the beach. He stood briefly next to his boat in knee deep water watching the enemy searchlights scour the area. He knew that if a beam found his boat a torrent of gunfire would quickly blow it to pieces. Tense minutes passed, then an hour went by, but nothing happened.

After Gamble sped away on the attack, John Clagett kept the 111 boat on track to strike his original contact. His prey was most likely the destroyer *Kawakaze*.[229] Bristling with four five-inch cannons and an assortment of light automatic guns, the 2,000-ton destroyer immediately opened fire.[230] Clagett gave the order to fire two torpedoes when the PT closed to within 500 yards of her target. He let loose with the remaining two fish about 100 yards closer. The volume of gunfire coming from the destroyer was so heavy he could not determine if any of the torpedoes hit.

PT-111 suffered a direct hit shortly after the last torpedoes leaped away, causing the boat to burst into flames. Clagett was thrown to the deck and sustained extensive burns to the face and arms. He managed to escape the flaming inferno by crawling over the side. Unable to swim due to his injuries, two shipmates helped to keep him afloat while other crewmen fended off nearby sharks. The group attempted to make a slow swim towards Savo Island.[231] Clagett survived the night and was rescued the following morning. Although some sustained injuries, most of his crew was saved. However, two sailors perished in the inferno and *PT-111* was a total loss.

The three boats led by John Searles were the next group to join the action. Searles was riding in *PT-59* and was accompanied by Bartholomew Connolly in *PT-115* and *PT-37* under the command of Ensign James Kelly. The force was moving through the passageway between Cape Esperance and Savo Island during the late evening hours when it was abruptly attacked by float planes. The aircraft made a strafing run and unleashed at least one bomb, but none of the PT's was damaged.

The sudden air attack scattered the PT group. About an hour later the boats spotted an enemy destroyer. The initial sighting was rapidly followed by many more. Searles and his fellow boat captains were quickly in a precarious position. "... the three boats found themselves completely trapped by enemy destroyers on three sides of them with the Guadalcanal coast on the other," explained Hugh Robinson. "As many as twelve destroyers were counted encircling them at one time." The situation looked to be a vicious trap, prompting each boat captain to search for a way out.

The first to act was Bartholomew Connolly in *PT-115*. He singled out one destroyer and fired two torpedoes after closing to about 500 yards. "He is certain that both hit," Robinson reported. "The ship slowed down abruptly and started to list."

Just as Connolly reversed course to retire, a second destroyer appeared close on the horizon about 2,000 yards away. He immediately fired his two remaining torpedoes and then reversed course again. The PT boat was now under intense gunfire that seemed to be coming from all directions. Seeing no easy way out Connolly cut his speed in a calculated gamble to throw off the enemy. The ruse worked. The Japanese gunfire became inaccurate, presumably due to the gunners losing sight of the PT boat's wake.

At about the same time an intense rain squall developed in the immediate area. Connolly seized the opportunity as his way out of the trap and pointed *PT-115* directly towards the storm. The sudden weather change allowed him to slip away from the pressing danger. Connolly went to Savo Island where he beached the 115 on the western coastline.

The commanding officer of the patrol group used the same rain squall to escape the closing ring of enemy destroyers. John Searles in *PT-59* moved north of Savo Island and remained there until dawn. He was never in a position to fire torpedoes.

The last boat of the patrol group did not survive the trap. James Kelly fired all four torpedoes before turning *PT-37* to retire. He then suffered every PT sailor's nightmare—a direct hit to the fuel tanks. A tremendous blast followed that reduced the torpedo boat to splintered wreckage. "The brilliant, blinding flash of the explosion lit the whole sky in the vicinity of Cape Esperance," Robinson later reported. Machinists Mate First Class Eldon Jester was blown through the side of the boat by the blast. Burned and wounded, he spent about three hours in the water before a passing PT picked him up to become the sole survivor of *PT-37*.[232]

The last group to join the battle was the two boat patrol under the command of Clark Faulkner. Ensign Ralph Richards in *PT-123* accompanied Faulkner's *PT-124*. The patrol was attacked by float planes en route to their assigned area three miles south of Savo Island, but suffered no damage.

At about 10:49 p.m. Faulkner spotted a destroyer moving through the channel between Savo and Cape Esperance. He took the 124 in for an attack firing three torpedoes at a range of 1,000 yards. "Two torpedoes hit sending up two large columns of fire," Robinson wrote of the strike. "The ship broke into flame and continued to burn for more than three hours. It is believed that it finally sank." Faulkner conned his boat back to Tulagi after the attack, but his accompanying boat captain did not fare as well.

Ralph Richards in *PT-123* was directly behind Faulkner's boat during the torpedo run. As he lined up to attack a second destroyer, Richards was unaware that a silent killer was stalking just above. Before he could fire any torpedoes, a float plane silently glided in from behind. With precise aim it dropped a bomb that landed perfectly on the fantail of the PT. Flames sprouted at once and quickly spread across the boat, turning the craft into a burning inferno.

Richards knew the boat could not be saved and wasted no time in ordering her abandoned. Once in the water crewmen faced new danger when the plane returned to make a strafing run. The boat never exploded, but slowly settled by the stern before disappearing into the sea. Four crewmen were lost and three sailors seriously injured with a gruesome assortment of shrapnel wounds, burns, and fractures.[233]

The two remaining patrol groups did not fire any torpedoes during the battle, but stayed in Iron Bottom Sound to search for survivors once daylight arrived. Robert Searles in *PT-47* and Stilly Taylor in *PT-39* diligently patrolled southeast of Savo Island, but never found the Japanese. The next morning Taylor recovered three Japanese landing scows with outboard motors attached. It appeared the small boats were abandoned in haste as each contained an assortment of rifles, knapsacks, and the personal effects of Japanese soldiers.

It was 10:15 p.m. when *PT-109* arrived at her patrol station. Rollin Westholm and Brian Larson heard the reports of enemy ships in the area as the boat plied the waters off the Guadalcanal coast and Savo Island. When gunfire and flashes were seen in the vicinity of Cape Esperance, the 109 headed in that direction.

The boat had only a brief encounter with an enemy warship. "Our patrol area was off Savo Island, some distance from the main action," Bryant Larson remembered of the night. "In the middle of a heavy rain squall, a shell exploded just off the bow of the 109. We turned to see a destroyer bearing down on us." The officers on the boat had to make a quick decision. "Having no position for a torpedo shot, we made a fast turn, hit the smoke generator and again got the hell out of there under scattered fire."[234]

Crewmen sighted a burning object thought to be a sinking enemy ship as the hours of the night transitioned into February 2.[235] At 4:10 a.m. the boat began searching for missing PT boats and survivors. With the help of daylight *PT-109* later found two boats beached on Savo Island. At 6:40 a.m. she pulled off Bartholomew Connolly's *PT-115*. Twenty minutes later she helped free *PT-48* before resuming her search for survivors.[236] The only sailor the 109 found was dead. Crewmen pulled aboard the badly burned and shrapnel riddled body of Chief Gunners Mate John Brown just before 8:00 a.m. The body was later transferred to another PT boat for transport back to Tulagi.[237] Unable to find any survivors, *PT-109* returned to Tulagi just after noon.

The combination of floatplanes and escort destroyers again proved effective for the Japanese. One of the float Zeros attacked a total of eight PT boats during the operation, while the second located Briscoe's destroyers early enough to foil his plans for a surprise attack.[238] The only Japanese loss occurred when *Makigumo* ventured east in pursuit of a PT boat. Admiral Koyanagi quickly ordered her back fearing she was encroaching on Tulagi. The destroyer was rocked a by a large explosion on her return trip west. Most likely caused by a mine, the blast left *Makigumo* motionless. Her surviving crew of 237 was later removed by *Yugumo*, before she fired a single torpedo to sink her sister ship.[239]

Six American dive bombers rose from Henderson Field at about midnight for a surprise night attack. The planes reported hitting two burning

Japanese ships, but the targets were likely one and the same, the damaged *Makigumo*. The planes actually caused no damage.

The pick-up operation was completed just before 2:00 a.m. when the last Japanese soldiers set foot aboard the destroyers off Cape Esperance. Koyanagi then ordered his ships to head north. The force escaped damage in an 8:00 a.m. air attack and made Bougainville about noon.

————

The February 1–2 night battle was the largest and last encounter between Japanese destroyers and torpedo boats in the Guadalcanal area. The PT sailors paid a heavy price in the action. The fight left three boats sunk and two moderately damaged from beaching. For Bryant Larson it was the loss of another friend as John Duckworth was among those killed on *PT-37*. "Duck was the only PTer to lose two boats," he later wrote, concluding the officer's luck just ran out.

Believing they had disrupted a routine reinforcement mission, the PT men were confident of victory. Nineteen torpedoes were discharged at the enemy. Hits were claimed on four destroyers with two thought to have been sunk.

The Japanese considered the evacuation mission a success. Destroyer *Makigumo* was lost, but the other warships transported 4,935 weary soldiers out of Guadalcanal.[240] The remaining Japanese troops on the island were now in a battle against time. In the February 1 operation during which *DeHaven* was sunk, American infantry landed on the west side of the island. Those troops started pushing up the coast towards Marovovo, the last stopping point before Kamimbo. With General Patch's offensive pushing along the coastal area on the north side of the island, the Japanese troops were on the verge of becoming trapped.

The Americans still did not know the Japanese were leaving. The movement of enemy barges between Guadalcanal and the Russell Islands was noticed, but thought to be part of a reinforcement operation.[241] The capture of a Japanese base near Tassafaronga, including a radio station and artillery pieces, also did not reveal what was really happening.

The second evacuation run took place on February 4 when twenty Japanese destroyers steamed the gauntlet down the Slot to the same two pick-up points. Air attacks damaged four ships, two only slightly, but failed to further disrupt the operation. Captain Briscoe's destroyers were no longer in the area and PT boats did not venture out. After about two hours of loading passengers, the destroyers returned to base without incident.

One last trip down the Slot was needed to fully complete the extraction mission. The final Tokyo Express run began with a high level of uneasiness. Japanese naval commanders worried about the location of enemy ships as well as time. Fears of a large scale battle began after reports placed American carrier and surface ships southeast of Guadalcanal near San Cristobal. Meanwhile, American troops on Guadalcanal were closing in on the last remaining Japanese ground units.

Eighteen destroyers left Shortland on February 7 bound for Cape Esperance and the Russells. Thirty-six American planes found the force and battled through escorting Zeros to attack. Bombs moderately damaged one destroyer causing her to turn back with two escorts. The Japanese force was otherwise not challenged. The Cape Esperance unit was fully loaded by 1:30 a.m. on February 8.[242] The last Tokyo Express pulled out of Iron Bottom Sound, linked up with the warships from the Russells, and set a course for the Slot. Their return to Bougainville marked the official end of Operation KE.

Injured Japanese soldiers or those too feeble to make it overland to the pick-up points were left behind to help slow the advancing Americans. Various figures have been offered over time as to the total number of Japanese troops removed by the three destroyer runs, with 10,652 being accepted by many historians as the most accurate.[243]

American forces on Guadalcanal woke up on the morning of February 8 to find the coastal areas on the northwest end of the island littered with small boats and debris. It soon became clear that the last Tokyo Express runs had not been bringing in reinforcements, but taking soldiers out. On the morning of February 9, the two advancing groups of American ground forces met southeast of Cape Esperance at the coastal village of Tenaro.[244] The brutal and bloody battle for control of Guadalcanal was over.

PART TWO

KENNEDY AT THE HELM

CHAPTER **11**

LULL

The Japanese evacuation of Guadalcanal ushered in four months of calm to the embattled sea lanes around the island. "That was the end of the PT action in Guadalcanal waters," Bryant Larson recalled. There would be no more Tokyo Express runs to Cape Esperance or night battles in Iron Bottom Sound. The weary PT sailors relished the slower pace of operations after enduring months of constant activity. However, most knew the lull would only be temporary.

The boat captains had been under tremendous strain during the night battles, wanting to produce results while keeping themselves and crews alive to fight another day. The pause in combat offered them a time to reflect on the previous three months of bitter fighting. "We were awfully glad when it was over," said boat captain Lester Gamble summing up the feelings of many.[245]

Torpedo boat captains reported sinking a total of seven major Japanese warships in the time from the first PT battle in mid-October 1942 to the last encounter with the Tokyo Express in early February 1943. The tally was comprised of five destroyers, one submarine, and a cargo vessel.[246] The number proved to be far from reality with the confusion of night battles and faulty torpedoes combining to create the flawed claims. Analysis of post-war records revealed PT boats caused much less damage than was originally thought. The boats were credited with sinking only two large Japanese ships, both in December. The victims were the submarine *I-3* and the large destroyer *Teruzuki*.

Looking back at the results, Bryant Larson later pondered, "How could we miss at point blank range? I do know that many of our torpedoes were defective—they either didn't run true or didn't explode when they hit," he continued. "I do know that aiming torpedoes on a black night without any speed or firing angle track (such as a submarine has) is a very crude system."[247]

Larson's beliefs about the torpedoes were correct. The PT men often had to contend with unreliable torpedoes—essentially, another enemy besides the Japanese. The culprit was the outdated Mark Eight torpedoes used by the boats. The weapons required constant maintenance and were regularly plagued by a variety of problems, including not running at a fixed depth.[248]

Although causing less damage than initially reported, the PT boats played a vital role in the Guadalcanal Campaign. "We didn't sink many ships, but we messed up a lot of attempts at reinforcement and supply," Larson noted. Although his squadron suffered a high number of boat losses, he was surprised more sailors were not killed in action. "We must have been more aggressive, or just lucky; maybe more skippers should have carried lucky beans!"

Hugh Robinson further elaborated on the PT's role in the campaign. "If we were not interdicting their line of supply, we were certainly interrupting it," he said. "It wasn't the number of Japanese destroyers sunk as much as the fact that we were out there firing on them, and they knew and didn't waste any time staying around. That was important."[249]

General Patch made a trip across Iron Bottom Sound a short time after the fighting ended. "He came over to Tulagi and decorated a number of our PT officers and men," Rollin Westholm remembered. "I received a Silver Star."[250] Patch used the visit to express his personal gratitude to the sailors who had fought valiantly to help keep enemy supplies and reinforcements out. "A wonderful and touching sight," the general commented as he handed out some of the well deserved medals. "All these fine young men, ready to go anywhere and do anything. Makes you feel humble."[251]

The Silver Star was for Westholm's actions in the January battle that resulted in the sinking of *PT-112*. The citation spoke of the encounter with the destroyer: ". . . [He] daringly maneuvered to within very close range and opening fire, scoring one known torpedo hit which sank or seriously damaged an enemy destroyer, before his own boat was put out of action by enemy fire." The award also highlighted subsequent actions taken by Westholm after his rescue: ". . . despite dangerous proximity to the enemy coast, [he] directed a persistent search for the survivors of an abandoned sister ship and succeeded in rescuing all but two members of the crew. His outstanding courage and gallant fighting spirit were in keeping with the highest traditions of the Naval Service."[252]

Whether it was those singled out for their individual acts of heroism, the unsung sailors who endured grueling night patrols, or the base force that kept the boats going in harsh conditions, the PT men greatly contributed to winning the battle for Guadalcanal. The reported sinking of enemy warships, no matter how inaccurate at the time, served as a great moral boost for the soldiers and airmen locked in the intense struggle. The boats filled a gap larger warships could not by helping close down the enemy supply line. Although not accurately measured, the contribution was significant.

The end of the fighting on Guadalcanal coincided with some administrative changes among the PT sailors at Tulagi. Even though Motor Torpedo Boat Flotilla One had been activated in December 1942, many headquarters positions were not immediately filled. Allen Calvert subsequently reached into the pool of veteran boat officers at Tulagi to add to his staff. One such move affected *PT-109* when Rollin Westholm was tapped to fill the role of Calvert's operations officer.

It was an ideal opportunity for Westholm, who was known for meticulous recordkeeping. "He wrote everything up like he was the commanding admiral," recalled one boat captain. "He had records of everything."[253]

In completing the paperwork for the transfer, Allen Calvert recorded that Westholm "has demonstrated consistently his outstanding personal and military character. His decisions have been sound, their execution faultless. He is probably the best informed officer on the subject of motor torpedo boats in the Navy today."[254] Westholm was given high marks in ability to command, ship handling, and administrative duties. Calvert also noted an independent command was most likely in Westholm's future.

There was additional good news awaiting Westholm shortly after the transfer took effect. On March 1 he was promoted to the temporary rank of lieutenant commander. The rank later became permanent.

Although the orders for Westholm's detachment from Squadron Two were recorded as effective on February 1, 1943, he stayed aboard the 109 through a transition period and left the boat and squadron during the middle of the month.[255] Lieutenant Allan H. Harris took over command of the unit.

The Japanese never again attempted to land troops on Guadalcanal as was often feared by some in the American command during the early months of

1943. *PT-109* joined other boats in making regular security patrols in the waters around Iron Bottom Sound during the early part of February. The voyages were routine and largely uneventful. No signs of the enemy were encountered.

The 109 left Tulagi with Rollin Westholm at the conn for an evening patrol late in the day on February 12. At 6:45 a.m. the next morning she pulled up to the wreckage of beached *PT-43* along the Guadalcanal shoreline. Crewmen took a close look to determine what was left of the boat. "Found to be unworthy of salvage," Bryant Larson recorded in the boat's deck log.[256]

The overnight voyage was the last time Westholm skippered *PT-109* on a patrol. When he departed to assume his new duties on Calvert's staff, Larson took command of the boat. On February 17, Ensign Samuel K. King reported aboard from Squadron Eight to serve as the executive officer.

Westholm wrote one last review of his executive officer before his departure. "An outstanding young officer with high leadership ability," he noted of Larson. "One of the best PT officers observed. Exceptionally cool under fire."[257] In the same review Larson listed his next duty preferences as either a destroyer assignment in the Atlantic or flight school in Florida.

American forces did not sit idle after securing Guadalcanal. The next offensive move was the occupation of the Russell Islands. American commanders had long feared that the island group, just thirty miles northwest of Cape Esperance, could be used by the Japanese as a staging area for further attacks on Guadalcanal. The islands were also eyed for a variety of uses, including as a staging point for future operations up the Slot, construction of airfields, a landing craft station, and small PT boat base.

The Japanese stationed troops on the Russells during their Guadalcanal evacuation runs, but it was unclear if the islands were still occupied. Admiral Halsey issued the order to invade the Russells on February 7. The operation was planned with a sizable force because of unknown enemy intentions and disposition. Rear Admiral Richmond K. Turner, who led the amphibious portion of the Guadalcanal action, was tapped to lead the Russells occupation. The mission was dubbed Operation Cleanslate.

As the invasion troops assembled on Guadalcanal, a small landing party was on its way to the Russells. A small scouting group consisting of marine officers and army personnel was transported to the islands on the evening of February 17 by the New Zealand corvette *Moa*. The soldiers went ashore in a small landing boat and set out on foot to determine the composition of the enemy, find suitable landing sites, and scout locations for future base facilities.

The men found no sign of the enemy and the island's natives assured them that the Japanese had departed and not returned.[258]

The PT boats at Tulagi were directed to help in the scouting operation and Bryant Larson was soon on his way to the Russells. "The 109 was assigned a pick-up mission; leave Tulagi at dusk, run to the Russells, find (in the dark) a particular cove off a particular bay to rendezvous with the marine scouts, and bring their [commanding officer] back to Guadalcanal for a report," he later wrote. *PT-109* pulled up to the *Jamestown* just after 1:00 p.m. on February 18 to begin the long process of filling her depleted fuel tanks with 1,000 gallons of high octane gasoline. At 7:40 p.m. the boat started the voyage across Iron Bottom Sound.

Larson's unfamiliarity with the area ensured that the mission was not an easy undertaking. "It was a navigational challenge using dead reckoning and coastal piloting skills," he recalled. Arriving late in the evening the boat pulled into Renard Sound, a small inlet on the eastern side of one of the two large main islands. Larson climbed aboard a Higgins boat at 11:45 p.m. for the short voyage to the beach. The PT idled in the sound as her boat captain waited for orders ashore. He returned about an hour and a half later with a Colonel Farrell and some members of the scout party. The trip back to Tulagi was uneventful and included dropping off the passengers at Koli Point, Guadalcanal right on schedule.[259] "Hairy times at best, but very satisfying," Larson later wrote of the mission accomplished.

The next morning *PT-109* took aboard another load of fuel in preparation for a return trip to the Russells. She was one of eight Squadron Two boats assigned to assist the invasion force.[260] The boat left Tulagi at 7:00 p.m. with Larson at the conn. The force proceeded directly to the Russells and commenced patrols off the northeastern portion of the island. The mission was to secure the flank of the invasion force and block the approach of any Japanese warships that might venture down from the north to challenge the operation. No enemy forces were encountered during the patrol.

Admiral Turner's small invasion fleet was comprised of four destroyers, four destroyer transports, five minesweepers, and an assortment of landing craft. The group departed Guadalcanal after dark on February 20. The flotilla arrived off the Russells at dawn the next morning to start the invasion. About 9,000 troops eventually went ashore in a landing that was entirely unopposed. The Japanese were unaware of the invasion for almost two weeks and did not launch an air attack on the island until March 6.[261]

The Russell Island group consists of two large islands surrounded by an assortment of smaller ones. The two main land masses, Pavuvu on the west and Banika on the east, are separated by a narrow waterway known as Sunlight Channel. A collection of small islands adjacent to the south end of Pavuvu creates the sheltered area of Wernham Cove. The location was chosen for a small PT base, the first of many to be established as American forces advanced out from Guadalcanal. The base became fully operational on February 25.[262]

———————

After completing its patrol on the night of February 20–21 in support of the invasion, *PT-109* moored in brushes along the shoreline of Renard Sound. Later in the day she shifted to the more spacious Wernham Cove. The boat made nightly patrols around the Russells for about a week but found no sign of the enemy.

One voyage gave Bryant Larson quite a scare, however. "I led a two-boat patrol north of the islands one bright, moonlit night that was supposed to be a milk run," he recalled. "But here comes Cactus Control [Guadalcanal headquarters] with a coded message that always meant action pending." Boat captains dreaded receiving such messages as they were often an ominous sign of great danger. "As I decoded it, the first words were 'two DD's [destroyers] sighted,' then a position that placed them very close to us—so close that I ran to the bridge to see if I could spot them visually."

Larson was well aware that a close encounter with Japanese destroyers on a bright night would not be in the best interest of his PT boat. Neither he, nor anyone else aboard his boat, was able to locate the enemy. "Then it dawned on us," he continued. "The coastwatcher that sent the report had spotted our two boats in the moonlight—we were the two DD's!" *PT-109* completed her stay at the forward base and returned to Tulagi on February 28.

On March 1 the 109 went into dry dock for some routine maintenance work. Over the next few days the boat's mufflers were changed and the bottom was scraped and painted. She was put back in the water on March 4 and went directly to Macambo Island for torpedo tube adjustments. Two days later the boat resumed night patrols out of Tulagi.

Even though no action was taking place at sea around Guadalcanal, the Japanese still made their presence known through occasional air attacks. Henderson Field and whatever shipping happened to be in the area were common targets. However, on the night of March 5 a lone enemy plane unleashed four bombs on the Tulagi PT base. Three landed harmlessly in the water, but the fourth scored a direct hit on the operations office. Four sailors were killed and two were wounded in the brief attack. One unlucky boat, *PT-118*, happened to be moored alongside the office and was riddled with shrapnel.[263] The boat was repaired and eventually returned to service.

Samuel King was detached from *PT-109* on April 1 to return to his original squadron. On the same day Ensign Leonard J. Thom assumed the duties of executive officer. Larson remembered him as "a huge, blonde, Viking-type linebacker from Ohio State."

The oldest of eight siblings, Thom was born in Sandusky, Ohio in 1917.[264] He was a tall man with a muscular build. A talented football player, he was a member of an undefeated high school team in 1936. Thom went on play college ball at Heidelberg College before transferring to Ohio State University. He had a brief stint with a semi-pro football team, the Columbus Bulls, after graduation.[265]

Thom decided football was not in his future. Like most young men of the day, he saw the war clouds gathering on the horizon. After declining an offer to play for the Chicago Bears, he volunteered for the navy and was assigned to the V-7 Program at Notre Dame University. Thom attained the rank of ensign upon graduation and volunteered for PT boats. He shipped off to the South Pacific in March 1943 after completing training at Melville.

Thom reported for duty just after *PT-109* completed a couple of days in drydock. On his first day of keeping the logbook, the new executive officer recorded that the boat satisfactorily completed a test run after returning to the water. Thom was accepted by the other PT officers and seemed to fit in well with the group. One boat captain remembered him as a funny guy who was always ready with a joke.[266]

The 109 resumed making occasional routine night security patrols shortly after Thom came aboard. The boat left its longtime base at Tulagi for the Russell Islands on the morning of April 13. Operating out of the new base for the next week, she ventured out on patrol every other night.

————

The slow months of early 1943 saw the arrival of more boats, sailors, and materials to the South Pacific. The remaining two echelons of Squadron Six pulled into Tulagi in March with the last group of new boats.[267] The base force received additional help when the PT tender *Niagara* arrived on February 17.[268]

The influx of new men allowed many of the old hands to be given time off or rotated out. Some of the experienced officers involved in the long stretch of combat were granted a ten-day leave to Auckland, New Zealand for rest and recuperation. Bryant Larson was among the chosen group. He boarded a ship for the voyage south.

The leave was an opportunity for Larson to visit a place he had never been to before. "So what do you do in a strange city," he later wrote of the trip, "you start by strutting along Main Street, eyeing the girls." Many of the young New Zealand men were off fighting on the European front, leaving an abundance of females. "Then you hit the bars and what next? For me it was a break away from the group so I could wander around the city on my own."

Meandering around Auckland, Larson soon found out it was hunting season. "When I indicated an interest in bird hunting to the proprietor of the hardware store, he told me to come back as soon as possible with some shotgun shells and he would do the rest—did he ever! When I returned he handed me (a total stranger) reservations and travel instructions to reach and stay with a family in the back country." It was a surprising turn of events for the native Minnesotan. Adding to Larson's astonishment, the store owner also gave him a shotgun to use on the trip. "Off I went and for the next week I enjoyed not only great hunting, but also a wonderful time with a New Zealand family and their friends."

The trip was only a prelude to more changes in store for Larson. Shortly after returning to Tulagi he was notified of a pending transfer back to the United States. He was going home. A new officer would be taking over command of *PT-109.*

———————

The slowdown in action following the conclusion of the Guadalcanal campaign was not the end of large-scale operations in the Solomons. Both adversaries used the time to prepare for the next stage of fighting.

The Japanese did not attempt to retake Guadalcanal, but instead focused on strengthening positions further north to form a defensive network capable of blocking an expected American advance through the Solomons. A string of airbases already ringed Rabaul and surrounded Bougainville. The labyrinth was extended south with the addition of two new bases in the Central Solomons. Airfields were built in the middle of the island chain at Munda Point on New Georgia and Vila on the southern edge of nearby Kolombangara. The new bases substantially reduced flight time to Guadalcanal. Both remained operational in spite of heavy American bombardment from the air and sea.

Air defenses around Rabaul were strengthened to better withstand the growing American air attacks. The Imperial Navy used destroyers and small boats to ferry troops and supplies among the various islands of the region. Island garrisons were strengthened as the Japanese prepared for the next American invasion.

Fresh off the Guadalcanal victory the Americans were looking to advance up the Slot, and their next target was New Georgia. Admiral Halsey began initial planning for the invasion operation in January 1943.[269] However, months of preparations were needed before the operation could commence. Supplies were stockpiled on Guadalcanal to prevent logistical problems. More planes, including new types, were brought into the theater. An airstrip was built on the Russells and operational planes at Henderson Field swelled to over 300 by March 1.[270] The Japanese knew it was only a matter of time before American forces would again be on the move.

———

On December 7, 1942, the same day Bryant Larson and Rollin Westholm were facing the Tokyo Express for the first time in the South Pacific, half a world away in Melville a young naval officer took command of his first PT boat.[271] Lieutenant (Junior Grade) John F. Kennedy was destined to become the last boat captain of *PT-109* and the most famous PT skipper of all time.

CHAPTER 12

ENTER KENNEDY

John Fitzgerald Kennedy was born on May 29, 1917 in Brookline, Massachusetts.[272] He was the third of nine children born to Joseph P. and Rose Kennedy. The new son was often called Jack from an early age. The family rose in wealth and political notoriety as the young century progressed.

The elder Kennedy had amassed a fortune in the 1920s through an assortment of business dealings and skillful stock transactions. He later left the business world to work in President Franklin Roosevelt's administration. Kennedy was appointed to the coveted position of ambassador to England near the end of 1937. The high-profile job put him in regular contact with top-ranking leaders in the political and military spheres, and the position increased in importance when World War II began in Europe during the fall of 1939. Kennedy held the position until 1940 when his isolationist views clashed with the Roosevelt administration's slow drift towards war.

The family's wealth allowed John Kennedy to grow up in privileged surroundings. As a young man he attended Choate, a private boarding school in Connecticut, and then he entered Harvard University in 1937. During his college years he was active in student groups and sports, participating in football and swimming. Academically, he initially attained only slightly above average grades, though he made improvements during his later years of study.[273]

His father's ambassadorship also opened the door to international travel. Kennedy visited England, a variety of European countries, and a number of other locations abroad. The trips bolstered his interest in politics and world affairs. By the time he graduated from Harvard in June 1940, the war in Europe was well underway and England was fighting for her very survival. For his senior thesis Kennedy wrote about why England had been unprepared for the war. The paper was later published as a book titled *Why England Slept*.

The young Kennedy was often sick and suffered from a variety of ailments during his early years. Visits to the hospital were not uncommon. He suffered a serious back injury while playing football at Harvard, rupturing a disk in his spine. Kennedy would continue to be plagued by back problems for many years.

Kennedy took time to enjoy life after his graduation from Harvard. His interests included chasing girls, attending house parties, and relaxing.[274] He traveled extensively during the first half of 1941 to an assortment of places across the United States and South America.

With America slowly moving towards war, Kennedy decided it was time to join the service. His inclination to enter the military was partially motivated by his desire not to be upstaged by his older brother, Joe Jr., who was training to become a navy pilot.[275] However, he faced a formidable stumbling block in the form of a poor health record and bad back. It has been reported that he was first rejected by the army and then by the navy, both as a result of failed physicals. Kennedy was accepted into the navy on a third attempt, likely due to behind the scenes string-pulling by his father.[276] He was appointed an ensign in the United States Naval Reserve on September 25, 1941.[277]

Having been around the water for much of his life, it was only fitting that Kennedy should end up in the navy. In addition to the residence in Hyannis Port, Massachusetts, his family had a home in Palm Beach, Florida. He was a good swimmer and an experienced sailor of small boats.

Kennedy's first assignment was an administrative job in Washington, DC at the Office of Naval Intelligence. He worked normal business hours collecting and summarizing information from around the world to help prepare daily intelligence briefings. The position also allowed the young officer to experience the Washington social life, an opportunity that he relished. The office shifted to around the clock operations after the Japanese attacked Pearl Harbor in December 1941, thus hurling the United States into war. Kennedy drew the night shift working seven days a week.

On January 15, 1942, Kennedy was transferred to the Sixth Naval District in Charleston, South Carolina.[278] The move was likely the result of the officer's romantic involvement with Igna Arvad, a European-born journalist suspected by the FBI of being a spy.[279] His new responsibilities included instructing workers at local war plants how to prepare for an air raid and deciphering routine messages now sent in code due to wartime security precautions. The assignment was largely a desk job and Kennedy found it to be dull and boring. His back was again giving him problems. He nonetheless applied for sea duty in the hopes of escaping the boredom.

The Charleston duty lasted until July when Kennedy was accepted into the V-7 Program in Chicago. He reported to Northwestern University on July 27 to begin the coursework. The program was now shortened to sixty days due to the urgent need for wartime officers.

The navy was looking for men to fill classes at the Melville Training Center due to the large number of PT boats under construction. The service again turned to the V-7 schools to find volunteers. John Bulkeley made a recruiting stop at Northwestern near the end of summer to pitch the PT opportunity with the same glamour that snared Bryant Larson earlier in the year. Bulkeley came looking for men who "want to get into a scrap without delay and who have plenty of guts."[280]

With many volunteers to choose from, prospective candidates were now selected on the basis of an interview. Out of almost 1,000 student officers at Northwestern, 178 volunteered for the fifty openings.[281] Bulkeley brought along John Harllee, an officer from Melville, to help with the workload.

Decades later Bulkeley revealed that Joseph Kennedy, Sr. had previously asked him for help in getting his son assigned to the PT service. Bulkeley agreed to interview the younger Kennedy during his next trip to Northwestern. "If I thought Jack could measure up, I would recommend his acceptance, I told Joe," Bulkeley recalled. The conversation took place in New York over lunch in Kennedy's ornate suite in the Plaza Hotel.[282]

John Kennedy savored the opportunity to rid himself once and for all of administrative work and have command of his own boat. He excelled in the interview and was among the selected candidates. Bulkeley did as promised to the Kennedy patriarch. Harllee later recalled that Kennedy's sailing experience, appearance, and personality stood out during the interview.[283] No physical exam was required.

Naval records indicate Kennedy reported to Melville on September 27, 1942. Four days later he was promoted to lieutenant (junior grade).[284] The eight week training course extended throughout the fall with final completion on December 2. Most graduates were sent to the war zone as replacements or assigned to newly organized PT squadrons, but not Kennedy. He found out, much to his anger, that he was staying put. His orders were to remain in Melville as an instructor.

Kennedy became attached to PT Squadron Four as a result of the assignment. The training unit was stationed at the base. At least his desire for a boat command was fulfilled on December 7, when he became commanding officer of *PT-101*. The seventy-eight foot boat was built by the Huckins Yacht Company and was among the assorted craft assigned to the squadron.

Kennedy worked in his new capacity at Melville for much of the next month. *PT-101* made regular cruises as a training boat, some lasting as long as twelve hours. The teacher, though, was about to catch a break that would get him one step closer to the war front. After only four weeks of instructing at Melville, Kennedy and *PT-101* were ordered south to become part of a new unit.

Squadron Fourteen was forming at Jacksonville, Florida, but was in need of boats. The 101 proceeded south under her own power in the company of four other PT's. The journey included navigating through a patch of foul weather off the coast of North Carolina where one boat ran aground. Kennedy made a visit to a nearby naval hospital after falling ill, most likely the result of swimming in icy water to help free the stuck boat. *PT-101* continued south under the command of its executive officer, and Kennedy later rejoined the group in Jacksonville.[285]

Longing to get to the action in the Pacific, Kennedy again applied for a transfer in early 1943. "It is requested that I be reassigned to a Motor Torpedo Boat Squadron now operating in the South Pacific," he wrote to the Chief of Bureau of Personnel.[286] At the same time he was working family connections with an influential senator from Massachusetts who sat on the Naval Affairs Committee. The transfer was quickly approved.[287] He received orders to proceed to the South Pacific and report for duty to the commanding officer of Squadron Two.

The long journey to war began with Kennedy making his way to the West Coast. In early March he left the United States aboard the old transport *Rochambeau* bound for the South Pacific. The former French liner was packed full with replacement personnel and a variety of cargo. Slowly steaming west, she arrived at Espiritu Santo after an eighteen-day voyage. The front lines were now only a short boat ride away.

———

The sound of roaring propellers filled the air at bases across the Northern Solomons during the late morning hours of April 7. Scores of Japanese planes were taking off and circling over air bases forming into groups. The large air armada then turned south towards the Slot. Allied coastwatchers, always quick to spot large movements, reported the developments to American authorities. The planes were part of a massive air offensive the Japanese were directing at Guadalcanal and New Guinea in the hopes of reversing some of their recent setbacks in the region.

Sixty-seven dive bombers covered by 110 fighters, 177 planes in total, were bound for Iron Bottom Sound. It was one of the largest Japanese air attacks mounted to date in the war, with the group only a few planes short of equaling the size of the first wave that attacked Pearl Harbor.[288] A large bounty of targets was thought to be waiting at the end of the Slot. The planes hoped to find the twelve warships and fourteen transports Japanese intelligence reported were in the Guadalcanal area.

The day began as a routine morning for the crew of *PT-109*. The boat spent the previous night patrolling the waters between Savo Island and Sandfly Passage. She took aboard fuel shortly after returning to Tulagi in the early morning. The crew then checked her guns and torpedoes before the boat moored in the brush along the Maliali River at 11:00 a.m.

At 2:00 p.m. the radar station on the Russell Islands was a swarm of activity after it picked up the approaching enemy planes. Guadalcanal radio immediately broadcasted a "condition red" alarm, warning all in the area that an air attack was imminent. Seventy-six American fighters rose from Henderson Field and rushed towards the enemy to meet the onslaught. As opposing fighters battled each other in the sky above the Southern Solomons, the bombers slipped past and dove to attack.

A group of American cruisers and destroyers, likely the bulk of the American ships reported by Japanese intelligence, were in Tulagi Harbor during the morning hours. Heeding the radio warning the task force moved out of the harbor area to open waters just in advance of the approaching planes. However, many inviting targets remained for Japanese bombsites in Tulagi Harbor and spread around in the waters near Guadalcanal. An assortment of vessels ranging from tankers to minesweepers to landing craft braced for the attack.

Fifteen PT boats were scattered among various locations around the area. Many boats were sparsely manned with a large number of their crews at base facilities ashore. The tender *Niagara* was moored along the same river bank as *PT-109* with her bow pointed downstream towards the harbor. The old tug *Rail* was tied up alongside the tender.

At about 2:45 p.m. a group of nine low-flying Japanese planes followed the river upstream, apparently after having already dropped their payloads over the harbor area. Crewmen aboard *Niagara* opened fire with twenty-millimeter cannons, while the *Rail* added machine gun fire. The first plane burst into flames and crashed into the trees about 1,000 feet behind *Niagara*. Two attackers attempted to strafe the ships, but the gunfire was inaccurate. Several more were seen leaving the area trailing smoke.

Seaman Second Class James Bartlett aboard *PT-109* opened fire with a fifty-caliber machine gun as the planes approached. Leonard Thom recorded in the deck log that Bartlett "reports hitting one plane, which caught on fire."[289]

No PT boats or associated support ships were damaged during the attack. Other vessels in Tulagi Harbor, however, did not fare as well. A New Zealand corvette and an American tanker were sunk.

By early April John Kennedy was close to completing his long journey to the war front. He boarded *LST-449* on April 4 for the run up to Tulagi after a short stay in Espiritu Santo. The amphibious landing ship was packed full with men and a large load of ammunition. The passenger list included men from all branches of the service en route to Guadalcanal as replacements. A maximum speed of just twelve knots prompted crews to give LST's the nickname of "large slow targets."[290]

The three-day voyage was nearing an end late on the morning of April 7. *LST-449's* final approach to Guadalcanal was almost perfectly timed to coincide with the arrival of the massive Japanese air attack. As the amphibious boat was nearing land, an assortment of vessels was leaving the area at high speed. The passing destroyer *Aaron Ward* signaled a warning of the impending air attack at about the same time a similar message was received from land. Lieutenant Carl Livingston turned *LST-449* south and attempted to leave the area. He eventually joined *Aaron Ward* and a group of other small boats that huddled together in flight from Iron Bottom Sound.

The flotilla was moving away from Guadalcanal in the direction of Espiritu Santo when it was attacked by nine Japanese dive bombers just after 3:00 p.m. *LST-449* maneuvered radically as her anti-aircraft guns opened fire. The sudden action aroused John Kennedy out of his bunk below deck. Bombs were hurling down from the sky by the time he made it topside. A series of near misses straddled the boat throwing up geysers of water. "The nearest on the port quarter lifted the stern and listing ship to starboard about twenty degrees," Livingston reported.[291] The action was the first taste of real combat for Kennedy after months of training.

The LST and her passengers survived the attack, but *Aaron Ward* was not as lucky. The destroyer was hit by a bomb that tore apart her after engine room. Two near misses added additional peril by flooding both fire rooms. She later sank after a valiant attempt to save her failed.

With the situation around Guadalcanal uncertain, *LST-449* continued to move away from the area as a precaution against further air attacks. She eventually arrived at Guadalcanal on April 13 to unload army troops and supplies. The boat crossed Iron Bottom Sound to Florida Island the next day. Kennedy disembarked and made his way to the flotilla command center at Sesapi. After officially reporting for duty, Flotilla Commander Allen Calvert introduced Kennedy to those in the room.[292] The new officer was later assigned to Squadron Two's commanding officer, Allan Harris.

Although Kennedy had plenty of training time under his belt and was a junior grade lieutenant, giving him seniority over many officers in the unit, he was new to the South Pacific. Harris assigned him to spend time with an experienced boat captain, George Wright in *PT-47*. Kennedy accompanied Wright out on a few routine patrols serving as an unofficial executive officer. "After a short time, we saw he was competent and qualified for his own command," Harris later recalled.[293] The shortage of boat captains at the time may have contributed to the quick assignment. Kennedy was given command of *PT-109*.

The 109 left the Russells on the afternoon of April 20 after a weeklong stay, and returned to Tulagi and was moored under the cover of riverside brush by 5:45 p.m. It was to be Bryant Larson's last day of duty aboard the boat. He and seven enlisted men departed the PT late in the day. The exodus left little in the way of experienced crewmen for the new boat captain.[294]

Larson had the opportunity to meet his replacement before he headed off Tulagi. He took Kennedy down to the PT and made several short trips around the harbor area.[295] Kennedy had not yet officially taken command of the boat. "Before I took off for home . . . I got to know Jack a little and many of my mates knew him very well," Larson later recalled. Through the interactions he judged the new man to be a competent officer.[296]

Larson was now a combat veteran with months of frontline experience. His journey back to the United States began with a short ride on a destroyer. "It was appropriate that I should leave Guadalcanal on a destroyer for I had arrived on a destroyer tow line, and had spent my time trying to sink destroyers," he later wrote. The ship was rolling while at anchor when Larson boarded. "I got seasick as I came aboard and stayed that way for the three days into Espiritu Santo. As a PT skipper I was always too busy to be sick—as a passenger, it took ten minutes!"[297]

PT-109 left her hiding spot under the brush along the Maliali River on the morning of April 25 and traveled to Sesapi with Leonard Thom at the conn. The deck log records Kennedy came aboard at 11:00 a.m. to assume command of the boat.[298] Thom stayed on to serve as the executive officer.

Three sailors boarded the 109 on same day as Kennedy, but the boat was still far short of a full compliment. More enlisted men trickled in during the coming weeks as Kennedy filled out the crew. Many of the sailors who came aboard were replacements recently arrived from the United States, providing good expertise but little battle experience.

The crew was at full capacity in less than a month. It was up to Kennedy and Thom to get the men ready for action. "It's been good training," Kennedy wrote at the time. "I have an entirely new crew and when the showdown comes I'd like to be confident they know the difference between firing a gun and winding their watch."[299]

Some sources have *PT-109* in a state of disrepair at the time Kennedy took command.[300] Although the boat was considered combat ready, she was likely in need of some work after months of operations in harsh and primitive conditions with less than adequate repair parts available. Kennedy joined the crew in giving the boat a thorough cleaning as base mechanics gave the engines an overhaul. The bottom of the PT was scraped clean of barnacles as she sat in drydock. A new coat of dark green paint provided the finishing touch.

The 109 ventured out on a test run on the morning of April 29. That evening she patrolled between Savo Island and Cape Esperance in the company of *PT-47*, and the two voyages showed the overhaul work to have been satisfactorily completed. In the coming weeks *PT-109* resumed occasional night patrols in the Guadalcanal area. Aside from the sporadic sightings of a light or flare, the voyages were routine and there were no encounters with the Japanese.

The rotation of PT boats and officers that began in February continued during the month of May. Lieutenant Alvin Cluster replaced Allan Harris as commanding officer of Squadron Two. Only twenty-four years old, Cluster had graduated from the Naval Academy with the class of 1940. In spite of his age, he had a good amount of experience aboard PT boats. Cluster assisted in the initial startup of the school at Melville before overseeing the transfer of four boats from Pearl Harbor to Palmyra Island. However, he had not yet seen combat. Cluster fit the PT officer mold well because he was easy going and did not like the strict naval mentality often found aboard larger warships. Cluster and Kennedy worked well together over the next few months.

While American forces were enjoying the break from action in the Solomons, heavy fighting was underway directly west in New Guinea where troops under the command of General Douglas Macarthur were advancing across the northern coast of the large island. PT boats had joined the fighting with a new base established at Milne Bay on the eastern end of the island.

The need for more PT boats in New Guinea resulted in the reassignment of the tender *Niagara* and six PT's to Milne Bay. While the torpedo boats were preparing for the voyage, one was damaged at the fuel dock. Allen Calvert needed to find a replacement on short notice. Two boats were identified as possible candidates: Kennedy's *PT-109* and *PT-110*, under the command of Lieutenant (Junior Grade) Patrick Munroe. Both recently underwent maintenance at the dry dock facilities and were considered to be seaworthy and in good shape. Calvert called both boat captains to his tent and asked which one wanted to go to New Guinea. The theater was rumored to have more action, prompting both to volunteer. "Calvert said we should step outside and flip a coin," Munroe later recalled. "I won the toss."[301] John Kennedy and *PT-109* stayed at Tulagi.

The New Guinea group departed on the afternoon of May 22 for the voyage west. Japanese bombers found the small flotilla the next morning about 230 miles out from Tulagi. *Niagara* was set aflame by a direct bomb hit during the ensuing attack. Additional damage was caused by several near misses. The doomed tender was later scuttled by a single torpedo fired from a PT boat. After initially returning to Tulagi, *PT-110* eventually made it to New Guinea on a later trip. The boat was sunk less than a year later with a great loss of life.

Kennedy seemed to fit in well among the PT sailors at Tulagi, mixing with both the newly arrived replacements and the old guard who had been through the worst of the fighting.[302] He moved into his own hut at Calvertville, eventually sharing it with Leonard Thom and two other officers. The accommodations were spacious enough for the men to comfortably move around and put up occasional visitors. The officers used a small boat to make the daily commute to the operations base on Tulagi.

The time ashore gave Kennedy an opportunity to interact with the locals. "Have a lot of natives around here and am getting hold of some grass skirts, war clubs, etc.," he wrote in a letter to his parents dated May 14, 1943. "We had one in today who told us about the last man he ate. 'Him Jap him are good.' All they seem to want is a pipe and will give you canes, pineapples, anything, including a wife."

Kennedy also shared additional experiences about his first month at the front. "We had a raid today but on the whole it's slacked up over the last weeks. I guess it will be more or less routine for another while. Going out every other night for patrol. On good nights it's beautiful—the water is amazingly phosphorescent—flying fishes which shine like lights are zooming around and you usually get two or three porpoises who lodge right under the bow and no matter how fast the boat goes keep just about six inches ahead of the boat"

In the same note he assured his mother that he was still meeting his religious obligations. "P.S. Mother: Got to church Easter. They had it in a native hut and aside from having a condition red 'Enemy aircraft in the vicinity' it went on as well as St. Pat's."[303]

Rollin Westholm had some interaction with Kennedy while both were based at Tulagi. He recalled Kennedy showing him a letter from his sister and asking for advice about a family situation. "A couple of days later he was watching me play acey-deucey, a navy dice game," Westholm later wrote. "After the game he asked me to teach him the game and said he would teach me backgammon." Westholm agreed to do the exchange on his next free night. "I did and we played both games many evenings thereafter."[304]

PT-109 departed Tulagi for another trip to the Russell Islands on the morning of May 30. She arrived at 12:30 p.m. and immediately moored in the brushes. The boat left her hiding place only for a few hours to refuel later in the afternoon.

The picturesque Russell Islands were covered with a lush green jungle. An occasional stream meandered into the dense foliage. The surrounding blue-green waters were alive with tropical fish of assorted sizes and colors. Below the mirrored surface was a coral ocean bottom, and the island was home to a coconut plantation developed by Lever Brothers before the war. Regular tropical rain showers turned the ground into a mud that sailors were constantly tracking aboard their boats.

The PT base on the Russells was now home to more than ten boats with various squadrons rotating in and out. Operational control of the base was given to John Searles, one of the few battle-scarred Guadalcanal veterans yet to be transferred out. The facilities were even more primitive than Tulagi. Instead of mooring dockside, boats hid under trees along the banks of Sunlight Channel. Enlisted sailors lived aboard their boats due to the lack of housing. Officers lived in an abandoned plantation house a short distance up a hill from the water.

A rectangular concrete pit previously used to store coconuts was converted into a radio shack. The base force set up a mess facility complete with a galley, meat locker, and bakery. A noisy evaporator worked around the clock to keep the base supplied with fresh water.[305] One small dock on Wernham Cove served as both an unloading point for sailors going ashore and as a fueling station. For safety's sake, torpedoes and depth charges were stored on a small nearby island. The base did not have any repair facilities. Some scattered anti-aircraft guns manned by marines provided security should the Japanese strike from above.

Officers not out on patrol frequently spent their evening playing card games at the plantation house and sipping a drink concocted from combining torpedo alcohol with fresh lime juice. Used for powering torpedoes, the pure grain alcohol was readily available in fifty-five gallon drums.[306]

Kennedy brought ashore a record player to help pass the off hours. His supply of records, however, was limited. He was known to regularly participate in the cribbage games.[307]

PT-109 made occasional night patrols through the early part of June, often in the company of another boat. When returning to Wernham Cove after a night at sea, boats first stopped at the dock for fueling. The pier was positioned parallel to the shore and contained a small storage shed used to hold tools. Each boat had to be filled with fuel pumped by hand from fifty-five gallon drums. The slow and laborious process frequently caused long wait times as multiple patrols often returned in close proximity. Boats regularly rushed to the dock vying for an early position in line.

The 109 was returning from patrol one morning when Kennedy decided to race another boat to the refueling station. The boats were nearly even until the final approach, when PT-109 pulled into the lead. Kennedy hoped that throwing the engines in reverse during the final moments would stop the boat, but the motors sputtered out sending the 109 continuing forward at a high rate of speed crashing into the dock. The collision sent tools flying in all directions, with some going overboard into the water, much to the anger of a nearby work party.[308]

Fortunately the damage to the boat was minor. Then the situation was somewhat diffused when some PT boats broke free of their moorings, distracting the attention of the angry dockside sailors. Kennedy offered a quiet apology, before sneaking away from the scene of the accident.

After spending nearly two weeks in the Russells, *PT-109* returned to Tulagi for a short stay on June 13. The boat underwent engine maintenance and returned to Wernham Cove just three days later.[309] The 109 remained in the Russells for the remainder of the month, but only ventured out on a single night patrol. By this time the routine voyages from the forward base were largely curtailed due to the lack of serious enemy activity and the ongoing threat from Japanese float planes.[310]

Aside from the lack of combat experience, Kennedy was doing well in his new environment. "Feeling O.K.," he wrote. "The back has really acted amazingly well and gives me scarcely no trouble and in general feel[s] pretty good. Good bunch out here, so all in all it isn't too bad . . ."

The bases at Tulagi and the Russells were no longer on the front lines, leaving the young officer still aching to get into the fight. The battle for the Solomons was about to move north to a new arena, however, and in only a matter of a few short weeks, Kennedy and *PT-109* would be in the thick of the action.

CHAPTER 13

MOVING UP THE SLOT

The next large American offensive operation in the Solomon Islands was ready to begin in late June after months of planning and preparation. An invasion fleet under the command of Admiral Richmond Turner departed from Guadalcanal on June 29 and set a course northwest. Its destination was New Georgia, home to a new Japanese airfield at Munda Point. Although under regular American air and sea bombardment since early 1943, the base remained largely operational. Capturing the air base was the ultimate goal of the mission.

The main assault began on June 30 and included landings at four locations. The largest and most important took place at Rendova. A small island adjacent to the larger New Georgia, Rendova stood directly across a narrow channel from Munda. The American strategy was to bombard the airfield with heavy land-based artillery guns before using Rendova as a staging area for a direct attack. The island was quickly secured after the landing took place without opposition.

Twelve PT boats of Squadron Nine accompanied the invasion force, under the leadership of Lieutenant Commander Robert Kelly of Philippines fame. Kelly was charged with establishing a forward PT base.

The island of Rendova is home to a 3,400 foot high mountain peak with coastal plains radiating out among various areas along the coastline. The inlet forming Rendova Harbor is on the northwestern portion of the island, and is partially protected from the open sea by a series of smaller islands and reefs forming a sheltered area suitable for anchoring large ships. Home to assorted coral reefs and an abundance of aquatic life, the harbor quickly became the center of American naval operations in the area.

Kelly chose Lumbari Island near the western entrance to Rendova Harbor as the location of the new PT base. The small kidney-shaped land mass was crowded with palm trees. It measured a mere four hundred yards long and half that distance in width. The station was very primitive with a square dugout set back from the beach with sandbag walls and a tent roof serving as base headquarters. Additional tents nearby functioned as the mess hall, sick bay, and housing facilities for the base force.[311]

There were constant reminders for the PT men of just how close they were to the front lines. The most prominent was the assortment of foxholes and gun emplacements spread around the immediate area. Crews lived aboard their boats. The base was soon christened Todd City in honor of Leon Todd, the first PT sailor to be killed in the area.

Unlike the PT bases at Tulagi and the Russells, Rendova featured sloping beaches that prevented the boats from mooring right up against the shore. The PT's had to moor in clusters around buoys in the open water of the harbor.[312] The arrangement made for little protection against air attacks.

It was not uncommon for afternoon rain clouds to gently move down from the mountain peak on Rendova and enshroud the harbor with rain. The area then became bathed in sunlight once the showers moved out to sea. The conditions left a thick humid air hanging over the PT base.

The first major event associated with the new PT base was an unfortunate case of mistaken identity. On the day of his arrival, Robert Kelly was initially told by area commanders that there would be no evening voyages. The PT boats spent much of the day fueling from fifty-five gallon drums moved to the area on a landing craft and searching for a suitable anchorage since no patrols were planned.[313]

The situation, however, changed and Kelly was later directed by the local naval authorities to send his torpedo boats out on a night patrol to intercept and destroy enemy forces expected to venture into the area from the north. When Kelly inquired about friendly ships operating in the region, he was specifically told that all American vessels were well clear of his patrol area.[314] Unfortunately, it was not the case. The squadron commander took all twelve of his boats out during the evening hours, dividing the force into smaller patrol groups.

Kelly ordered his boats to attack when a group of PT's found what was thought to be an enemy transport under escort in hazy weather about five miles off the western tip of Rendova. The strike was executed in near perfect form with one or more evenly spaced torpedo hits sending the target ship to the bottom.

The enemy transport turned out to be Admiral Turner's flagship *Mc-Cawley*. The vessel was leaving the area under tow and escort after suffering serious damage from an air attack earlier in the day. The only men aboard were a salvage crew. Fortunately, the sailors had just transferred to a nearby destroyer over fears of the vessel's stability. The transport sank in less than a minute without any loss of life.[315] Luckily the encounter did not escalate, perhaps due to the weather conditions. None of the escort ships were hit and the PT boats were not taken under fire.

The costly mistake was the result of poor communications among the various American commands. Operational control of the PT boats was then given to Admiral Turner in the hopes of preventing additional problems. Turner promptly added a PT liaison officer to his staff to ensure that appropriate operational information reached all of the area naval commanders in a timely manner.

The first real encounter with the enemy for the Rendova PT boats was a sea battle similar to those fought in Iron Bottom Sound. Kelly led a three boat patrol out of the harbor as daylight was fading on July 3 to patrol off the western tip of Rendova. A midnight radio message urgently warned of Japanese destroyers heading into the area. About an hour later Kelly sighted distant flashes of gunfire, which he took to be the enemy.

The gunfire marked the first appearance of the Tokyo Express in the region. A Japanese force comprised of the light cruiser *Yubari* and nine destroyers had slipped into the area to give the Rendova beachhead a heavy pounding. However, the shelling completely missed the mark due to poor targeting and the entire bombardment fell harmlessly into the nearby jungle.[316]

With the *McCawley* incident just days old, Kelly cautiously approached the ships, not entirely sure if the vessels were friend or foe. As he passed through the enemy formation, four destroyers detached from the main group, encircled the PT boats, and opened fire. A furious battle at close quarters followed with the torpedo boats under constant fire. The PT's made smoke and radical turns to escape the onslaught.

The battle was inconclusive. Kelly's boats managed to fire six torpedoes but all of the shots missed. The PT's were able to slip away without suffering any serious damage.

With reports of the Tokyo Express on the move, the PT boats stationed at the Russell Islands ventured out on a security patrol to guard against the possibility that the enemy destroyers could move further south to threaten the Guadalcanal area. John Kennedy was among the boat captains heading out into the night.

The PT's were under orders to ply the open waters between the Russell Islands and New Georgia. No sign of the enemy was found, but the boats ran into rough seas. The conditions continued to worsen as the night progressed. It was difficult for topside crewmen to stay standing aboard PT-109. The sailors below deck fared little better as they remained confined in their bunks for safety.

Squadron commander Alvin Cluster was riding in PT-48, using her as his flagship for the patrol. The 48 boat had the misfortune of suffering damage to the bottom of its hull and started taking in water. The flagship's situation continued to worsen in the poor weather conditions. Her crew fired all four torpedoes to lighten up the boat, and a mattress was stuffed into the hole as a temporary patch. The fixes, however, proved inadequate and more help was needed.

Kennedy responded to a distress signal and came to the aid of the stricken boat shortly after dawn. He then left to hail a distant destroyer to borrow a bilge pump. Transferring the pump proved to be a precarious undertaking. Both the PT and destroyer struggled to stay in close proximity amid the swells and dips of the rough ocean. The 109 would be in immediate peril or even sinking condition if her wooden frame crashed into the destroyer's steel hull. Kennedy was able to keep his boat at a safe distance and get the pump aboard.[317]

The pump, however, was not enough to stabilize PT-48. When doubts began to emerge as to whether the damaged boat could make it back to the Russells, the decision was made to leave the 48 on Buruku Island for a repair crew to retrieve. Her crew crowded aboard PT-109 for the trip back to base.

Kennedy's torpedo boat did not escape the patrol unscathed. On the way back to the Russells a wave slammed into its port side hitting with tremendous force. It jarred a torpedo causing it to start a hot run in the tube. Lenny Thom stuffed toilet paper into the impeller on the warhead's exploder to keep the weapon from arming itself.[318]

The torpedo eventually broke loose from the tube, causing a depth charge to break free of its mounting and crash through the deck into the crew's compartment below landing on a bunk. The berth had just been vacated by a crewman. Fortunately, neither weapon exploded as it would have been a certain end to *PT-109*. However, the incident sent one crewmen to the hospital and the boat back to base for repairs.

From its unfortunate beginnings with the *McCawley* incident, the Rendova PT base continued to grow throughout July with the arrival of more boats, including those of Squadrons Five and Ten. The base soon became home to a large group of boats from an assortment of squadrons. The 109 was the sole representative from Squadron Two sent north.

––––––

The first two months in the Solomons allowed John Kennedy to learn what had been happening on the front lines in the South Pacific. He heard of the vicious land fighting for Henderson Field on Guadalcanal. "The Marines took a terrible beating but gave it back," he told his parents in a letter. He also speculated on when the war would end. "As far as the length of the war, I don't see how it can stop in less than three years, but I'm sure we can lick them eventually. Our stuff is better, our pilots and planes are—everything considered—way ahead of theirs and our resources inexhaustible though this island to island stuff isn't the answer. If they do that the motto out here 'The Golden Gate by 48' won't ever come true."[319]

PT-109 and *PT-106* departed the Russells on July 10 for a brief run to Guadalcanal, returning on the same day. It may have been the last voyage the 109 made before new orders sent the boat north to Rendova. The exact date of the move is unknown due the final month of *PT-109's* log book being lost with the boat, but the transfer occurred sometime in the middle of July. The voyage from the Russells took ten hours to complete.[320]

The move took *PT-109* away from Al Cluster's jurisdiction and put her under the operational control of the Rendova PT base commander. Kennedy was looking forward to serving under the popular Kelly.[321] The squadron commander had a good reputation and was recalled by one boat captain as a "forthright and fearless leader."[322] However, Kelly had already departed Rendova by the time Kennedy arrived.

Early operations revealed that the Rendova boats could only effectively cover the western areas around New Georgia. A second base was needed to extend PT coverage to the northern and eastern coastal areas. The station was established at Lever Harbor on the northeast coast of New Georgia, and Kelly was sent north to command the new base. His replacement was Lieutenant Commander Thomas G. Warfield.

The new commanding officer was a 1932 Naval Academy graduate who saw action in the Philippines early in the war before escaping the Japanese onslaught and transferring into PT boats. He put Squadron Ten into commission and continued to serve as her commanding officer. Warfield was a no-nonsense officer who did things by the book and tended to keep a distance from his men. Kennedy was now operating at a new base, in unfamiliar geography, with a different set of boat captains, and a commanding officer very different from the easygoing Cluster.

The newly arrived PT boats operated in a network of islands and waterways to the north and west of Rendova covering a distance spanning almost fifty miles.[323] Kolombangara stood directly northwest of New Georgia with the two islands separated by Kula Gulf. The jungle-covered circular island is dominated by a large extinct volcano rising to a height of almost 6,000 feet. Vella Lavella was the next island northwest of Kolombangara with Vella Gulf situated between them.

A narrow string of small islands including Gizo and Wana Wana are positioned along the southern boundaries of Kula Gulf, Kolombangara, and

CENTRAL SOLOMON ISLANDS, 1943

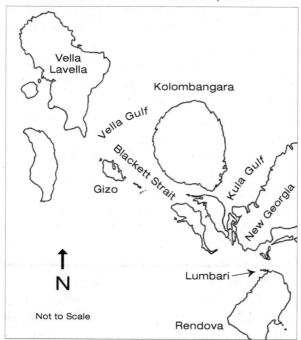

Vella Gulf. The narrow passageway of Blackett Strait runs between the island string and Kolombangara. Ferguson Passage, a tight gap near Gizo Island, links Blackett Strait to the much larger Solomon Sea to the south.

The opposing sides were locked into fierce land combat on New Georgia by the time *PT-109* arrived in the middle of July. Heavy American artillery on Rendova pounded the Munda air base as ground forces clashed with stubborn Japanese defenders. Imperial leaders knew an American breakthrough in the Central Solomons would threaten bases further north and were committed to providing the New Georgia garrison the reinforcements and supplies needed to hold out.

The Rendova PT boats were charged with accomplishing dual objectives. First, the boats were to engage Japanese naval traffic operating to bring reinforcements to the front lines. Second, the PT's would guard the Rendova area against possible attack from any Japanese surface ships that might venture south to strike American amphibious forces. Torpedo boats were prohibited from operating north of eight degrees south latitude so Allied planes could safely assume any small craft north of the line were Japanese.[324]

A typical night patrol had the boats departing Lumbari after sunset and initially moving straight west. Depending on the particular mission, the PT's turned north at various locations to travel into the heart of Japanese territory. When attempting to disrupt the Japanese supply line, the boats went through Ferguson Passage, Gizo Strait, or Wilson Strait to gain access to the southern coastal areas of Vella Lavella and Kolombangara. The PT's hunted barges or made ready to tangle with Tokyo Express runs during patrols in the southern portion of Vella Gulf and Blackett Strait. The boats took up blocking positions south of Ferguson Passage if the mission was to protect against possible enemy movements against Rendova.

The enemy was not the same Japanese Navy encountered in the waters of Iron Bottom Sound. The balance of power in the Solomons, both at sea and in the air, now favored the Americans. Allied planes roamed the area attacking any enemy target daring to show itself during daylight hours, while American surface forces regularly used the cover of night to patrol the Slot and points beyond.

The Japanese supply line to New Georgia was a multi-step process, causing the Imperial transporters to dodge American naval and air power on at least two separate occasions. The enemy base at Vila on the southern end of Kolombangara was the key middle point in the supply chain. Tokyo Express ran from the north, moved through either Kula Gulf or Vella Gulf to trans-

BLACKETT STRAIT AREA

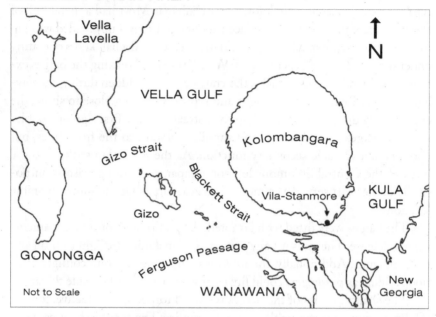

verse Blackett Strait, and delivered their cargos to Vila. Barges then ferried the troops and supplies across the southern end of Kula Gulf to the northwest coast of New Georgia. The final step was an overland journey to reach the beleaguered Munda garrison.

American cruisers and destroyers twice clashed with the Tokyo Express during early July. Both actions took place near Kolombangara in the vicinity of Kula Gulf. The Battle of Kula Gulf (July 6) and the Battle of Kolombangara (July 12 & 13) were largely draws from a tactical perspective. The Japanese lost a total of one light cruiser and two destroyers in the actions, while American losses amounted to a light cruiser and one destroyer with additional ships suffering heavy damage.[325]

The PT's stayed on the sidelines during both fights. Not wanting to risk a repeat of the *McCawley* incident, the American cruiser commanders had insisted the PT boats remain in port.[326] In both battles, however, the Japanese destroyer transports successfully delivered their cargos to Vila.

The sea battles, coupled with the growing threat from the air, helped convince Japanese naval leaders to begin to abandon using destroyers to transfer troops and supplies directly to the front lines. Barges soon began to take over a larger portion of the transportation role.

The Japanese barges used in the Solomons did not conform to a standard type. The small vessels were known as a Daihatsu. Most had a metal hull of about fifty feet in length and displaced about eight tons. Fully loaded with up to ninety troops, the small vessels could make seven and a half knots operating under the power of a diesel motor.[327] With slow speed making the barges extremely vulnerable to air attacks, the craft kept well-hidden during the daylight hours. Moving about at night and typically keeping close to shore, the craft quickly disappeared inland up river streams at the first sign of trouble.

The barges moved troops and supplies forward to the front lines, but also served a valuable secondary function. As the American strike into the heart of the Central Solomons left some Japanese island garrisons outpositioned, the craft served as a method to evacuate troops to more favorable locations.

The barges were fitted with armored plate for protection and armaments for self defense. The guns usually consisted of an automatic light cannon and machine guns. Additionally, the interior compartments were configured so troops riding as passengers could fire their weapons against outside threats.[328]

The shallow drafts of the barges rendered torpedoes ineffective, forcing PT boats to engage the small craft with gunfire. The torpedo boat captains soon learned it was not an even fight. The armor gave the barges protection not afforded to the PT's, and the light guns of the torpedo boats often did not have enough firepower to swiftly knock out the enemy.

The Japanese also relied on help from the air to keep the supply line moving. The float plane menace, used so effectively in the waning days of the fight in Iron Bottom Sound, was now a serious everyday threat. Operating from several area bases and equipped with machine guns, bombs, and flares, the planes prowled the area almost nightly looking for the telltale phosphorescent wakes of the PT boats. Swooping in low to bomb and strafe, the planes also used flares to warn nearby vessels of the torpedo boat threat. The illuminations sent barges close to the shoreline with gunners alert for action. Some daring Japanese pilots even lurked off Rendova in fading daylight to follow torpedo boats departing for evening patrols.[329]

Although impossible to completely eliminate the float plane threat, the Rendova boat captains quickly developed countermeasures. The typical patrol speed was often reduced to five or six knots to minimize the trailing wakes. The speed reduction was accomplished by running on only one engine with the remaining two kept in neutral. Although the procedure was widely used, not all experienced PT sailors agreed it was good.[330] Boat captains could be

PT boat hulls are seen under construction at the Elco factory in Bayonne, NJ. Contrary to popular belief, the hulls were not constructed of plywood, but were made of mahogany planks. —*National Archives*

The launching of *PT-103* in Bayonne, NJ on May 16, 1942 marked the debut of a new type of torpedo boat. The Elco 80-foot boats were larger, heavier, and better armed than the two proceeding production classes built by the manufacturer. —*National Archives*

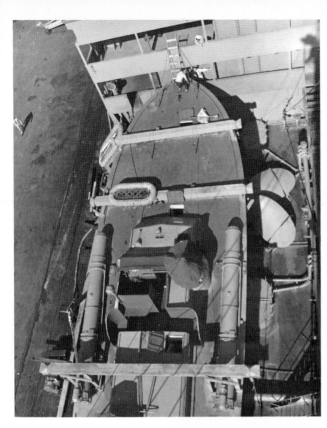

Looking down on the forward half of an Elco 80-foot PT boat shows the small bridge area known as the conn. Typically manned by the boat captain, the area contains the wheel and an assortment of gauges and controls.
—*National Archives*

The overhead view of the back of an Elco 80-foot boat shows an open hatch near the end of the boat leading to the lazarette. Located at the very back of the boat, the compartment contained a work bench, spare parts, and ammunition.
—*National Archives*

John Bulkeley became a national hero after using a PT boat to evacuate General Douglas Mac-Arthur from the Philippines in early 1942. His exploits helped convince many young naval officers, including Bryant Larson and John Kennedy, to volunteer for the PT boat service. —*National Archives*

Bryant Larson volunteered for PT boat service while attending naval officer training at Northwestern University in Chicago in 1942. He eventually took *PT-109* to the front lines of the war in the South Pacific. —*Courtesy of WW II PT Boats Museum and Archives, Germantown, TN and Karen Hone*

Rollin Westholm used *PT-109* as his flagship while commanding a squadron of torpedo boats during the battle for Guadalcanal. He worked closely with his executive officer Bryant Larson during a series of horrific night battles near the embattled island. —*Courtesy of USSBush.com and Ted Mayhugh*

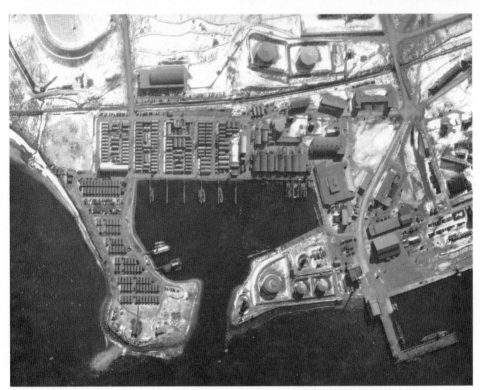

An aerial photo taken near the end of World War II shows an expanded Motor Torpedo Boat Squadron Training Center in Rhode Island. The facility was much smaller in 1942 when Bryant Larson and John Kennedy graduated among the early classes. —*National Archives*

A sailor cleans a fifty-caliber machine gun on an unidentified PT boat in a 1944 photograph taken in the Philippines. The double-barreled weapon could fire rounds at a rate of 550 per minute.
—*National Archives*

PT-105 is seen among a group of PT boats on maneuvers in the Atlantic shortly after completion in July 1942. The initial group of boats had no armament forward of the conn area, but the space was used later in the war for more firepower. —*National Archives*

A side view of *PT-107* off the East Coast in July 1942 reveals the sleek lines of an Elco 80-foot PT boat. The depth charges fitted in place of the after torpedo tubes was rarely done during wartime conditions in the South Pacific. —*National Archives*

Left: The single barrel Oerlikon twenty-millimeter cannon could send a small shell up to 5,500 yards against an air or surface target. The weapon was fed by a sixty-round magazine mounted on top of the gun. A bag below the barrel collected the spent cartridges. —*National Archives*

Below: The back end of a torpedo tube is seen up close on an unidentified PT boat. A black powder impulse charge located at the top rear of each tube electronically fired the torpedo, but a sailor with a mallet regularly stood by in case the electronics failed. —*National Archives*

Above: A navy photographer snapped a series of pictures on August 20, 1942 of *PT-109* sitting on the deck of the Liberty ship *Joseph Stanton* in preparation for the voyage to Panama. The photo was taken at the Norfolk Navy Yard in Virginia.
—*National Archives*

Right: Engine exhaust exited out of six pipes on the back of *PT-109*'s squared off stern. Each pipe was covered with a muffler to deaden the engine noise, but the system could only be used when the boat was traveling at a low rate of speed.
—*National Archives*

PT-109 (left) and *PT-107* sit on the deck of *Joseph Stanton* just prior to the voyage to Panama. When transported on the deck of a cargo vessel, PT's could float free in the event the ship sank. —*National Archives*

A PT boat lays a smoke screen as part of training maneuvers near Panama in 1943. The smoke generator proved to be a life-saving device in the South Pacific, helping many boats to escape from angry Japanese destroyers. —*National Archives*

An aerial view of the Tulagi PT base shows a number of PT boats moored in clusters and an assortment of buildings used as base facilities. Note the three boats in floating dry docks for repairs and maintenance. —*Courtesy of WW II PT Boats Museum and Archives, Germantown, TN*

PT sailors prepare to load a torpedo into a tube. The outdated Mark Eight torpedoes used by the boats in the Solomons required constant maintenance and were regularly plagued by a variety of problems, including not running at a fixed depth. —*National Archives*

PT-109 returns to Tulagi on December 1, 1942 loaded full with survivors from the sunken cruiser *Northampton*. The damaged heavy cruiser *New Orleans* is in the background. —*National Archives*

The phosphorescent wake behind a speeding PT boat could be seen miles away by Japanese float planes lurking in the dark South Pacific night sky. The planes often attacked boats from behind with bombs and machine guns without warning. —*National Archives*

PT boats moored in the Russell Islands. Both Bryant Larson and John Kennedy took *PT-109* to the advanced base in 1943, but the boat only made routine security patrols and saw little action.
—*National Archives*

The deck log of *PT-109* for April 25, 1943 records that John F. Kennedy took command of the boat at 11:00 a.m. He replaced Bryant Larson who received orders to return to the United States after enduring months of arduous combat near Guadalcanal.
—*National Archives*

Log of the PT 1∅9   Attached to the _____
_____ Naval District, Apr 25, 1943

Hour	Wind		Barometer	Temperature		State of the Weather by Symbols	Clouds			Condition of the Sea
	Direction	Force	Height in Inches	Thermometer, attached	Air, dry bulb	Air, wet bulb		Forms of, by symbols	Moving from—	Amount covered, tenths	
A.M. 4											
8											
12 M.											
P.M. 16											
20											
24											

REMARKS

∅850 Under way for Sisapi
1100 Lt(jg) J F Kennedy assumed command of boat
1145 - Moored at usual berth in tender.
1500 - L.E. Trewith F1/c - L.E. Drawdy F1/c, C.R. Harris Cm2/c reported aboard

Examined and found to be correct.

Ens. L.J. Thom, U.S.N.R.
Commanding.
Exec.

A crane prepares to move a torpedo onto a PT boat at Rendova. The loading of torpedoes and the refueling of boats were both manual processes often requiring hard labor by base force sailors and boat crews alike.
—*National Archives*

John F. Kennedy began his navy career with a desk job in Washington, DC. He volunteered for PT boat service while attending officer training in Chicago and eventually made his way to the South Pacific. —*National Archives*

Groups of PT's are moored in clusters in the open water of Rendova Harbor. Unlike the bases at Tulagi and Russell Islands, the sloping beaches of Rendova and Lumbari prevented the boats from mooring right up against the shore. —*National Archives*

Two floating drydocks in Rendova Harbor were used to repair and maintain PT boats. Dedicated base crews kept the small boats operating in spite of harsh front line conditions and a constant shortage of spare parts. —*National Archives*

The Japanese increasingly relied on small barges after their defeat at Guadalcanal, such as the one seen in this photo, to move troops and supplies around the Central Solomons. The small craft became formidable opponents for PT boats after the enemy added guns and armor. —*National Archives*

Above: Crewmen aboard *PT-109* pose for a picture sometime in July 1943. The sailors are assembled around the charthouse with the photographer positioned near the bow. Boat captain John F. Kennedy is farthest to the right.
—*National Archives*

Left: Sailors work to overhaul a PT boat engine at the Rendova base. The boats were powered by three Packard 1,200 horsepower motors each weighing about 3,000 pounds. The engines often remained in use long after their recommended service life, resulting in constant maintenance issues.
—*National Archives*

A late-war photo shows Rollin Westholm aboard an unknown warship. He had a long career in the navy after World War II and retired from the service in 1964. —*Courtesy of USSBush.com and Ted Mayhugh*

William Liebenow (right) receives a Bronze Star from Assistant Secretary of the Navy H. Struve Hensel in Washington, DC on April 3, 1945. Liebenow commanded *PT-157* in August 1943 during the rescue of John F. Kennedy and *PT-109* survivors. —*National Archives*

A full length view of the destroyer *Bush* was taken off the Mare Island Navy Yard, California in June 1944. Rollin Westholm was the boat's commanding officer when she was sunk near Okinawa by Japanese suicide planes in 1945. —*U.S. Navy / Courtesy of the Floating Drydock*

Bryant Larson took command on *PT-529* in 1944 and remained aboard until the end of the war. Although of similar design to *PT-109*, the new boat was outfitted with the newest technology and weaponry. The boat is seen underway off the coast of Borneo near Tarakan in 1945. —*Courtesy of WW II PT Boats Museum and Archives, Germantown, TN*

confronted with a combination of float planes, armored barges, or destroyers on any given night.

The Japanese began to jam commonly used radio frequencies to further hamper PT operations. "Communication between boats and base were generally satisfactory," Thomas Warfield reported in late July.[331] However, he also acknowledged that instances of radio jamming were increasing and suggested a rotation of frequencies to help remedy the problem.

Torpedo boat operations continued to increase during the second half of July with a total of about fifty-two PT's eventually operating from the two New Georgia area bases.[332] A limited number of the newer boats now had radar. Unfortunately, mistakes and costly errors involving PT's increased along with the number of boats in the area.

The next unfortunate incident occurred as part of a large PT boat operation on the night of July 17–18. Twelve boats left Rendova to move against Japanese destroyers thought to be en route to Blackett Strait. Operating in three groups to saturate the area, some boats made contact with as many as six destroyers and made torpedo runs during the ensuing skirmish. "All torpedoes fired ran true, and all boats observed a torpedo hit on the leading destroyer just abaft her bridge, amidships," Thomas Warfield reported.[333] One PT saw a torpedo hit a second destroyer. However, as with many of the battles near Guadalcanal, the reports were inaccurate as no Japanese warships reported damage.[334]

Three of the PT boats patrolling west of Kolombangara later strayed from their assigned area, moving too far north. An Allied reconnaissance plane reported the craft as Japanese destroyers, setting off additional alarms among area naval commanders. Five American destroyers patrolling off the northern coast of New Georgia raced to the reported sighting. The warships opened fire at 20,000 yards after spotting the boats at extreme range.[335] The PT's returned fire with torpedoes and scurried south. The destroyers did not pursue. Fortunately, no damage was suffered among any of the participants. The same would not be the case during the next incident only a few days later.

A trio of boats, PT's 164, 166, and 168, were en route to Rendova on the morning of July 20 after conducting a routine evening patrol. Their progress was slowed after one boat hit a log during the night causing the entire group to reduce speed. A flight of four B-25 medium bombers was passing through the area after conducting an early morning patrol farther north. Morning sweeps around the Central Solomons were a common procedure with the planes hoping to catch any unsuspecting Japanese stragglers from the previous night. The airmen were told no American surface ships would be operating in the region during daylight hours.[336]

The planes dove towards the targets for a strafing run after sighting the torpedo boats just south of Ferguson Passage. The PT sailors easily identified the approaching bombers as friendly and were horrified when machine gun bullets started flying. Emergency radio calls, frantic arm waving, and the firing of signal flares did nothing to dissuade the attacking planes. The boat captains gave no order to fire, but inexperienced gunners on two of the PT's opened up with machine guns.

The brief exchange had deadly results. All three of the boats were hit. *PT-166* was rocked by an explosion and had to be abandoned. Some of her crew were wounded. One B-25 left the scene trailing smoke and crashed about five miles away. Crewmen on *PT-168* battled a fire on board as the boat raced to the crash scene to rescue three of the six airmen. The disastrous episode resulted in the loss of a PT boat, a B-25, and three American servicemen. It created a high level of animosity among the PT sailors and airmen, with each group blaming the other for the sad episode.

———————

John Kennedy entered the world of the Central Solomons as he pointed the bow of *PT-109* towards Lumbari Island after the boat reached the confines of Rendova Harbor. A makeshift sign made of painted oil drum covers became visible as he approached the PT base. It was strung between two palm trees near a small dock and read "Todd City." Once ashore Kennedy reported to base commander Thomas Warfield. He was introduced to a number of officers, including executive officer Lieutenant Arthur Berndston and communications officer Lieutenant James Woods.[337]

As with any new officer, Kennedy needed to be brought up to speed as to what was happening in the area. The group talked about the tactical situation and some of the challenges facing the boat captains. Kennedy then took the 109 to a mooring buoy assigned to him by Warfield. Between fifteen and twenty boats were at Lumbari at the time the 109 arrived.

Kennedy and his men had little time to rest, as they were ordered out to patrol, along with another boat, on their very first night at Lumbari. Although the voyage was routine, it was the first time the 109 moved among the various islands of the unfamiliar geography. The crew was tense and apprehensive about what the night would bring.

Kennedy moved his boat cautiously, keeping careful watch not to become separated from the lead boat. When the machine guns on the first PT opened fire on a nearby island, Kennedy ordered his gunners to do the same. A stream of bullets leapt out from the 109 hitting the distant shore with unknown results. There was no return fire and the shooting stopped almost as quickly as it started. Tension among *PT-109's* sailors began to ease when the boats set a course for Rendova ending the patrol.

Kennedy and his men soon fell into an exhaustive routine of regular night patrols, not unlike what Rollin Westholm and Bryant Larson experienced during the fight for Guadalcanal. Tension surrounding night patrols, the threat of air attack both while at sea and in port, and limited sleep combined to put an exhaustive strain on officers and enlisted men alike. The boat continued to have nocturnal encounters with both friendly and enemy aircraft.

With the B-25 incident still fresh in the minds of the Lumbari PT sailors, Kennedy set out for an evening patrol in the vicinity of Gizo Island. During the night lookouts spotted two planes positively identified as friendly PBY's. The Black Cats were operating in close proximity to *PT-109*. Kennedy asked his radioman to try to raise the pilots on the airwaves just as an explosion was heard in the general vicinity. A confusing series of radio exchanges followed that included a report of Japanese floatplanes in the area.

In an attempt to head off any additional problems, Kennedy told his radioman to warn that the PT would open fire on the next plane to overfly her.[338] The American planes moved off after apparently heeding the notice. *PT-109* did not encounter any additional aircraft during the remainder of the patrol.

The afternoon of July 19 found *PT-109* getting ready for another evening patrol. She later departed Lumbari in the company of *PT-105*, *PT-107*, and *PT-163*. The 107 boat was equipped with radar. The group had orders to patrol the area west of Kolombangara, and the night featured thick low-hanging clouds.

The boats became separated shortly after arriving on station. When *PT-107* made radar contact with what was thought to be three enemy destroyers, boat captain Bill Barrett radioed the other boats to congregate for an attack. None of the PT's were able to pick up the message. Just then a star shell burst above, illuminating the immediate area around the 107, and inaccurate gunfire from the destroyers began to splash around the boat. Barrett ordered smoke and turned to run for cover.

As *PT-107* was coming under attack, the other three boats ended up close together near Gizo Island. Without the benefit of radar, none had located the Japanese destroyers. The first sign of trouble occurred when a lookout on *PT-109* sighted flashes on the distant horizon. Kennedy radioed a contact report and turned the boat in the direction of the sighting. He then poured on speed with the two other boats following close behind. The trio of PT's arrived in the area of the presumed battle only to find nothing. By that time *PT-107* had successfully escaped to the south and the destroyers had moved away in the opposite direction. The PT sailors, though, were not alone. Just then a Japanese float plane found the torpedo boats.

An alert lookout aboard *PT-109* sounded the alarm, yelling, "Plane coming in at two o'clock. Can't see the type."[339] Kennedy looked to the sky, but was barely able to see the approaching aircraft. It seemed to be heading directly towards the boat and closing fast. He gave the order to open fire. A stream of machine gun bullets jumped skyward from the 109. The other two boats also opened fire. The plane made a sharp bank and disappeared into the night. No bombs were dropped in the aborted attack.[340]

The three boats lowered speed to reduce their wakes and continued to patrol. Nothing seemed out of the ordinary several hours later when the PT's were southwest of Gizo. The boat captains, however, had no idea they were again being stalked from above. A star shell suddenly burst overhead without warning, with the brilliant white light clearly illuminating the boats below. Increasing speed and ordering smoke, Kennedy started zigzagging in the hopes of slipping away unnoticed.

The gunners on *PT-163* were the only ones to open fire. A string of bombs exploded among the boats shortly after the shooting started. One landed close behind *PT-109*, partially showering her with shrapnel and hitting two crewmen. Kennedy told Lenny Thom to take the conn and then raced to the first aid kit. He administered aid to the wounded men.

The plane did not return for a second attack, but vanished into the darkness not to be seen again. The 109 returned to Rendova after morning light. Although their wounds were not thought to be serious, both of the injured crewmen left the boat for further medical attention. Damage to the boat was considered minor and included some splintered deck planks.[341]

Five days passed before *PT-109's* next float plane encounter. On July 25 the 109 was part of a six boat patrol. The group was on station southeast of Wana Wana Island when a float plane dropped out of the darkness to attack without warning. None of the boats opened fire, but all sped up to take evasive action, zigzagging to avoid the night menace. A total of six bombs fell among the group. One exploded twenty yards off the starboard quarter of

PT-105. The boat's executive officer was hit in the head with shrapnel as he stood at the conn and killed instantly.

The attack ended almost as quickly as it began with no other boats sustaining damage. *PT-109* escaped unharmed to fight another day.

CHAPTER 14

THE LAST DAYS AT RENDOVA

Six American destroyers suddenly appeared off the southern coast of New Georgia during the early morning hours of July 25, 1943 to mark the beginning of a new offensive. The area just east of Munda Point was soon subjected to a heavy pounding as the destroyers poured nearly 4,000 rounds of five-inch shells onto Japanese positions.[342] The seaborne attack was barely complete when scores of planes arrived to deliver one of the strongest bombings of the campaign. The final stage of the barrage occurred when heavy artillery batteries from nearby islands joined the fight. The combined-arms bombardment marked the resurgence of the American drive towards Munda.

While the troops slowly advanced closer to the enemy airfield, the PT sailors at Lumbari continued to carry out their dual mission of protecting the Rendova area from attack and disrupting the Japanese supply line. The enemy seaborne threat to Rendova appeared to decline as the month of July progressed, allowing the PT's to focus on attacking the Japanese supply operations. The boats made almost continuous evening runs into Blackett Strait during the last days of the month.

The incidents of mistaken identity also subsided late in July. New procedures were established to better help area commanders share operational information. Base commander Thomas Warfield sent a daily report of proposed PT boat operations to Admiral Turner's staff. The information was then distributed to all air and surface commands associated with the New Georgia operation. "The PT's are likewise warned of the presence of friendly units in the daily dispatch of operation orders from Commander, Task Force

31. This is only a step towards the goal," Warfield wrote, explaining the improved communications."[343]

The large number of available PT's at Rendova now allowed for a rotating schedule of boats for the evening patrol duties. Some of the boats remaining at the base for the night often stayed on alert in case emergency action was needed to defend the harbor area. Following the rotation system, *PT-109* remained in port on the night of July 26 while six boats departed Lumbari during the early evening for a voyage into Blackett Strait. With the eastern portion of the waterway home to the busy enemy base at Vila on Kolombangara, the area was considered hostile waters and a hotbed of Japanese supply line activity. The patrol marked one of the first substantial encounters between PT boats and Japanese barge traffic.

Three of the boats, *PT-106, PT-117,* and *PT-154,* were patrolling the area west of Makuti Island when they sighted a group of enemy barges moving away from Kolombangara in the direction of Gizo Island. The barges had just moved parallel to Gizo and were close to the shore when the Japanese spotted the PT's. The American boats then closed to attack with gunfire.

The battle that followed clearly illustrated the limitations of the torpedo boat's light armament against the armored barges. Warfield described what happened during one encounter in his battle report. "One hundred fifty rounds of fifty-caliber were fired at the center barge with no visible effect. Most all shots seemed to ricochet harmlessly off."[344] The squadron commander attributed some of the problems to poor supervision and weapon upkeep, but also added, "Tactics are under revision for barge strafing."

John Kennedy's next turn to make the run into enemy waters took place on the night of July 27. *PT-109* was one of eight boats departing Lumbari for operations in the Gizo Strait area. The voyage was a rescue mission to extract a group of American servicemen from the island of Vella Lavella.

The boats left the Rendova area traveling northwest past Wana Wana and Ferguson Passage before turning north to pass through Gizo Strait. All the boats arrived on station at 9:00 p.m. The weather conditions were favorable for the mission. Scattered rain squalls from earlier in the evening had dissipated, leaving an overcast sky. A flare was sighted about two miles south of Gizo Strait about twenty minutes after the boat passed through the area. A second one appeared much closer a short time later, temporarily illuminating all of the boats. However, the PT's were not attacked from the air.

The boats operated in two separate groups to carry out the rescue operation. *PT-109* joined four other PT's patrolling two miles north of the strait.

They did not encounter any signs of the enemy. Three boats led by Lieutenant George Cookman in *PT-107* comprised the rescue force and proceeded north to the southeastern coast of Vella Lavella. Planes passed near Cookman's boats on four separate occasions over the next few hours, but never closed to strike. Sailors were even able to clearly identify one intruder as a single engine float plane, clearly a Japanese aircraft.

The rescue took place when two sailors departed one of the boats to go ashore at a predetermined location. The pair returned at 2:10 a.m. with seventeen men for the trip back to Rendova. "Eleven of the seventeen were survivors of a Black Cat forced down at sea on July 16 off [the] northwest coast of Vella Lavella, while the other six were members of a returning reconnaissance party," Warfield explained.[345] All boats departed the area at 4:30 a.m. and were back safely at Lumbari by 7:00 a.m.

Torpedo boats ventured out on patrol the next couple of nights, but *PT-109* remained in port. Eight boats prowled the waters of Blackett Strait on the night of July 28–29, but made no enemy surface contacts. Aside from a brief float plane attack and the sighting of a friendly native canoe, previously advised to be in the area, the voyage was uneventful.[346]

One night later four boats exchanged fire in poor weather conditions with several barges in the vicinity of Blackett Strait with inconclusive results. The small battle was discontinued when the PT's were directed to investigate a possible ship near Wana Wana Island. The potential target was one of three picked up by radar at Rendova. The contact report turned out to be negative, prompting the boats to return to base.[347]

The night of July 30 marked the last patrol of the month by *PT-109*. John Kennedy guided his boat out of Rendova Harbor during the early evening hours in the company of seven other PT's for the voyage into Blackett Strait. It was a routine patrol, but the voyage also included searching for a pilot reported down at sea about ten miles southeast of Gizo Island. However, bad luck befell Kennedy and his crew. "On the way to station *PT-109's* rudder failed and it returned to base," Warfield explained.[348]

PT-109's crew had to contend with whatever food was available as the boat rotated between evening patrols and time in port. Fresh food was a rare commodity at the Rendova PT base by the last days of July. The sailors aboard the 109 were surviving on a diet consisting mostly of Spam and other canned foods. Anything beyond the canned staples was a rare treat.

Kennedy was not able to enjoy one of his favorite foods due to the lack of available ingredients. He was known to like pancakes and had the boat's cook prepare the meal whenever possible. It was not often while at the front lines.

At about this time Kennedy heard of several landing craft arriving in the area to deliver supplies to New Georgia. He rushed over to the lead ship, *LCT-161*. In conversation with the boat's commanding officer, who recognized him as a former ambassador's son, he was able to get some New Zealand mutton in exchange for a promise to buy the officer a lobster dinner should the two ever be together in Boston.[349] Although it was not much, some fresh food at the front lines was better than nothing.

———

The beginning of August 1 marked the start of another month, but the day promised to be nothing more than routine for the PT sailors on Lumbari Island. The highlight of the morning was the arrival of *PT-164* from Tulagi. She was carrying a load of critical spare parts, often in short supply at forward operating bases. Sailors from the boat and base force began the slow unloading process shortly after her arrival in Rendova Harbor.

PT-109 was one of many boats moored out in the harbor. Her crewmen were in good spirits as the boat was not planning to go out during the evening. She had recently completed several patrols and was scheduled to take the night off.[350]

John Kennedy was using the day to add some firepower to his boat. The increased Japanese reliance on barges for transportation was now clear to American naval commanders. The initial skirmishes in Blackett Strait confirmed the growing belief among Rendova boat captains that PT boats, in their current configuration, were not well suited for barge hunting. Most suspected it was only a matter of time before a torpedo boat fighting a barge at close range would meet a fiery end when Japanese bullets pierced the wooden hull to set the fuel tanks aflame.

Kennedy decided to take matters into his own hands as the navy brass explored ways to add more firepower to the boats. The broken rudder incident on July 30 gave him time to act. He went ashore looking for armament and found it in the form of a small army gun.

The weapon was an antiquated thirty-seven millimeter anti-tank gun mounted on a small steel cart complete with wheels and bracing legs. The weapon was a little larger than anything currently on the boat, but it came with a big disadvantage—it was not automatic. Each shell had to be loaded and fired as a single shot.

Kennedy brought the gun to the 109 in a small Higgins landing craft at about noon. Crewmen used brute strength to haul it aboard along with a couple of large wooden planks. To mount the weapon the planks were laid on deck near the bow, and the gun was put on top with its wheels removed. The improvisation required the temporary removal of the boat's small rubber raft normally positioned on the foredeck. The plan was to have the gun securely bolted to the wood boards by base force carpenters. Although it was purely experimental, Kennedy felt comfortable knowing his boat would have some added punch when he inevitably crossed paths with an enemy barge.

The first indication of an evening encounter with the Tokyo Express occurred when a secret message from Admiral Theodore Wilkinson came to Thomas Warfield. Wilkinson had recently taken over as amphibious commander from Admiral Turner. "Indications express may run tonight one dash two (1–2) August," the coded message began.[351] The next lines outlined the countermeasures to be taken. It directed Warfield to deploy the maximum number of PT boats in the Blackett Strait area and Robert Kelly to send his Lever Harbor boats to the southern area of Kula Gulf.

It appeared the torpedo boats were only backups, for the message also notified the PT commanders that Captain Arleigh Burke was taking six destroyers up the Slot to operate north of Kolombangara. After examining the document Warfield concluded that Vila was the destination of the Japanese ships. Although the route of the express was unknown, Burke's destroyers were in a good position to intercept the enemy on either side of Kolombangara.

The message also included an ominous warning: "Jap air out to get Peter Tars [PT Boats.]" There was little time for Warfield to determine the meaning of the statement before the base was thrust into chaos.

Ensign George Ross was playing poker with some fellow officers in a tent when he was startled by a nearby commotion. "We heard this air raid siren and nobody paid much attention to it because we'd never had an air raid at that particular island—we were sort of isolated from the main base there, and we didn't figure they would ever raid us," he later recalled.[352] Ross, whose fate would soon be intertwined with those of Kennedy and the other *PT-109* crewmen, was dead wrong.

A flight of eighteen Japanese bombers were fast approaching Rendova Harbor. Their target was Lumbari Island. There was little time to react before the planes were almost overhead. The warning siren was soon supplemented by the sound of machine gun fire rattling in the distance.

The base was taken by complete surprise. Some boats were in the process of refueling, while others were moored at various locations near the island. The base force sailors on land raced to get to the safety of foxholes. PT men scrambled to get their boats moving.

John Kennedy jumped into the conn and ordered *PT-109* to get underway. The boat captain looked skyward to see a Japanese plane trailing smoke before crashing into the water off Rendova, sending a column of water high into the air. Crewmen opened fire with the forward machine gun and twenty-millimeter cannon at the stern shortly after the boat began to move. The 109 was among several PT's to move away from the base and out of harm's way. Other boats, however, were not as lucky.

A bomb exploded among a small cluster of boats moored together at a dock, causing severe damage to two. *PT-117* suffered a gaping hole in the hull near her bow and was beached. Still carrying some of the spare parts from Tulagi, *PT-164's* bow was demolished by the blast. The detonation not only tossed some of the remaining repair parts into the water, but also dislodged two of her torpedoes. The underwater missiles fell into the water and began to run erratically around the harbor before beaching without exploding. Both boats were considered total losses and two sailors were killed.[353] A third boat suffered slight damage.

Kennedy brought *PT-109* back near Lumbari after the all clear sounded. Looking around he saw the harbor was a scene of chaos and destruction. Materials were floating in the water and men were swimming about trying to find their way to shore or back aboard boats.

Warfield wasted no time in calling his boat captains together in the aftermath of the attack for a meeting in the operations bunker. To the base commander, the air attack was a clear signal the Japanese were intending to reach Vila through Vella Gulf. The strike intended to knock the PT boats out of service for the night. The ominous warning in the secret message now made perfect sense.

Kennedy used a small boat to row ashore on Lumbari. Boat captains gathered around Warfield in the operations center sitting in chairs or on the ground. Some maps were posted nearby for planning purposes. Base executive officer Arthur Berndston began the meeting by asking for a tally of damage and casualties. Warfield then read excerpts of the secret memo before asking how many boats were in operational condition. It was clear that the base survived the air attack in good shape and was still able to amply contribute to the night's operation against the Tokyo Express.

With fifteen boats available for patrol, the possible battle would be

ORDER OF BATTLE
AMERICAN PT BOATS VS. JAPANESE DESTROYERS
AUGUST 1–2, 1943

JAPANESE (Captain Katsumori Yamashiro)

SCREEN: Amagiri

TRANSPORTS: Hagikaze, Arashi, and Shigure

AMERICAN (Lieutenant Henry Brantingham)

DIVISION B: Off Vanga Vanga

PT-159 Henry Brantingham
PT-157 William Liebenow
PT-162 John Lowrey
PT-109 John Kennedy

DIVISION A: Off Gatere

PT-171 Arthur Berndtson
PT-169 Phillip Potter
PT-172 Stuart Hamilton
PT-163 Edward Kruse

DIVISION R: East of Makuti Island

PT-174 Russell Rome
PT-105 Richard Keresey
PT-103 Joseph Roberts

DIVISION C: South of Ferguson Passage

PT-107 George Cookman
PT-104 Robert Shearer
PT-106 David Payne
PT-108 Sidney Hix

among the largest PT operations in the Solomons to date. Warfield used a map to explain his belief that the Express would come through Vella Gulf. "And I stressed that it would not only come down but go back again, so they would have two shots at it," he later recalled of the meeting.[354]

The next step was to develop an operational plan. Although it was possible Burke's destroyers would do the fighting, there was no guarantee he could find the enemy. An additional factor to effect the planning was that only four of the available PT's were equipped with radar. The primitive sets were still new to the boats and not yet in widespread use.

The arrangement Warfield developed divided the PT's into four separate groups with each led by a radar-equipped boat and a senior officer. Three of the groups would be stationed in an approximate north-south line in or near Blackett Strait along the likely Japanese approach route. The plan offered the boats multiple points to make contact with the enemy, assuming the Japanese traveled through Vella Gulf as Warfield believed. The fourth group was to be stationed further south as a backup. Warfield referred to each patrol force as a division for planning purposes. He explained the overall plan to the boat captains and then provided the division leaders with detailed instructions.

The plan called for Division B to be comprised of four boats and led by Lieutenant Henry Brantingham in *PT-159*. Stationed the farthest north of the four divisions, the group was assigned to patrol in Vella Gulf off the west side of Kolombangara near Vanga Vanga. The division included *PT-109*.

The second group was designated Division A and included four boats under the command of Lieutenant Arthur Berndston in *PT-171*. The force was to patrol in Blackett Strait off the southwest coast of Kolombangara near the village of Gatere. Division R was to take position just east of Makuti Island in the heart of Blackett Strait. The southernmost of the three groups near Kolombangara, it was comprised of a trio of boats under the command of Lieutenant Russell Rome in *PT-174*.

The only boats stationed outside of Blackett Strait were the four PT's of Division C. The force was directed to patrol the area south of Ferguson Passage and was led by Lieutenant George Cookman in *PT-107*. The group was essentially a reserve unit put in place to guard against a possible seaborne attack on Rendova should the Tokyo Express turn out not to be a supply but an attack operation. Cookman could easily move north from his location to join a battle in Blackett Strait after the enemy was located.

Warfield gave the officers explicit instructions closely following his general operating philosophy of sending out a large number of boats and restricting radio communications to contact reports.[355] Division leaders were directed to immediately radio out a report after picking up a target on radar, and then move to attack. Other boat captains were to visually follow their leader's movements. Additional radio conversations were discouraged to prevent confusion and possible interception by the Japanese.[356]

"When the leading boat saw something and attacked, the other boats were to follow right along without further ado and no further conversation," Brantingham later said. "That was the practice of our squadron."[357] Boat captains who were new to the area, such as John Kennedy, were at great disadvantage, as this attack method was not used by other squadron commanders.

Warfield's restrictions on radio use may well have been based on the increasing number of attacks from the air. "It has been noted that attacks on PT's by enemy planes has usually closely followed periods of PT radio activity on the assigned frequency, which state of facts leads to the conclusion that Jap planes have been aided in detecting patrolling PT's by the use of RDF [radio direction finder] bearings," he wrote just prior to the operation in a recent action report.[358]

The squadron commander's directions did not fully appreciate the difficulty of maintaining visual contact at night. The situation was frequently made worse by poor weather conditions. The radio restrictions and resulting confusion would have deadly consequences during the night ahead.

Unlike other squadron commanders, such as Rollin Westholm during the fight for Guadalcanal, Warfield did not go out on patrol with his boats. He preferred to stay back at Lumbari in the base operations center and keep in contact with boats by radio while a mission was underway. As a result, Henry Brantingham was given the dual responsibility of leading a division and the entire operation. He was not only the most senior officer afloat, but had a good amount of PT boat experience, including fighting alongside Bulkeley in the Philippines during the early days of the war.[359]

Brantingham faced a great challenge in leading the operation. He was commanding PT's from four different squadrons, and most of the boat captains had never operated together. Some were not yet used to the geography or Warfield's operational rules.

The planning meeting ended with Warfield telling his officers to get their boats ready for action. For the boat captains originally scheduled to stay in port, it was something that would have to be done in a hurry.

American intelligence was again correct in anticipating the Japanese ship movements in the Central Solomons. Tokyo Express runs were now operating directly from Rabaul with no intermediate stops. After the two naval battles in the vicinity of Kula Gulf during the first half of July, Japanese commanders at Rabaul decided to try something new by sending the Tokyo Express around Kolombangara from the opposite direction.

On the night of July 21 a group of Japanese destroyers proceeded south through Vella Gulf before entering Blackett Strait to safely deliver their cargo at Vila. The force returned via the same route completely unmolested. Pleased with the operation's success, the Japanese decided to repeat the operation with another group of destroyers.[360]

The next supply mission was ready for departure on August 1 with the date selected to correspond with a moonless night. Control of the operation rested with Captain Katsumori Yamashiro. The commander of the Eleventh Destroyer Flotilla, he was an experienced officer, having participated in the conquest of Hong Kong and the fighting around Guadalcanal.

Yamashiro had four destroyers at his disposal for the mission: *Amagiri*, *Hagikaze*, *Arashi*, and *Shigure*. Only *Amagiri*, Yamashiro's flagship, served as a screen, carrying no cargo. The remaining three vessels carried a total of 900 troops and 120 tons of supplies.[361]

The force departed Rabaul at noon, setting a course for the Bougainville Strait. The passageway between Bougainville and Choiseul marked the northern end of the Slot. Lookouts aboard the destroyers carefully scanned the sky for Allied warplanes as the ships moved closer to the front lines.

———

John Kennedy had now spent about three months in the South Pacific, but had not yet proven himself in an actual battle. He was known to get along well with the other boat captains and was accepted as a peer after spending several weeks at Lumbari. Although the PT men knew Kennedy was a former ambassador's son, he seemed to be treated like just another officer.[362] After reporting to the easygoing Al Cluster at Tulagi, Kennedy now had to deal with Warfield's strict by-the-book command style. The squadron commander generally kept his distance from his men, and as a result was unpopular among many of the boat captains.[363]

Kennedy headed back to his small rowboat at the conclusion of the planning meeting, for the short trip back to *PT-109*. Along the way he came across George Ross. Kennedy knew of him from some previous contact they had had back in Melville, but the two did not know each other well. Ross had graduated from Princeton University in 1941 and had attended the V-7 officer's school at Columbia University before volunteering for PT duty.

Ross was currently a man without a boat and getting bored with his time ashore. He had been serving as the executive officer of *PT-166* when the boat was mistakenly attacked and sunk by American B-25's ten days earlier, but he was not aboard at the time of the incident. Ross asked Kennedy if he could ride along on *PT-109* for the night. Kennedy had a full complement of sailors, but figured he could use an extra man for the added weapon. He inquired if Ross knew how to fire a thirty-seven millimeter gun. The officer replied he did not, but was willing to learn. Kennedy then readily agreed to let him come aboard.

The boat captain broke the news of the evening patrol as soon as he returned to *PT-109*. The unexpected announcement brought initial disappointment, followed by a flurry of activity to get the boat ready for departure. Kennedy quickly gave Ross some basic instructions on how to operate the improvised cannon. He then assigned the guest passenger the gun as a battle station. His role would be a forward lookout as well as a gunner.[364] The sudden presence of new man on board made some of the crewmen uneasy, even prompting the idea that it was a bad omen.[365]

Time did not allow the thirty-seven millimeter cannon to be properly mounted as planned. Crewmen used ropes to lash it to the planks after no base force carpenter could be found. The rubber raft was not returned to the boat in the rushed preparations prior to departure. It was not uncommon for a PT boat to be without a raft and none of the 109's sailors gave it a second thought.

As *PT-109* made ready for what would be her final voyage, her enlisted crew was a mixture of veterans and new hands. Most had come aboard when John Kennedy and Lenny Thom reformed the crew shortly after the new boat captain's arrival. However, there were a few recent additions.

Four sailors were among the first group who came aboard after Kennedy took command of the boat: Gunner's Mate Third Class Charles Harris, Torpedoman Second Class Andrew Kirksey, Radioman Second Class John Maguire, and Quartermaster Third Class Edgar Mauer. Harris was only twenty years old and came from Watertown, MA. Kirksey was a native of Reynolds, GA. Enlisting on July 1, 1942 he was twenty-five, married, and father of an infant son.[366] Maguire hailed from Dobbs Ferry, NY. He volunteered for the PT's on the advice of his brother, who was already serving with the torpedo boats. Quartermaster Mauer had survived the sinking of the PT tender *Niagara* with little more than the clothes on his back. Aboard *PT-109* he served as the quartermaster, cook, and signalman.[367]

Motor Machinist Mate First Class Patrick McMahon was the oldest crewman aboard the 109 at thirty seven years old. A native of rural Wyanet, Illinois, he worked as a mechanic before the war and chose to enlist in the navy even though he was not required to serve in the military due to his age.[368]

THE BATTLE OF BLACKETT STRAIT: AUGUST 1–2, 1943

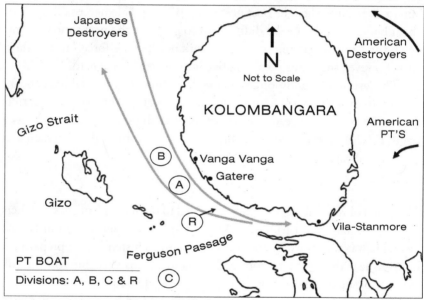

Joining McMahon in the engine room was Motor Machinist Mate Second Class William Johnston. Born in Scotland, his family had moved to the Boston area while he was very young. He was a veteran who had been in the Pacific for some time and had hoped to be rotated out.

The remaining crewmen were newcomers, all having recently come aboard as replacements. Torpedoman Second Class Ray Starkey of Garden Grove, CA had transferred from another PT boat. Seaman First Class Raymond Albert of Akron, Ohio was a young recruit with little experience. Motor Machinist Mate Second Class Harold Marney came from Springfield, Massachusetts. He was the youngest man on the boat at nineteen years of age and had just come aboard the 109.[369] A native of Belleville, Illinois, Motor Machinist Mate First Class Gerard Zinser was a career navy man. He had served aboard several warships since joining the service in 1937.

Kennedy was aware of a problem with one of his sailors, Andrew Kirksey. The torpedoman's behavior had recently changed as he became increasingly nervous.[370] Kennedy wrote about the situation in a letter home about six weeks later. "He had been somewhat shocked by a bomb that had landed near the boat about two weeks before. He never really got over it; he always seemed to have the feeling that something was going to happen to him."[371] The boat captain knew the sailor had a wife and kids and thought about transferring him to shore duty when the boat next went to Tulagi. "He never said anything about being put ashore—he didn't want to go—but the next time we came down the line I was going to let him work on the base force." In the short term, however, there was no alternative but to keep him aboard.[372]

The last minute addition of George Ross brought the total men aboard *PT-109* to thirteen. No one turned in the daily muster sheet to headquarters during the rush to get ready for departure after the surprise air attack. As a result, *PT-109* would depart leaving no written record of the crewmen and passenger aboard.[373]

———

The island of Kolombangara had been added to the network of coastwatchers when Australian Sub Lieutenant Arthur Reginald Evans arrived in March 1943. He was welcomed by friendly natives who assisted him in preparing a hideout near the southern end of the island. Evans was able to overlook Blackett Strait and the Vila area from two separate outposts.

Known by his middle name of Reginald, he had become familiar with the Solomons Islands while working in the region for a trading company during the late 1930s.[374] He was later joined by American Corporal Frank Nash of the U.S. Army Air Communication Service.[375] Evans would soon play an important role in the lives of John Kennedy and the crew of *PT-109*.

CHAPTER 15

SUNK

T he sun dropped low on the horizon behind Lumbari Island as the daylight of August 1 began to slowly fade away. The fifteen PT's around Rendova Harbor getting ready for departure came alive and the haven was soon filled with the roaring sound of boat engines.

Crewmen aboard *PT-109* worked to complete the final preparations for the patrol. Guns were uncovered and loaded with ammunition. Equipment in the engine room was checked over, as was the boat's fuel supply. John Maguire worked below deck to make sure the radio was in proper working order and locked onto the frequency designated for the evening.[376]

The torpedo boats rumbled out of Rendova Harbor in order of division. Henry Brantingham's boats were among the first to leave as his group was traveling the farthest north. The clusters of boats departed in different directions to confuse any watching Japanese eyes.[377] It was the start of *PT-109's* final patrol.

The four PT's of Brantingham's division traveled in a loose formation as the island of Rendova slowly faded into the background of the approaching night. Each was positioned to avoid the wake of the boat ahead. The group traveled northwest, passing through Ferguson Passage into Blackett Strait before continuing up the west side of Kolombangara to an area approximately even with the village of Vanga Vanga. The other divisions moved into their assigned positions to the south and east.

All fifteen PT boats were in the Blackett Strait area by 9:30 p.m. ready to meet the Tokyo Express.[378] The clear skies of the early evening had given way to overcast, and the resulting poor visibility created ideal conditions to mask a small force of enemy destroyers.

Brantingham broke from Warfield's plan of keeping each group together once on station to better the chances of locating the enemy and of launching coordinated attacks. He split his division into two even sections with his *PT-159* and *PT-157* patrolling separately from *PT-109* and *PT-162*.[379]

It is unclear if the division leader created a sub-command arrangement after dividing his boats.[380] Kennedy was ordered to stay close off the starboard quarter of John Lowrey's *PT-162* at all times. Since both boats were equipped with short-range radios for inter-boat communication, the echelon could remain in contact while staying off the main radio network. With Brantingham's flagship the only radar-equipped boat of the group, orders to limit radio use, and poor visibility conditions, it is clear the arrangement almost ensured it would be difficult for all the PT's to be able to find the enemy.

As the PT boats moved into position in Blackett Strait, Captain Yamashiro's destroyers were operating about one hour ahead of schedule.[381] The force passed through the northern end of the Slot undetected, arriving at the entrance of Vella Gulf at about 11:30 p.m. The timing put them well ahead of Arleigh Burke's six destroyers. Still steaming up the Slot, Burke would never make contact with the enemy.

John Kennedy manned the wheel as *PT-109* slowly idled in the pitch black night. Lookouts scanned the horizon in search of the enemy. Her crew was tense, as was usually the case in the hours leading up to a battle. Although occasional conversation broke the silence, there was little the men could do but wait. Time seemed to pass slowly, but the clock eventually reached midnight ushering in the start of August 2.

Warfield's operation plan ensured that the Tokyo Express would have to run through a gauntlet of torpedo boats to get to Vila. The following series of battle sequences occurred in rapid succession and were as confusing as many of the night encounters in Iron Bottom Sound. It proved to be one of the last major confrontations between PT boats and large Japanese warships during the war. It was also to be one of the most poorly coordinated and executed torpedo boat attacks in the South Pacific.

By midnight the Japanese destroyers were running parallel to the west side of Kolombangara heading towards the entrance to Blackett Strait. At the same time Henry Brantingham's division was still idling in two separate groups off Vanga Vanga. Lowrey and Kennedy were positioned further west with the flagship unit between them and the coast.

The first sighting of the approaching enemy was made at midnight when radar on *PT-159* showed five contacts heading south along the Kolombangara coast at about fifteen knots. Brantingham concluded the targets were barges owing to the timing and their proximity to the island. He ordered his boat and *PT-157* to close for a strafing run. Conflicting information exists as to whether the division leader directed Lowrey and Kennedy to stay put and what, if any, communication Brantingham had with his other boats prior to moving towards the enemy.

Lookouts on *PT-159* made out four shapes, while the men on *PT-157* only saw half the column, as the two boats moved towards the enemy. The PT sailors soon learned that they were not attacking barges, but were closing in on destroyers. The enemy saw the approaching PT boats also. The Japanese warships turned on searchlights before opening fire with heavy guns.

Brantingham quickly switched to a torpedo attack as enemy shells splashed around the boats. *PT-159* unleashed a full spread of four torpedoes after closing to about 1,800 yards, but one started a fire in the tube temporarily illuminating the boat for Japanese gunners. William Liebenow then sent two torpedoes from his *PT-157* scurrying towards the enemy. "A large explosion was seen at the target by personnel on both of these boats," Warfield recorded in his report of the battle.[382] However, as was often the case in previous night encounters, no Japanese ships were hit.

The two PT's turned away to escape under the cover of smoke after making their torpedo runs. "We zigzagged for ten or fifteen miles, I have no idea what direction we went," Liebenow later recalled. "We were just going."[383] The boats moved northwest, eventually ending up far from the action.

The Tokyo Express was now fully alert to the presence of torpedo boats in the area, but not all of the PT's knew of the enemy's arrival. Brantingham either did not radio a contact report to Lowrey and Kennedy, or it was not picked up at any time during the attack or subsequent retirement. The 157 and 159 boats rendezvoused near Gizo Island. Warfield explains what happened next. "It was decided that PT-157 should return to station and that PT-159 should return to base, as it was out of torpedoes, all of which was done."

The move was inexplicable. The flagship of Division B, the group's only radar-equipped boat, was heading home without any communication with the other two patrolling PT's. The Tokyo Express continued on course for Vila. The battle had only just begun, but the unfolding events would not get much better for the American boat captains as the flawed action of Brantingham's division was set to be repeated.

Continuing south into Blackett Strait, the Japanese destroyers soon encountered the boats of Division A. Under the command of Arthur Berndtson aboard *PT-171*, the four boats were prowling the waters off the southwest coast of Kolombangara approximately even with the village of Gatere.

Contacts first appeared on Berndtson's radar screen a few minutes after midnight. Although unaware of Brantingham's earlier strike, he concluded the targets were destroyers and moved forward to attack. "When *PT-171* got in position it was abeam the first destroyer," Warfield reported of the move. "Estimating its speed at thirty knots, the *PT-171* closed to 1,500 yards, at which point the destroyers fired starshells and opened fire, straddling the *PT-171* and splashing water on its deck."

Berndtson aimed for the second destroyer in column and released four torpedoes as the area around him was illuminated with a dull glow from above. All of the tubes flashed during the firing process, causing at least one of the destroyers to turn directly towards the PT boat. With shell splashes getting closer, Berndtson turned to make a hasty retreat. *PT-171* raced across Blackett Strait under the cover of smoke, passing across the bows of the other three division boats.

Thinking an enemy destroyer might be blocking Ferguson Passage, the division leader turned towards Gizo Strait.[384] He exited the area through the waterway and set course for Rendova. In a striking repeat of the first encounter further north, Berndtson failed to update the three other boats in the division of his actions. He then left the area, taking his radar with him.

PT's 169, 172, and 163 all visually spotted the destroyers while still idling, but could not close to attack with Berndtson's flagship interposed between them. The latter two boats escaped to Ferguson Passage after turning to take evasive maneuvers while coming under enemy fire. They were also attacked by Japanese floatplanes, but slipped through unharmed into the open waters to the south. The boats later returned to the area, but had no further contact with the enemy.

All three engines on *PT-169* simultaneously failed, leaving the boat temporarily stranded in a precarious position. However, quick work restarted the motors allowing for a timely escape. She moved northwest out of the area, though was unable to locate the other two boats.

The four boats of Division C under the command of George Cookman in *PT-107* were patrolling south of Ferguson Passage. Two contacts suddenly appeared on the boat's radar screen at about five minutes after midnight. "No previous contact report had been received, but a searchlight and gunfire had been seen to the north,"Warfield wrote. *PT-107* dashed forth to attack, leaving the remaining boats of the division behind. Cookman fired a spread of four torpedoes by radar, but none hit the targets. "Course was reversed and the *PT-107*, apparently undiscovered, proceeded south through Ferguson Passage, en route to base, its fish expended,"Warfield explained of the flagship's departure.

The division leader again left without providing a contact report or instructions to his other boats. The three remaining PT's were attacked by a floatplane as they moved towards Kolombangara. The boats found no sign of the enemy and eventually set out for Rendova.

Only the three boats of Division R remained between the Japanese destroyers and their destination. Led by Russell Rome in *PT-174*, the group was patrolling in the heart of Blackett Strait near Makuti Island. He knew the battle was heading his way when the boats observed gunfire and searchlights for about ten minutes.

The faint shape of a warship came into view at 12:25 a.m., indicating that the enemy had finally arrived. The ship was moving slowly about a mile off the Kolombangara coast. Rome closed to attack, surmising she was guarding Blackett Strait from the Ferguson Passage entrance. The destroyer better revealed her position when she turned on a searchlight and opened fire on something to the west.

The division leader fired four torpedoes at a range of about 1,000 yards before turning away. He dodged return fire and a strafing attack from the air, but was soon on his way back to base. *PT-103* fired four torpedoes from long range and left the area. The last boat of the group, *PT-105* under the command of Richard Keresey, let loose a pair of torpedoes. He then searched for his division leader. None of the torpedoes found a Japanese hull.[385]

The first phase of the Battle of Blackett Strait was over. Captain Yamashiro's destroyers had successfully dodged a horde of torpedoes without sustaining the slightest damage. The force arrived at Vila at 12:30 a.m.[386] The three transports cut their engines and slowly drifted to a stop at the designated rendezvous point about a thousand yards offshore. Dozens of barges then scurried out to begin unloading the passengers and supplies. *Amagiri* cautiously guarded the area as the unloading work moved along at a swift pace. In what seemed to be record time *Hagikaze's* hooded signal lamp flashed "Let's go home."[387] The second part of the battle was about to begin.

———

When Henry Brantingham rushed off to attack what he thought were some Japanese barges, he left behind the second echelon of his division. The distance between the two boat sections was perhaps as far as one mile.[388] Separated from their division leader, *PT-109* and *PT-162* continued to patrol in the assigned area. John Kennedy definitely knew something was happening as he could plainly see distant flashes of gunfire in the direction of Kolombangara. Lowrey turned his boat away from the island with *PT-109* following suit. The 109's radio occasionally picked up snippets of frantic conversation indicating a battle was taking place somewhere, presumably further south.

Kennedy called his men to battle stations and eventually pulled his boat alongside *PT-162* to discuss the situation. Lowrey had not received any communication on the short wave radio from the flagship. In short, neither boat captain had any idea of what was happening, nor that the other boats of their division had already attacked the enemy destroyers. They were not certain that the Tokyo Express arrived earlier than expected and had no idea it had already passed them by.

The two concluded the other PT's were under fire from shore batteries. They decided to move further away from Kolombangara, concerned their boats might soon come into range of the same guns. The PT's moved in the direction of Vella Lavella.

The radio airwaves were filled with scattered fragments of an unfolding battle, creating a confusing picture for the boat captains not directly engaged with the enemy. Richard Keresey in *PT-105* later remembered it with frustration: "We were under radio silence, but then these people come on the radio and start shouting how terrible it is, they are under attack, they are retreating," he later recalled. "It was totally useless information, you couldn't make any sense out of it, who it was or where they were. It was scaring the hell out of me."[389]

Thomas Warfield tried to follow the developments as best he could from the operations center on Lumbari as the night battle unfolded. The squadron commander never sent out an intelligence update to ensure all the boat captains were armed with the most current information. He suspected that the Tokyo Express had safely made Vila and would return on the same route. Warfield later redirected some of the boats' captains still in the area to new positions.[390] Kennedy and Lowrey were literally left in the dark after receiving no direct communications from anyone.

The pair found no sign of the enemy and continued with their patrol. The group unexpectedly increased to three at about 2:00 a.m. when *PT-169* suddenly emerged from the darkness. Under the command of Lieutenant (Junior Grade) Phillip Potter, the boat had been part of Berndtson's Division A. He became separated from the other PT's when the division leader departed the patrol area after making a solo attack on the Japanese destroyers.

The new group patrolled the northern reaches of Blackett Strait. None of the boats were equipped with radar, but each had a full complement of four torpedoes. The night was so dark the boats had difficulty staying in visual contact with each other. Some time passed before the boat captains decided to break radio silence and call Lumbari for further instructions. The terse reply was to resume patrol on the normal station.[391]

Unbeknownst to the three captains, a fourth PT was also in the general area. *PT-157* under the command of William Liebenow moved north after attacking the Japanese destroyers with Henry Brantingham on their inbound run. The boat ended up further north than the others and never made contact with the three boats of Lowrey's group.

Lowrey was not sure of his current position. He asked Kennedy to lead the group back to the original patrol area where they became separated from their division leader. Kennedy agreed it was a good idea. All three PT's turned to the left. The maneuver put the 109 at the head of the formation. The boats spread out to form a picket line across the strait.[392] The three PT's searched for the enemy and waited.

As PT's 109, 162, and 169 patrolled the northern end of Blackett Strait, the Tokyo Express was once again on the move further south. After successfully unloading the precious cargo, Captain Yamashiro decided to return to Rabaul via Vella Gulf, the same route on which he arrived. He did not want to take any chances, given reports earlier in the day from Rabaul indicating the possible presence of American destroyers in Kula Gulf. The decision meant he would again have to pass through a gauntlet of torpedo boats.

The destroyers departed Vila slowly, initially moving through dangerous waters infested with reefs and shoals. Ten minutes after getting underway the group increased speed to a thirty knot clip. The warships were fully blacked out in a tight column formation. Only about 550 yards stood between each vessel.[393]

Richard Keresey's *PT-105* was the first boat to encounter the outbound Tokyo Express. She was patrolling just inside Blackett Strait near Ferguson Passage when flashes of gunfire were seen in the vicinity of the Kolombangara coast. It was sometime before 2:30 a.m. "All of this showed the outline of a destroyer 2,000 yards away to the east moving slowly to the north at about ten knots," Warfield wrote in his report of the battle. "*PT-105* was abeam this vessel. Two torpedoes were fired, but no explosion was observed."

Out of torpedoes, Keresey headed south through Ferguson Passage where he passed three boats going north. Unlike the division leaders, though, he radioed out a contact report.[394]

The three PT's Keresey saw were the remaining members of George Cookman's Division C. Attracted by the same flashes in the vicinity of Kolombangara at about 2:15 a.m., the boats raced into Blackett Strait, only to find no sign of the enemy. The Japanese destroyers were probably already past the area by the time of their arrival.

As the enemy force continued to move northwest, it passed through the area off Gatere previously occupied by the boats of Division A. However, the patrol station was now empty. The division leader left for home and *PT-169* stumbled upon Kennedy and Lowrey after becoming lost. "PT's 172 and 163 which had retired well to the south of Ferguson Passage did not resume station until after 2:55 a.m. and were too late to make contact," Warfield explained.

Captain Yamashiro had unknowingly dashed through three of the four PT groups designed to stop his trip back to Rabaul. As the destroyers veered to the north, roughly paralleling the Kolombangara coast, only four PT boats stood between the Tokyo Express and the open waters of Vella Gulf.

At 2:15 a.m. PT's 109, 162, and 169 were still in the northern end of Blackett Strait patrolling the passageway between Gizo Island and Kolombangara. The boats had recently shifted position in the hopes of finding additional members of the division, but neither the other PT's nor the enemy was located. *PT-109* was the furthest east and closest to the Kolombangara coast. The opposite end of the rough picket line was occupied by *PT-169* near Gizo Island. *PT-162* was approximately in the middle of the others, almost halfway between Gizo and Kolombangara. About one mile separated each of the boats.[395]

Kennedy, Lowrey, and Potter had no clear knowledge of the battle that had taken place earlier in the evening. None of the boat captains knew that the Tokyo Express was again on the move and barreling down upon them at a high rate of speed.

PT-109 moved slowly and quietly through the night. Kennedy idled the boat using only the center engine to minimize the motor noise and keep down the phosphorescent wake. It was a common procedure among boat captains. Since the center propeller was positioned slightly deeper in the water than the remaining two, it produced less of a wake when operated alone.[396]

Although the practice of idling on one engine provided the advantage of helping to conceal the boat's position, especially from the air, it also had some clear drawbacks. The lag time needed to engage the other two engines would prevent the boat from quickly ramping up speed. One boat captain later recalled it took about thirty seconds to really get the boat moving fast after engaging the other two engines.[397]

As the clock passed 2:00 a.m. the crew was no longer at general quarters. Sailors were spread out across the ship at various locations. Kenney, Thom, Maguire, and Marney were all clustered in or around the conn. George Ross was on deck near the front of the boat close to the thirty-seven millimeter cannon. Raymond Albert was on watch near the port side machine gun. Patrick McMahon sat in the engine room below deck near the back of the boat surrounded by equipment, gauges, and dials.

Various accounts disagree as to the exact location of *PT-109's* remaining crewmen. Most were likely in various positions in the middle or rear part of the boat behind the conn. Charles Harris was not on duty and may have been along the starboard side sleeping on deck between a torpedo tube and the dayroom using his life jacket as a pillow. Gerard Zinser, Edgar Mauer, and Andrew Kirksey were all likely also on or near the dayroom. William Johnston and Raymond Starkey were probably on deck near the stern close to the twenty millimeter gun.[398]

The entire crew was taken by complete surprise when the *Amagiri* suddenly appeared out of the night at about 2:30 a.m. With only seconds to react, Kennedy's attempt to turn the boat failed and *PT-109* was cut in two by the menacing bow of the Japanese destroyer.

The angle of the impact likely saved Kennedy from immediate death. The narrow margin was perhaps only a couple of feet. The violent force of the collision knocked the boat captain from his feet in the conn. It is unclear if he reinjured his already bad back.[399]

Two sailors close to Kennedy also lived through the terrible ordeal. John Maguire was slammed down to the deck where he heard the sound of cracking wood. Lenny Thom was tossed from the boat captain's side, but survived. Two other crewmembers were not as lucky. Harold Marney was manning the forward machine gun near the initial point of impact and was certainly crushed to death instantly. The second sailor to perish was Andrew Kirksey, probably also a victim of the initial impact.

Although it is unclear why no one aboard *PT-109* saw the approaching destroyer until the last seconds, the two other boats patrolling in the area did
spot *Amagiri*. Those boat captains had a key advantage over Kennedy. Given
their greater distances from the destroyer, each was able to get a somewhat
clear picture of the enemy with enough time to do something.

The boat initially farthest from the action was *PT-169*. Phillip Potter
recalled seeing *Amagiri* from a distance of about two miles. It seemed to be
heading directly towards the 109. He radioed out a frantic warning.[400] The
message was either not picked up by Kennedy's boat or arrived too late.

Potter reported firing two torpedoes before turning away as the destroyer
passed at a distance of about 150 yards. The torpedoes missed and probably
did not even have time to properly arm at such a short range. The action took
place just before *PT-109* was hit. The destroyer briefly straddled the 169 boat
with gunfire before disappearing into the night. Not taking any chances, Potter fled behind Gizo Island.

Lookouts on John Lowrey's *PT-162* sighted the warship about 700 yards
away heading north at a high rate of speed and correctly identified her as a
Japanese destroyer. Lowrey turned his boat to fire torpedoes, but for an un-
recorded reason nothing happened. "The *PT-162* finally turned to the southwest upon getting within 100 yards of the warship to avoid collision," Thomas
Warfield reported. "At the time of the turning, *PT-109* was seen to collide
with the warship . . ."[401]

Further north than the other three boats, *PT-157* also had a brief brush
with the enemy. Lookouts sighted a ship close to the Kolombangara coast
moving north. It is not known if the warship was *Amagiri* or one of the other
members of the Tokyo Express. William Liebenow fired his two remaining
torpedoes, but saw no explosions. The attack resulted in no response from
the destroyer and she continued on into the darkness. Out of torpedoes,
Liebenow headed back to base per Warfield's instructions.

Sailors on the other boats saw the burst of an explosion when the 109
was run down, and assumed the PT was sunk. The ferocious blast led them
to believe there could be no survivors.

After slicing through the torpedo boat, crewmen aboard *Amagiri* felt a
slight thud and saw the flash of exploding gasoline. It was initially unknown
if the PT boat had successfully fired a torpedo into her hull or if the forward
area of the destroyer was on fire. It soon became clear that the PT fared the
worst in the encounter.

The destroyer suffered minor damage in the form of a dented bow and a portion of a propeller blade was sheered away, the latter causing the vessel to vibrate. The effect of the propeller damage was mitigated when the ship reduced its speed by a couple of knots.[402] No crewmen were injured. Captain Yamashiro's destroyers completed the voyage back to Rabaul without incident to bring the Tokyo Express run to a successful conclusion.

The Battle of Blackett Strait was one of the most poorly executed PT boat operations in the South Pacific. Dogged by unsound operating procedures, poor judgment among division commanders, and possibly just plain bad luck, the Americans failed to score a single hit on two passes of the Tokyo Express.

CHAPTER **16**

SHIPWRECKED

There was no chance of saving *PT-109*. Many historians believe the boat broke into two pieces.[403] Weighted down by
the remaining two engines, the rear portion sank into the
water immediately. The forward part managed to stay afloat with the bow
protruding out of the water at a sharp angle, most likely due to an air pocket
trapped in one of the forward compartments.

John Kennedy realized he was alive after *Amagiri* departed into obscurity.
He pulled himself up off the deck. The immediate area was quiet except for
the sound of burning gasoline. Although it ignited in a flash at the time of
the collision, the force of the passing destroyer and her wake spread out the
flaming fuel. It was now burning on the water in patches with one not more
than twenty yards from the bow.

The boat captain wanted to locate and rescue any of the remaining crew
who were alive, but his immediate concern was the fire. He ordered the few
sailors still aboard into the water fearing the lingering gasoline in the tanks
could explode at any moment. John Maguire and Edgar Mauer followed him
over the side. The group swam a safe distance from the boat. The trio went
back to the bow when the flames seemed to subside after about ten or fifteen
minutes. Kennedy now focused on saving his men.

Eleven of the boat's sailors miraculously survived the collision. Most,
however, were spread out in the water at various distances from the boat with
some unconscious. Kennedy wanted to collect all of the survivors at the bow.
When he called out into the night, a response came from Charles Harris.
"Mr. Kennedy! Mr. Kennedy! McMahon is badly hurt."[404] The boat captain

took off his shoes, shirt, and sidearm before diving into the water to follow the voice.

Patrick McMahon was the only member of the crew below deck when the collision occurred. A torrent of flaming gasoline rushed towards the sailor in the engine room before he was propelled into the water by an explosion. He was alive, but had suffered severe burns on his face, chest, arms, and legs.

"How are you, Mac?" Kennedy said as he approached McMahon about a hundred yards from the boat. "I'm all right. I'm kind of burnt," McMahon replied. Tormented by the burns, it was clear he could not swim because of the pain. Kennedy called out for others in the immediate area. Harris responded in a low tone that he had an injured leg. The boat captain assisted him in slipping out of a waterlogged jacket and sweater, before turning his attention back to the more seriously wounded shipmate.

Back on the bow Mauer was using a blinker light to guide those in the water back to the boat. Kennedy made ready to start the return journey. "Go on, skipper," McMahon muttered. "You go on. I've had it."[405] The boat captain would have nothing of it. He told McMahon to turn over onto his back and took him in tow by the strap of his life jacket. The group started to swim towards the boat using voices and Mauer's light as a guide. At one point Kennedy had to cajole Harris along who was slowed by his wounded knee.

An ocean breeze was blowing the remnants of the boat away from the group, making the swim a difficult undertaking. "McMahon and I were about an hour getting back to the boat," Kennedy recalled of the arduous ordeal. "There was a very strong current."[406]

As Kennedy was working to assist the two sailors, other rescues were taking place with crewmen slowly making their way back to the boat. With Mauer remaining on the bow, Maguire secured a rope to the hull and swam out in search of shipmates. He found George Ross, Lenny Thom, and Gerard Zinser. The group returned to the boat with Ross assisting Zinser part of the way.

Lenny Thom was not a strong swimmer, but he ventured back into the water to help William Johnston to the boat. The motor machinist mate somehow managed to make it up to the surface from the sinking stern, swallowing gasoline in the process. Raymond Albert returned to the boat under his own power. The last man to arrive was Raymond Starkey. Suffering burns on his face and hands, he initially clung to a floating mattress before swimming several hundred yards to the boat.

Kennedy took stock of the crew after arriving back with McMahon and

Harris. All eleven surviving sailors were together for the first time since the collision. The men were confident they would be quickly rescued. Certainly one of the other nearby boats saw the collision and might come to their aid. Lumbari PT boats or seaplanes would be dispatched to scour the area when *PT-109* failed to return.

In the short term, though, Kennedy and his crew had plenty to worry about. The list of the bow was slowly increasing, raising concern as to how much longer it could stay afloat. They were in Japanese-held waters. Any enemy ship or plane might spot them during a routine pass. All of the men were exhausted with several wounded and in need of medical help.

It was time to explore options. Kennedy asked the men, "What do you want to do if the Japs come out—fight or surrender?" Someone replied, "Fight with what?"[407] The response prompted Kennedy to take a count of the available weapons.

A single Thompson submachine gun, a handful of pistols, and a few knives were the only armaments they possessed. All other firepower was gone, including the thirty-seven millimeter cannon. It survived the crash, but was hanging in the water over the side of the bow.

Most of the other supplies were also gone. The boat's first aid kit was lost, as were the food provisions. The group did have a small lantern from the boat and a signal pistol. They knew the latter had to be used cautiously so as to not alert the Japanese. "There is nothing in the book about a situation like this," Kennedy told his men after looking over the weaponry. "Seems to me we're not a military organization anymore. Let's just talk this over."

The comments sparked a group discussion on the question of what to do if found by the enemy. No one was in favor of surrender, as it was well known the Japanese did not treat their prisoners well. However, there was no consensus of what to do next. Kennedy knew there had to be a leader if the men were to survive and came to an important conclusion. He would make the decisions and simply give orders going forward.[408]

"We seemed to be drifting towards Kolombangara," Kennedy later recalled. "We figured the Japs would be sure to get us in the morning, but everyone was tired and we slept."[409] The wreck was actually slowly drifting south deeper into Blackett Strait going towards Ferguson Passage.[410]

Daylight found the men still adrift in Blackett Strait. Rendova Peak was visible almost forty miles away. The survivors, though, could also see Japanese activity much closer on Kolombangara to the east and Gizo to the west.[411] No help was in sight.

The remainder of the hull overturned during the late morning. "We knew the ship would sink any minute, so we decided to swim for an island we knew was nearby," Kennedy later said.[412] He had to make the critical decision of what island. Kolombangara was closest, but out of the question as it was known to be occupied by thousands of enemy troops, and its coast was not regularly patrolled by American ships. Gizo was also not seriously considered. Kennedy decided to head for a group of small islands between Gizo and Ferguson Passage.

It was to be a demanding journey of about three and a half miles. The physical abilities of the group ranged from Kennedy, a Harvard swim team veteran, to several crewmen who could not swim at all. The wooden timber used to secure the thirty-seven millimeter cannon to the forward deck was pressed into service to help the sailors. Kennedy ordered nine of the crew to cluster around the wood with Lenny Thom in charge. The men tied their shoes to the timber and grasped it with one arm while using the other to stroke through the water. The makeshift arrangement seemed to work.

With the large group under Thom's control, Kennedy took the responsibility of getting Patrick McMahon safely to the destination. He clinched

ROUTE OF *PT-109*'s SURVIVORS: AUGUST 2–7, 1943

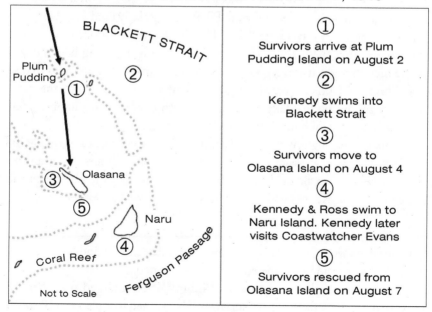

① Survivors arrive at Plum Pudding Island on August 2

② Kennedy swims into Blackett Strait

③ Survivors move to Olasana Island on August 4

④ Kennedy & Ross swim to Naru Island. Kennedy later visits Coastwatcher Evans

⑤ Survivors rescued from Olasana Island on August 7

the strap of the wounded man's life vest firmly in his teeth and swam with the shipmate in tow, taking occasional rest breaks when needed. It was a grueling ordeal made worse by the ocean salt water. Kennedy swallowed the liquid as he swam, and McMahon was further pained when his burns were exposed to the salt.

Kennedy and McMahon were the first to make landfall after a journey of nearly four hours. They landed on the southeastern tip of Plum Pudding Island at about 6:00 p.m. and crawled out of sight into the bushes after briefly resting on the beach. The remaining survivors arrived a short time later, after finding the swim a slow undertaking after struggling to coordinate their paddling.

Uninhabited Plum Pudding Island spans about forty yards in diameter and is positioned about four miles southeast of Gizo Harbor. It offered the survivors dry land and a place to hide from the Japanese, but little else. The small land mass was covered with a variety of low-growth foliage and trees. The fruit on the few coconut trees was green and inedible.

The island was overflown by a formation of planes shortly after the second group arrived. The sailors stayed low in the foliage, fearing they were Japanese, as the planes sped past low and fast. It was only when the planes were overhead did the men spot the white tails identifying the aircraft as from New Zealand.[413] By then it was too late to try to send off a signal.

Kennedy was tired, but knew the PT boats regularly used Ferguson Passage as an entry into Blackett Strait. He decided to swim out towards the waterway during the night in the hopes of signaling a passing boat. Not all of the men thought it was a good idea and some unsuccessfully tried to dissuade him. "If I find a boat, I'll flash the lantern twice," he told the men. Kennedy set out on his dangerous journey with the lantern, a life belt, pair of shoes, and a pistol hung around his neck with a lanyard.

Hopping among several small islands and reefs, he eventually made his way into Ferguson Passage. Staying in the channel for hours, he found no sign of the PT's. Six boats departed Rendova Harbor for the nightly patrol, but all went past Kennedy's location to the waters west of Gizo Island.[414]

————

The survivors were fortunate no Japanese craft came by to find them. However, Americans did not come either, or so it seemed.

In the aftermath of the sinking, Phillip Potter emerged from behind Gizo Island to look for *PT-109*'s survivors. He claimed to have spent between a half and three quarters of an hour searching the area before returning to base after finding nothing in the darkness. John Lowrey in *PT-162* assumed the 109 went down with all hands and departed the area.[415]

The PT commanders at Lumbari knew for certain the 109 was missing when she did not return to base. There was a discussion at the morning de-briefing about sending some boats back into Blackett Strait to conduct a search. The conversation ended with reports from the nearby boat captains of the boat blown to pieces by an explosion. The chances of survivors seemed doubtful.[416] "He was presumed to be dead," Richard Kersey later recalled of Kennedy.[417] The PT base later held a simple funeral service for the missing boat captain and crew.[418] Even though boats were not sent out to look for survivors, an air search was ordered.

A flight of New Zealand P-40 fighter planes overflew the area late in the day looking for survivors. The pilots found the hulk of the boat while flying at low altitude, but it was empty of people. The aviators did not see the survivors hiding in the brush on Plum Pudding Island.

Unknown to the *PT-109* crewmen, the demise of their boat attracted the attention of coastwatchers Reginald Evans and Frank Nash. The pair first spotted the fire of the boat's ramming from their position miles away on Kolombangara. Daylight then revealed floating wreckage in the same area.

Unable to discern the nature of the debris, Evans reported to his superiors it could possibly be the remnants of a barge. It was too dangerous to be investigated up close during the day due to the location in Japanese waters. He was actually looking at the forward part of *PT-109*, which was slowly drifting further away from him.

Evans was notified of the loss of the 109 by a coastwatcher on New Georgia at 9:30 a.m. on the same morning. The message requested information. He had nothing to report and did not immediately make the connection between his unknown object and the lost boat. He did, however, initiate his own search, notifying all native scouts to be on the lookout for survivors.

Exploration of the Kolombangara coast revealed nothing except spent American torpedoes washed up on shore. There was no sign of sailors in the vicinity of Gizo. If there were survivors, he was confident his scouts would find them.[419] Evans continued to watch the unknown object and communicate with other coastwatchers about the missing PT boat. The wreckage was last seen drifting south towards Ferguson Passage. A connection was eventually made between the lost torpedo boat and the mysterious object.

———————

Kennedy struggled to return to Plum Pudding Island as time slipped into August 3. The trip almost killed him as ocean currents pushed him into Blackett Strait and then back towards Ferguson Passage.[420] He arrived on Plum Pudding Island at about noon after making an intermediary stop on small Leorava Island. The crew was overjoyed when their boat captain crawled out of the water. Thinking he had perished in the expedition, many assumed they would never see him again.

The extremely exhausted boat captain was pulled up on the beach by his shipmates. Kennedy collapsed and slept for the balance of the day, only waking briefly to order George Ross to make the same trip during the night. Less than enthusiastic about the dangerous mission, Ross nonetheless departed at about 4:00 p.m. He made it to Leorava Island before deciding the undertaking was fruitless. After sleeping on the beach, perhaps the same one used by Kennedy the night before, he returned to Plumb Pudding Island the next morning. Ross would not have found any PT's even if he made it into Ferguson Passage, as the boats were far from his location with the nightly patrol battling Japanese barges near Vella Lavella.

The morning of August 4 found the mood among the survivors down-trodden. The men were suffering from hunger and thirst after being shipwrecked for two days. The lack of water seemed to have the greatest effect on the sailors. "I was always thirsty," Kennedy recalled of his time shipwrecked. "Guess I drank quite a bit of salt water. Somehow I couldn't get pineapple juice out of my mind and at the time would willingly have paid a year's pay for one can of it."[421]

The enlisted men vented anger at the navy for not coming out to rescue them. Kennedy felt a little better after his long sleep, but even his outlook started to dim. Two attempts to flag down PT boats failed, friendly planes passed by too quickly to identify and signal, and no American ships were spotted. The survival prospects for the shipwrecked sailors seemed to be getting worse.

Kennedy decided the group should move to Olasana Island in the hopes of finding food and water. "We're going to that small one," he told the men pointing to the land mass in the distance. "We'll have to swim for it. Everyone on the log. I'll take McMahon."[422] The group set out for the three hour trek using the same arrangement as before.

Kennedy gathered his men in the trees behind the beach shortly after arriving on the tip of the new island. He could see another island about a half a mile away. The sailors were too exhausted to do anything more. They kept largely out of sight, not wanting to be seen by any passing Japanese. No one attempted to undertake a journey into Ferguson Passage. The men did not know six torpedo boats were set to venture through the passage en route to patrol stations in Blackett Strait.[423]

About a mile and a half south of Plum Pudding Island, the new location brought them one step closer to Ferguson Passage. Olasana was larger with an abundance of vegetation and numerous coconut trees loaded with fruit ripe for eating. However, the island contained no fresh water much to the shipwrecked sailor's disappointment.

The small islet Kennedy saw in the distance was Naru Island (also known as Cross Island.) It fronted the western side of Ferguson Passage. Frustrated that all of his attempts to find friendly forces had thus far failed, he did not want to just sit and wait. He talked over the situation with his other officers on the morning of August 5. Kennedy and Ross decided to swim to Naru, leaving Thom behind in charge of the remaining men. A flight of P-40's was seen to pass near Naru just prior to the group's departure, with one making a strafing run on something.[424]

The two officers carefully explored the new territory after arriving on Naru at about noon. They proceeded with great caution, frequently hiding in trees and brushes. The island appeared to be deserted. The pair then made an important discovery on the far side of the land mass. There they found a Japanese crate containing hard candy and crackers. About twenty yards away was a small lean-to, a barrel of water, and a one man canoe. They indulged in a few pieces of the new found provisions and took a drink of water before saving the rest for their crew.

Kennedy and Ross then spotted the remains of a small Japanese vessel on an outlying reef off the eastern side of the island. Carefully moving down the coast to get a better look, the pair emerged from the brush to find what appeared to be two natives on the wreckage looking in their direction. The sailors jumped back in the bushes thinking they might have just come face to face with the enemy or unfriendly natives. The twosome were not Japanese, but were equally frightened. Startled by the encounter, the islanders bolted to a nearby canoe and paddled away.

Unknown to Kennedy and Ross, the natives were friendly and working as scouts under the direction of Reginald Evans. Biuku Gasa and Eroni Kumana were both only nineteen years old. After witnessing hundreds of Japanese troops landing on Gizo a few days earlier, they left their observation post on a nearby island in a canoe to report the news to Evans. The scouts did not encounter *PT-109's* survivors as they followed the reefs east before darting into Blackett Strait. The pair did find some floating debris from the 109, including a letter written by Raymond Albert, but they could not read English. The letter was dropped off to a native on an intermediary island before reaching Evans.[425]

The coastwatcher asked the scouts to be on the lookout for possible PT boat survivors on their return trip. Gasa and Kumana spotted the wrecked Japanese vessel on Naru during their trek west and decided to take a closer look. The two set out for home after the sudden encounter with Kennedy and Ross, whom they thought were Japanese.

Fate then intervened on the side of the stranded *PT-109* sailors. Gasa and Kumana decided to make a chance stop on Olasana to pick up some fresh coconuts. Lenny Thom emerged from the brush just as they approached the beach, causing the startled natives to paddle back a safe distance. Understanding only broken English, they listened with a high level of skepticism as the executive officer tried to explain he was an American.

Thom initially struggled to get through to them. "Me know Johnny Kari," he then said. Kari was a native scout who had previously visited Lumbari. "White star," Thom continued, pointing a finger to the sky. "White star."[426] Coastwatchers regularly instructed their scouts to help downed airmen from planes with white stars, the American insignia. The natives finally seemed to understand.

Gasa and Kumana slowly paddled ashore as more survivors materialized from the brush. "Some of them cried, and some of them came and shook our hands," Kumana later recalled of the meeting.[427] The groups communicated in the most rudimentary form. When the islanders motioned to Naru, indicating there were Japanese on the island, the survivors feared they would never see their two shipmates again.

Thom knew he had to somehow get a message of their existence back to an American base. An ill-conceived plan to canoe all the way to Rendova was abandoned after it became apparent the seas were too rough. Using the stub of a pencil and an invoice from a trading company, Thom wrote out a note for the natives to take with them.

Back on Naru, Kennedy and Ross waited in the brush until they were sure the two men were gone. Kennedy was determined to go out into Ferguson Passage in the one man canoe during the night for another attempt to flag down a PT boat. After the attempt to make contact again failed, he opted to take the food and water back to the men on Olasana, leaving Ross behind on Naru.

Kennedy was immediately greeted by his overjoyed crewmen upon his arrival on Olasana. The sailors told him they had been found by friendly natives and the boat captain rushed to embrace the two saviors. The men were able to determine they had seen each other, not Japanese, on Naru.[428] At about the same time, Coastwatcher Evans was moving to a new location. He was setting up camp on Gomu, a small island off the southern coast of Kolombangara, to be able to better cover Blackett Strait.

Kennedy departed with the natives in their canoe for Naru on the morning of August 6. They arrived after encountering Ross, who was swimming to Olasana. Kennedy used a knife to carve his famous message into the head of a coconut:

> NAURO ISL
> NATIVE KNOWS POSIT HE CAN PILOT
> 11 ALIVE
> NEED SMALL BOAT
> KENNEDY[429]

Gasa and Kumana showed Kennedy and Ross where a larger canoe was hidden on the island, before departing for help with Thom's note and the coconut message. They did not go directly to Rendova, but rather to Wana Wana Island, south of Kolombangara and west of New Georgia. They told English-speaking native Benjamin Kevu of the survivors, who immediately dispatched a messenger to Reginald Evans. Gasa and Kumana then set out with John Kari in a larger canoe with the messages for Rendova.

Kennedy and Ross were not fully sure if they could trust the natives. They used the newly found two-man canoe to again venture into Ferguson Passage in an unsuccessful attempt to hail a PT boat. Heavy seas overturned the canoe, causing the men to make a treacherous swim back to Naru. The two were cut by coral reefs, but made it to the island where they slept for the night.

As *PT-109's* survivors slept among the two islands, American and Japanese destroyers battled further north in Vella Gulf. The Americans ambushed a four destroyer Tokyo Express run, sinking three with no loss of their own in what became known as the Battle of Vella Gulf.

Plans to save the 109's men were well underway on the morning of August 7. When Reginald Evans learned of their existence he immediately dispatched a large war canoe manned by seven natives to Naru with a note for

Kennedy to return with them. He was soon in contact with the American authorities on Rendova to begin planning the rescue operation. The Americans had also received the note and coconut from Gasa and Kumana.

When the war canoe arrived at Naru, Kennedy and Ross read Evans' note before boarding it for the trip to Olasana. The natives brought food, water, coffee, cigarettes, and a small cooking stove to help the weary sailors. It was the first solid meal the survivors had in almost a week. Additionally, they built a small shelter of palm fronds for the injured McMahon. Kennedy then departed for the trip to Gomu, hidden in the canoe covered by fern leaves.

Reginald Evans went down to the beach when he saw the canoe approaching. "For a while I thought they had no one with them," Evans later recalled, fearing the native had returned empty handed.[430] "Hello, I'm Kennedy," the PT boat captain said after revealing himself. "Come to my tent and have a cup of tea," Evans replied.[431] The two discussed the rescue plan. The arrangement called for Kennedy to proceed to Rendova while PT boats rescued the balance of the survivors. Kennedy did not like it. As the sailors' commanding officer, he wanted to be personally involved in the operation. He was also familiar with the islands and reefs of the area. The plan was adjusted for the boats to first pick up Kennedy on Patparan Island in Blackett Strait before proceeding on for the others.

Thomas Warfield selected Henry Brantingham to lead the operation. The actual rescue would be done by *PT-157* under the command of William Liebenow, with the assistance of Arthur Berndtson in *PT-171*. Brantingham rode in the 157 along with the boat's regular crew, a pharmacist mate, three natives (Biuku Gasa, Eroni Kumana, and John Kari), and Al Cluster, who came up from the Russell Islands to help in the rescue.[432] Two war correspondents were also aboard to ensure the story received favorable press coverage.

Seven PT's departed Rendova Harbor during the early evening of August 7. Five boats proceeded to a patrol area on the eastern side of the lower end of Vella Gulf and arrived on station by 9:30 p.m. The weather was overcast with occasional rain and fair to poor visibility.[433]

PT's 157 and 171 proceeded directly to Patparan Island, traveling at slow speed so as not to be spotted by Japanese float planes. Kennedy departed Evans' hideout earlier in the evening with some natives to travel to the rendezvous point by canoe. He wore a pair of overalls borrowed from the coastwatcher to keep him warm during the cool night. Kennedy waited in the darkness as the appointed meeting time of 10:00 p.m. came and went with no sign of the rescue boats. More than an hour passed before he finally heard the rumbling sound of approaching torpedo boats.

Liebenow fired off the prearranged signal of four gun shots. Kennedy answered with three pistol shots, the only rounds he had left in the weapon, and one shot from a Japanese rifle given to him by Evans. The native canoe pulled up to the starboard side of *PT-157*. "Hey Jack," rang out from the PT. Kennedy angrily responded, "Where the hell have you been?" before he was pulled aboard.[434]

It was well after midnight before the boats reached Olasana. Berndtson kept *PT-171* lurking in the background, using her radar to scan the area as *PT-157* carefully nudged along a reef before moving through a break that Kennedy insisted was there. "[Kennedy] stood between me at the wheel, and the two natives," Liebenow later wrote of the tense moments. "He pointed out the direction, the natives agreed, and we headed out."[435] Kennedy, Cluster, and a native boarded a small wooden boat once near the island. It was lowered off the stern and the group paddled towards shore.

The remaining survivors were asleep when the boat came ashore with Kennedy calling out for Lenny Thom. "Here we are!" Thom finally answered.[436] With the help of a second small boat, several trips were made to bring all of *PT-109's* survivors off the island.

Once all of the shipwrecked sailors were safely aboard, *PT-157* followed the same course out of the area, heading for Rendova. *PT-171* departed to join the remaining boats on patrol in Vella Gulf.

The crew of *PT-157* comforted the survivors as best they could during the three-hour return voyage. The boat's cook prepared sandwiches and distributed brandy, while the pharmacist mate tended to the wounded and the reporters gathered information for their stories. The rescue boat arrived at Rendova Harbor at about 5:00 a.m. where the load of guest passengers departed. The natives were provided gifts before leaving for the journey back to their home island.

The *PT-109* sailors once thought dead received a stirring welcome at the Lumbari PT base. The men were sent to Tulagi after some initial first aid, with the most serious cases going on to a larger field hospital on Guadalcanal. Kennedy was put under doctor's care for about a week on Tulagi. During this time he was treated for cuts, lacerations, and fatigue. He then moved to a tent at Calvertville for rest and recuperation.

The loss of the two crewmen—especially Andrew Kirksey—during the ordeal weighed heavily on Kennedy. "When a fellow gets the feeling that he's in for it, the only thing to do is to let him get off the boat because strangely enough, they always seem to be the ones that do get it," Kennedy wrote at the time. "I don't know whether it's just coincidence or what. He had a wife and three kids. The other fellow had just come aboard. He was only a kid himself."[437]

The rescue of John Kennedy and his surviving crew members marked the end of the short battle career of *PT-109*. The boat's life had spanned little more than a year. Some early press reports of the rescue brought the story to the American public, and most of the articles focused largely on Kennedy, the former ambassador's son. The 109 then slipped into history. She was just one of many warships lost in action, as the Pacific War continued on at a fever pace.

PART THREE

BEYOND THE 109

CHAPTER 17

PT BOATS AND DESTROYERS

T he loss of *PT-109* marked the end of a torpedo boat that served with distinction during the bitter fighting in the Solomon Islands. However, World War II in the Pacific continued, and so did the naval careers of Rollin Westholm, Bryant Larson, and John Kennedy. Larson and Kennedy spent a short amount of time together when changing command of the 109. Westholm had some contact with Kennedy at Tulagi during his time as a staff officer in the flotilla command. Although sharing the common thread of having served aboard and commanded the same boat, there is no definitive information to suggest the officers had any additional contact with each other as the war progressed. Each followed a different path through the conflict and saw more action in the grueling months ahead.

———

Rollin Westholm became the operations officer of Motor Torpedo Boat Flotilla One after departing *PT-109* in February 1943. The duty lasted until late into the year. Flotilla leader Allen Calvert was more than pleased with his work. "His decisions have been uniformly sound and the success against the enemy attained by this command are to a great extent due to him," Calvert wrote. "He possesses a pleasing personality and a high personal and military character."[438]

The command apparatus grew along with the number of PT boats and squadrons in the Solomon Islands. Captain Edward Moran became Commander Motor Torpedo Boat Squadrons South Pacific Force in July 1943.

Although not having operational control over the boats, the command worked to improve logistical support, training programs, and to standardize operating doctrine.[439]

Westholm joined Moran's staff in late November 1943 to work on issues relating to boat operations, maintenance, and training. He achieved the highest possible rating by his superior when it came time for a formal review. "This officer has performed his duties in an outstanding manner. He is conscientious, thorough, and has a high sense of devotion to duty." Moran wrote.[440]

Even while serving with great distinction in the PT boat force, Westholm never forgot his destroyer days before the war. He consistently listed a new destroyer command as his first preference for next duty on the various performance reviews during his time in the Solomons. Calvert and Moran both felt he was well suited for such an assignment.

Orders arrived in early 1944 detaching Westholm from duty in the South Pacific and sending him back to Melville, Rhode Island. His time at the training center, however, was temporary. In April he moved to the Fleet Sound School in Key West, Florida for a short stay. Westholm was then sent west to take command of a destroyer. Unbeknownst to the young officer, the new warship he was to command had already seen action in the Pacific.

The destroyer *Bush* was commissioned on May 10, 1943.[441] She was named in honor of a fallen marine who perished aboard the venerable *Constitution* in 1812. The warship arrived at Pearl Harbor in December 1943 after several months of operating in Alaskan waters. She then moved to the South Pacific where she assumed a support role providing escort, patrol, and fire support duties. She participated in amphibious operations at New Guinea, New Britain, and the Admiralty Islands before it was time for the warship to take a break from the action. She had spent about five months on the front lines. The destroyer arrived at the Mare Island Navy Yard near San Francisco, CA on May 4, 1944 for repairs and upkeep.[442]

Rollin Westholm assumed command of *Bush* on May 27, 1944. The *Fletcher* class destroyer represented the latest in United States small ship technology. The warship displaced 2,100 tones and measured 376 feet in overall length. She had a main battery of five-inch guns and torpedo tubes.[443] An assortment of smaller guns provided anti-aircraft defense.

The destroyer was en route back to the front in early August to resume her support role. Westholm was promoted to the rank of commander about a month later. He now commanded a crew of twenty officers and about 300 enlisted men. Westholm certainly must have known that more fighting lay ahead.

The *Bush* participated in the conquest of the Philippines during the last part of the year. The destroyer was operating with friendly ships in Leyte Gulf on November 1 when the area came under a heavy Japanese air attack.[444] Westholm was awarded the Legion of Merit for his subsequent actions. The citation noted "[Westholm] expertly fought off an intense and determined attack of hostile aircraft, destroying at least two enemy planes with only minor damage to his ship."[445]

The Philippines operation came to a successful completion in January 1945, after which *Bush* continued to operate on the front lines as the American forces moved across the Pacific towards Japan. After participating in the Iwo Jima operation during February and March, the destroyer joined the naval forces preparing to invade Okinawa. She would meet her fate during the horrific battle to secure the island.

The enemy was determined to fight to the bitter end, even as American forces moved onto the doorstep of the Japanese home islands. The Japanese resorted to suicidal tactics during the last desperate year of the war. Pilots designated as Kamikazes were sent on one-way missions to crash their planes into American warships in a last ditch gamble to turn the tide of the conflict.

As American soldiers fought on land for control of Okinawa in early April, naval units stood ready to protect the area against threats from the air and sea. Intelligence reports suggested the Japanese were planning a massive Kamikaze attack. Radar equipped warships were positioned at numerous points around Okinawa to provide an early warning and to help vector friendly fighters to the suicide attackers. Manned largely by destroyers, the defensive network was a series of stations known as radar pickets.

Bush was assigned to radar picket station number 1 for much of the first week of April. Located just over fifty miles north of the center of Okinawa, it was one of sixteen picket ship locations near the embattled island.[446] The action started shortly after her arrival on station as *Bush* fired on several small groups of enemy planes as the enemy probed the American defenses. The main strike came on April 6 when the Japanese unleashed the first of ten large-scale Kamikaze attacks in the region.

The destroyer skirmished with several planes during the early morning hours and may have shot one down. The mass attack, however, did not start until later in the day. Four large groups of planes approached the area during the early afternoon. Friendly fighters and ship gunfire drove some planes away, but others kept coming.

Shortly after 3:00 p.m. a lone plane appeared dead ahead of *Bush*. It closed on the ship weaving between ten and thirty-five feet above the water. The destroyer opened fire as Westholm ordered evasive maneuvers. "All batteries were firing at maximum rate and despite heavy and what appeared to be accurate five-inch and forty-millimeter gunfire, the plane kept coming in," Westholm reported. "At the time it seemed unbelievable that it could do so."[447]

A last minute sharp turn by the destroyer failed to throw off the attacker. The plane crashed into the starboard side of the ship causing a tremendous explosion amidship between the two stacks. The plane's bomb or torpedo detonated in the forward engine room killing all of the occupants and many in the adjacent fire rooms.

The destroyer slowed to a drift with her position marked by a growing plume of black smoke. Flooding quickly caused a ten degree list. However, crewmen acted fast to get the situation under control and stabilize the ship. An auxiliary diesel generator was cut in to provide power, fires were extinguished with the help of escaping steam, and portable pumps were able to stop the flooding. Wounded sailors were treated on the fantail and in the wardroom. *Bush* suffered grievous damage, but was still afloat. "A careful survey of damage at this time led to the belief that the ship could be saved," Westholm wrote.

The Japanese planes continued to attack over the next few hours. The destroyer *Colhoun* closed to provide help, but was also struck by a Kamikaze plane. She was soon in the same condition as *Bush* and later sank.[448] Additional American fighters were dispatched to the area and clashed with enemy planes about fifteen miles south, preventing their arrival over the pair of beleaguered destroyers.

Help came in the form of two small support ships that closed to provide assistance as even more Japanese planes approached. Several aerial attackers were shot down before a second Kamikaze hit *Bush* at 5:25 p.m. The plane hit between the stacks, starting a large fire after narrowly missing the bridge. "The crash almost cut the ship in two," Westholm noted. "It is believed that bottom and keel were the only things holding it together."

Crewmen were close to having the fire under control about twenty minutes later when a third plane slammed into *Bush's* port side just above the main deck. It narrowly missed *Colhoun* and had evaded determined gunfire from several ships. Fire quickly swept the forward part of the warship as ammunition began to explode. Most of the wounded in *Bush*'s wardroom were killed in the blast. Rollin Westholm and his crew still did not give up in the face of great danger and continued their valiant fight to save the ship.

A heavy swell rocked the destroyer at 6:30 p.m. causing her to begin to cave in amidships. Westholm finally ordered her abandoned when it became apparent *Bush* would not last much longer. The warship jackknifed and sank just as the last men were leaving the stern. The sailors then faced a new struggle as they fought to survive in the heavy seas. Six vessels eventually helped rescue the *Bush* sailors. A total of 227 crewmen survived.

Westholm was awarded the Navy Cross for his skillful command of *Bush* and his heroic efforts to save the ship and its crew. "After giving the order to abandon ship, he supervised the evacuation of the crew and was the last man to leave the stricken vessel," the citation read. "Through his profound devotion to duty, he proved to be an inspiration to all."[449]

Westholm focused on administrative duties in the months immediately after the sinking. He wrote the final action report on *Bush*'s loss and spent time working on ship records. He later received orders to return to the United States. Westholm spent the final months of World War II in Norfolk, VA, serving as a liaison officer in the training command. His role involved forming and training crews for new destroyer escorts.[450]

———

Bryant Larson waited for transportation back to the United States after arriving in Espiritu Santo by destroyer. Only a short time had passed since he ceded command of *PT-109* to Lenny Thom and John Kennedy. The heavy fighting around Guadalcanal was months behind him. Larson was granted a twenty-day leave upon his return stateside.[451]

Larson was promoted to lieutenant (Junior Grade) just before departing the South Pacific.[452] He also had a chance encounter with a friend from back home in Minnesota. "Timer" Sutton was a bomber pilot waiting to go north to the front lines. "I told Timer I was heading home to marry his friend and neighbor, Gerry Smith," he later recalled of the meeting.[453] The two had been introduced before the war.[454]

The trip home began with a long ocean voyage east. Larson had no way of knowing that word of his marriage plans arrived back home before he did. Sutton included the information in a letter home to his mother and the news was out. "I did get home," Larson wrote, "and within three weeks (repeat, three) we were married in a full, formal church wedding, followed by a ten-day official honeymoon in northern Minnesota and an unofficial honeymoon that lasted for eleven months!" The honeymoon came about after Larson sent a telegram to the navy asking for the additional time off. "Being married on leave respectfully request ten days additional delay in reporting," the note read.[455] The request was granted.

Larson liked the PT's and wanted to stay in the small boat service, but preferred the duty to be on the Atlantic coast.[456] New orders granted his preference. "I was ordered back to Melville to wait reassignment, which could be either shipping out very quickly as a replacement, or drawing a new squadron. We took a chance on the latter and headed for [Rhode Island.]" The bet paid off when Larson was not selected to be a replacement.

In many ways the young officer was retracing the path he took to war more than a year ago. With more than thirty torpedo boat squadrons in operation and more boats on the assembly line, the PT Training Center had grown substantially in size and people since Larson's first visit. The squadrons were now operating on the European front, in addition to the Pacific, resulting in the need for a constant supply qualified sailors.

The newlyweds made their home in nearby Newport, a setting which allowed the couple to enjoy a lively social life. "Life in Newport was a ball," Larson related. A large number of PT officers brought brides along to live in the area. It seemed his wife would remind him of yet another evening party whenever he left each morning for the short trip to base.

The time at Melville was not all fun, however. "We did have some duties as instructors in patrolling and boat handling," Larson later wrote. "We also took some serious training in the operation and use of the new radar being installed on every boat. In particular, we practiced blind torpedo firing from a radar track."

Orders issued on January 25, 1944 assigned Larson to a new squadron. The couple took a train back to Minnesota for a short leave, before returning back to the East Coast. The new duty sent him to New York City.

The process of getting the new squadron running efficiently was much the same as what Larson previously experienced with *PT-109*, but with new people. "The officers of [Squadron] thirty-six were a mixed bag of veterans (four from Guadalcanal), transfers from other duty, and recent V-7 graduates (like us two years ago)," Larson wrote. "Neither the squadron commander nor the executive officer had had any prior PT or combat duty."

Motor Torpedo Boat Squadron Thirty-Six was commissioned on April

3, 1944 under the leadership of Lieutenant Commander Francis Tappaan. The unit received twelve newly constructed Elco eighty-foot boats.[457] Larson was given command of *PT-529* and a young crew. Most of his sailors were under twenty years old and had little experience. However, the men benefited from advanced specialty training based on their rating. "It was my job to turn them into an effective battle crew," Larson added. "Bit by bit we qualified."

Although the new boat was of the same basic design as *PT-109*, it was outfitted with the newest technology and weaponry. Gone were the torpedo tubes, along with the outdated torpedoes and revealing flashes that often gave away a boat's position during a night battle. PT boats now used aerial torpedoes designed to be dropped from bombers. The weapons were placed on racks and simply rolled over the side to fire.

A single barrel forty-millimeter gun was mounted on the stern. The new weapon gave the PT's some heavy firepower for use against the armored Japanese barges. "But best of all we had radar—eyes that could see in the night and so greatly reduce the stress of night patrols, at least for those of us that learned the trade with only binoculars and a lot of luck," Larson later wrote. Some things, however, did not change. "For all that, the new boats remained as vulnerable as ever—a floating gas tank that depended on darkness, stealth, rapid smoke-covered retirements, and large quantities of guts and luck."

Larson knew his time in the United States would now be limited. "There would still be time for some fun and games, but we would be always looking over our shoulder, for the bloody war was still out there and that's where we were headed," he recalled. He knew what to expect as a combat veteran. Larson's rank was elevated while still on the East Coast, as he was promoted to full lieutenant on July 1, 1944.[458]

Orders soon arrived sending the squadron south to Panama. On July 20 he put his wife on a train bound for Minneapolis and made ready to ship out. The honeymoon was over. After three weeks of training it was time to return to the war. The boats were loaded onto transport ships for the long voyage across the Pacific to the Admiralty Islands.

Much had changed in the South Pacific since Larson's departure. The tide of war was now favoring the Americans. The heavy fighting in the Solomon Islands was over. A new strategy, born out of the grueling island combat on Guadalcanal and New Georgia, was allowing Allied forces to advance much faster towards the interior of the Imperial Japanese Empire than was initially expected. Instead of conquering all enemy-held islands, heavily defended bastions were bypassed in favor of those occupied by a lesser number of troops. The front lines continued to move forward, cutting off the side-stepped islands from supplies, reinforcements, and rescue.

By early 1944 forces under the command of General Douglas Mac-Arthur were making substantial advances along the northern coast of New Guinea. The once feared Japanese fortress base at Rabaul had been attacked heavily from the air and then bypassed in a series of flanking moves. The maneuver was completed during the spring months when American forces landed on the Admiralty Islands and Hollandia on the northern coast of New Guinea. Positioned almost 400 miles northwest of Rabaul and more than 150 miles from New Guinea, the Admiralties became a forward naval operating base. The moves set the stage for the conquest of the Philippines.

PT boats continued to play an important role in the South Pacific both on the front lines and behind. The night battles with enemy destroyers Larson experienced in Iron Bottom Sound were largely a thing of the past. The boats regularly accompanied naval forces piercing ever deeper into Japanese territory. Missions varied to include disrupting the enemy supply lines, reconnaissance duties, and search and rescue. Torpedo boats also worked behind the front lines to keep the isolated Japanese island garrisons contained. It often meant long patrols and night gunfights with barges.

After arriving at Manus in the Admiralty Islands, the boats of Squadron Thirty-Six proceeded almost due west to Mios Woendi. The small island off the northwest coast of New Guinea was home to a forward PT operating base. Bryant Larson conducted his first night patrol since his days aboard *PT-109*. The young officer was now a section leader, meaning he led small groups of two or three boats on patrol. The first patrol was uneventful with no sign of the enemy in the immediate area.

One of Larson's most memorable voyages occurred when the 529 and one other boat were sent 250 miles down the New Guinea coast to conduct radar tests with a group of destroyers. "While moored at the base we discovered we could draw beer rations for the entire squadron—about 250 cases," Larson later explained. "Draw it we did—then took off for Woendi with beer lashed topside and stuffed below decks!" The clever boat captain and crew proceeded to keep about fifty-five cases for their own use before turning the remainder over to the squadron. "I thought it was very generous of us and it did keep the 529 well supplied for many, many months."

A large group of PT boats moved north when the American invasion of the Philippines began in October 1944. Squadron Thirty-Six contributed six boats to go with the main naval forces, but *PT-529* was not among the chosen. Larson and the remainder of the squadron initially stayed behind at New Guinea, but later moved north to the Leyte Gulf area of the Philippines.

The boats were charged with intercepting Japanese shipping in the vicinity of Ormoc Bay, the last large port available to the enemy on the west side of Leyte Island. "Over the course of many patrols the 529 had only one contact," Larson wrote of the time. "We fired two torpedoes at an enemy ammunition ship bound for Ormoc." The two fish missed, but Larson radioed the contact information to a group of nearby American destroyers. "They didn't miss," he added.

The American campaign in the Philippines moved north to the large island of Luzon with an amphibious landing on January 9, 1945. PT Squadrons Twenty-Eight and Thirty-Six came with a tender only four days later to begin operations in the area.[459] Larson was now under a new commanding officer as Lieutenant John Morrison, Jr. assumed leadership of the squadron in December 1944.

Larson witnessed the frightening sight of a Japanese Kamikaze crashing into an American ship shortly after arriving at Luzon. The boats patrolled the coastal areas north and south, but made few enemy contacts. With the west coast of Luzon facing the South China Sea, the boats often had to contend with rough seas.

A special mission sent *PT-529* to pick up an American serviceman who evaded capture after the fall of Bataan in 1942 and had spent the subsequent years hiding with the locals. Larson took the boat about a hundred miles south unescorted to a small bay near the Bataan Peninsula. The passenger climbed aboard from a small raft after an exchange of signals during the pitch dark night.

The boat encountered rough seas on the return trip. "The waves I could see by the foaming tops I could ride over—it was the ones I couldn't see (many if not most) that slammed us like a sledge hammer," he later recalled. Larson reassured the crew of their safe return as he reached for the lucky bean still in his possession from Guadalcanal. "We did make it, thanks to a very well built, seaworthy boat, and a very salty crew."

Larson's squadron was ordered to Borneo as the liberation of the Philippines drew to a close in early 1945. The large oil-rich island, located southwest of the Philippines, had been under British and Dutch control before it fell to the Japanese in early 1942. Only coastal areas had been developed, with much of the interior left to native control. A large portion of the island was a dense and swampy jungle.

American and Australian forces landed on the small heart-shaped island of Tarakan off the east coast of Borneo on May 1, 1945. The island was important due to oil fields and an airbase.[460] Waterways near the main port were known to be mined. Some of the underwater hazards were put in place by the Japanese for defensive purposes, while others were dropped by Allied planes to hinder the voyages of enemy tankers.

PT operations began in advance of the invasion to guard against Japanese suicide boats and to prevent enemy interference with Allied engineering teams who were clearing away obstacles near the landing beach.[461] "Our mission was to patrol around the island and along the Borneo coasts to prevent any escape," Larson explained. "Escape to where? There was nothing but salt water swamp land for hundreds of miles!"

The 529 boat was initially assigned to make one of the first patrols around the island. However, it was delayed to allow a minesweeper to ensure the route was clear. The sweeper was then sunk by gunfire from the shore. Larson quickly realized that he was again the beneficiary of some good luck. "The sea bean was still working," he later wrote.

With few targets available at sea, the squadron commander decided to send boats to patrol up some of the coastal rivers in the area. The boat captains with combat experience knew it would be a dangerous undertaking. "[Morrison] said it would look good on the squadron record," Larson remembered. "So we patrolled, but very cautiously for the end was near and we wanted to live."

Larson was not done fighting even as the war was winding down. He was to have one more brush with the enemy. "It was a night patrol just off Tarakan," he recalled. "Another very dark night." The boat's radar registered a contact. Although it was not uncommon in the area, most radar blips turned out to be nothing more than floating debris. Larson directed his companion boats to stay behind. He called his crew to battle stations and cautiously brought *PT-529* close to the target. Turning on the boat's small searchlight revealed the object to be a small raft, improvised of several oil drums tied together, with eleven Japanese aboard.

Larson was faced with a decision. "I had three choices—leave them alone to starve and/or drown, kill them all (an acceptable choice under the rules of our Tarakan war), or take them aboard as prisoners," Larson wrote. He decided on capture. The prisoners were individually pulled aboard under the barrels of guns. Each was stripped of clothing and forced to lay flat on the deck near the bow for the trip back to land. "These were the enemies I had hunted, chased, or been chased by, for all these months and years and finally we came face to face," Larson later reflected. "They didn't look very mean— just some naked, worn out men that wanted to go home. But for clothing, we had much in common."

Larson received a good review from his squadron commander on his final officer performance evaluation conducted in August 1945. "Subject officer is considered far above average in the PT program," John Morrison wrote. "Thoroughly capable and cooperative."[462] The end of the war was getting closer by the day.

The United States officially received notification of the Japanese surrender on the morning of August 16. It was closely followed by an Imperial order for all Japanese armed forces to cease fire.[463] The fighting was over.

The PT sailors were understandably overjoyed. "We made it! Time to go home," Larson wrote of the time. However, the squadron commander did not receive any directive to end patrols, so the boats were ordered out as usual. Larson explained how he handled the situation. "So we cleared the harbor, turned and ran north a short way, cut the engines, broke out the beer, and returned to the harbor base on schedule—the last patrol!"

CHAPTER 18

GUNBOAT SKIPPER

The sinking of *PT-109* and subsequent struggle for survival in the Blackett Strait did not mark the end of John Kennedy's PT boat service. He had been in the Solomons about five months and wanted another opportunity to fight the Japanese. It was a common practice for the survivor of a sunken ship to be granted a thirty-day leave to go home. Kennedy, however, declined squadron commander Al Cluster's offer for orders back to the United States. "He got to be more determined—and he was very determined before," Cluster later said about Kennedy's desire to get into a fight with the enemy.[464] The young officer was ready to step aboard a new boat after about three weeks of rest and recuperation on Tulagi.

Cluster assigned Kennedy to be the commanding officer of *PT-59*, a battle-scarred veteran of fights in Iron Bottom Sound. Her previous skipper had recently left for the States and much of her crew had been rotated out. The boat was manufactured by Elco, but was an older design than *PT-109*.

The 59 was part of an experiment to give PT boats more firepower against Japanese barges. She would no longer be a torpedo boat, but was in the process of undergoing conversion to a gunboat along with sister boats *PT-60* and *PT-61*. It was a radical and untried concept championed by Cluster. For Kennedy it meant the abandonment of the intense training on torpedo attacks he endured at Melville. He instead would likely participate in close-range gun battles with barges and other small enemy craft.

Among Kennedy's first duties as boat captain was to form a crew. The 59 boat required a large group of sailors to man the extra guns. Neither officer from *PT-109's* last voyage was available. Both were given new assignments, with Lenny Thom taking command of *PT-60*. Kennedy quickly found two available officers, one a former boat captain and the other a newcomer to PT's.

The enlisted men came from a variety of sources. Two sailors from the boat's old crew remained aboard. Five men who previously spent time aboard *PT-109*, including two survivors of the sinking, were the next to join. Most of the remaining enlisted sailors came from *PT-21*. The boat was recently damaged en route to the South Pacific and was scrapped for parts. Many of these men were Pearl Harbor survivors from sunken battleships. "Have a picked crew—all volunteers—and all very experienced," Kennedy wrote at the time about his new boat mates. "Every man but one has been sunk at least once, and they all have been in the boats for a long time."[465]

The conversion took place with the assistance of the repair ship *Argonne*, with *PT-59* moored alongside the vessel for much of the conversion work. The PT crew, including the boat captain, provided some of the labor. Kennedy lived at the Tulagi PT base during the construction period, but occasionally stayed overnight on the repair ship.

Kennedy shared thoughts on his current situation in two letters sent to his parents. "They will not send anyone back while there is fighting in this area. When it's over I'll get back. As a matter of fact, I am in a bad spot for getting out as I am now captain of a gun-boat. It's the first one they've ever had of its type. It's a former PT and is very interesting."[466] He also added a note about being the initial gunboat skipper. "It was sort of a dubious honor to be given the first, so I will have to stick around and try to make a go of it."

The young officer also wrote of how the struggle for survival after the 109's sinking affected his outlook on the war. "It certainly brought home how real the war is—and when I read the papers from home and how superficial is most of the talking and thinking about it. When I read that we will fight the Japs for years if necessary and will sacrifice hundreds of thousands if we must—I always like to check from where he is talking—it's seldom out here. People get so used to talking about billions of dollars and millions of soldiers that thousands of dead sounds like drops in the bucket. But if those thousands want to live as much as the ten I saw—they should measure their words with great, great care." He concluded with a note of hopefulness. "Perhaps all of that won't be necessary—and it can all be done by bombing."[467]

The renovation of *PT-59* required extensive changes to the boat's armament and the addition of a primitive radar set. The four torpedo tubes and twenty-millimeter gun were removed. The freed weight was used to add two forty-millimeter cannons and six additional fifty-caliber machine guns.

The boat was also given armor, something the PT sailors were not used to having aboard their small boats. Thin shields about a quarter of an inch thick were installed on the guns. Although not substantial enough to stop larger caliber shells, the armor offered a slight amount of protection against the small arms fire that seemed to regularly emanate from Japanese barges.

The conversion work proceeded at a slow pace throughout September. The approval from Admiral Halsey's headquarters for the use of armor plate had to make it through red tape. Workers from the repair ship were dealing with multiple projects of varying priority, including battle-damaged cruisers and destroyers needing to get fixed up to return to action.[468]

Most of the construction work was completed by the beginning of October, and Kennedy made a trial voyage around Savo Island during the first week of the month. The boat may have lost some speed as a result of the modifications. However, it was not deemed significant because Japanese barges were known to be slow movers. The high speed maneuvers needed to evade destroyers would no longer be needed.

The new *PT-59* was ready for action on October 9 after some final adjustments and a new coat of paint. It was finally time for Kennedy to return to the front lines. He took his new boat north to Rendova after making brief stops at Guadalcanal and the Russell Islands. Lumbari was no longer the most forward PT base by the time the new gunboat was ready for action. Kennedy stayed in the area for just over a week using the time for additional trials, equipment tests, and crew training.

Kennedy had been promoted to full lieutenant on October 1. It had been almost exactly a year since his last change in rank.[469] His new boat and crew were soon ready for action. "Got a real good boat now and a top crew—all very experienced men—and it helps a lot," he wrote.[470]

As much as Kennedy was ready for the next challenge in the South Pacific, he was also thinking about when it would be time to go home. "Feeling fine, but after this present fighting is over will be glad to get home," he wrote his parents at the time. "When I do get out of here you'll find that you have a new permanent fixture around that Florida pool. I'll just move from it to get into my sack. Don't worry at all about me—I've learned to duck—and have learned the wisdom of the old naval doctrine of keeping your bowels—your mouth shut—and never volunteering."[471]

The front lines in the Solomon Islands continued to move northwest while Kennedy was recovering from *PT-109's* sinking and subsequently working on his new gunboat. After winning a hard-fought battle for New Georgia and taking control of the Munda airfield, American amphibious forces bypassed heavily garrisoned Kolombangara to land on lightly defended Vella Lavella in the middle of August.

PT operations moved forward with the front lines. Seven torpedo boats of Squadron Eleven and a small transport arrived in Vella Lavella on September 25 to begin operations.[472] The group set up a forward operating base at Lambu Lambu Cove on the northeast coast of the island.

With the loss of the Central Solomons, the Japanese were scrambling to move into defensive positions further north. It required troops to be removed, if possible, from Kolombangara, and garrisons to be strengthened on Bougainville, Shortland, and Choiseul. Only the islands of the Northern Solomons now stood between the advancing American forces and Rabaul.

Kennedy maneuvered *PT-59* out of Rendova Harbor on the afternoon of October 18 for the trip to Vella Lavella.[473] The route through Blackett Strait took Kennedy near the area of his ordeal with *PT-109*. The boat continued north through Vella Gulf.

Passing through a narrow gap in coral reef allowed Kennedy and his boat to enter the hundred-yard-wide Lambu Lambu Cove. The 59 had arrived at the most primitive forward operating base yet. The meager facilities included a repair dock, a small command post, first aid station, and an assortment of tents. Kennedy reported to Art Berndston, who had recently moved up from Lumbari to become base commander.

The main role of the Lambu Lambu PT base was to interdict Japanese barge traffic near Choiseul Island. The large land mass is positioned southeast of Bougainville and directly north of Vella Lavella. The island represented the northwest terminus of the Slot during the struggle for Guadalcanal. The area was now a hotbed of enemy activity as the Japanese attempted to reposition troops around the Northern Solomons.

Kennedy was ordered out on patrol the very first night, joining five other PT's on a barge hunting trip to Choiseul. The mission was to block the southern and western approaches to the island. The force divided into two equal groups with the 59 boat joining *PT-169* and *PT-183*.

The night did not go well for Kennedy. His problems began when *PT-59* was plagued by engine trouble during the outbound voyage. Kennedy's section cautiously approached Redman Island off the Choiseul coast at about midnight. Lookouts scanned the bright moonlit night looking for any sign of enemy activity. A Japanese floatplane suddenly swooped out of the sky at 12:30 a.m. to attack the boats with bombs. The surprise strike failed when the bombs harmlessly fell well astern of *PT-169*, but it left Kennedy wondering why his radar set had failed to detect the intruder.[474]

The trio of boats then moved close to the coast in search of barge traffic. The group began the voyage back to base after no sign of enemy vessels could be found. However, the force was attacked from the air twice more during the return to Vella Lavella, resulting in slight damage to *PT-183*. The radar on Kennedy's boat again failed to detect the planes. It was the first opportunity for the guns of *PT-59* to take aim against the enemy. Gunners opened fire on the second plane, but apparently scored no hits.

It was a frustrating inaugural patrol for Kennedy's new gunboat. Plagued by engine problems and radar failure, the barge hunting voyage was a bust. It was the first of thirteen patrols he would undertake, all to the Choiseul area while operating out of Lambu Lambu Cove. However, less than a week later Kennedy's boat participated in a daring rescue operation of marines trapped on Choiseul by superior Japanese forces.

It began in late October when American amphibious forces again prepared to strike in the Solomons. Bougainville was the next island targeted for invasion, and American commanders decided to create diversionary attacks on Choiseul and the Treasury Islands in advance of the main strike. Dubbed Operation Blissful, the move was designed to keep the Japanese off balance in the Northern Solomons and divert resources away from the real target.

Marine Lieutenant Colonel Victor Krulak was charged with leading the operation. His orders were to take a reinforced battalion to the island for a limited time to launch harassing attacks on Japanese positions, but avoid any major battles. He was promised support from air units and PT boats based on Vella Lavella, two coastwatchers already stationed on Choiseul, and friendly natives.

One PT sailor departed with the marines as part of the operation. Lieutenant (Junior Grade) Richard Keresey, boat captain of *PT-105*, accompanied the soldiers to help find a suitable location for a PT base should the island eventually fall under American control.

The marine contingent would be up against a much larger enemy force. American intelligence estimated up to 5,000 Japanese soldiers were on Choiseul. However, many were thought to be stragglers from islands further south awaiting transport to Bougainville. The majority of the Japanese troops were thought to be in poor physical shape, lightly armed, and largely confined to coastal areas.[475]

The marines departed Vella Lavella in four destroyer transports under the cover of darkness on the evening of October 27, 1943.[476] The landing began shortly after midnight on an undefended beach along Choiseul's southwest coast. The destroyer transports left behind four small landing craft for use by the troops during their stay. Admiral Halsey later issued a press release announcing that 20,000 American troops had landed on the island to add credibility to the operation.[477]

PT boats continued to patrol around Choiseul, but proceeded cautiously as boat captains did not want to risk mistaking the marine landing boats for Japanese barges. Kennedy soon fell into the routine of nightly patrols. Most of his voyages, however, were inconclusive and he had little contact with the enemy.

While the Choiseul diversion was taking place, American forces landed at Empress Augusta Bay on Bougainville on November 1. The Japanese command wasted little time in dispatching a surface force from Rabaul to attack the invasion group. The torpedo boats were not called into action. Kennedy and his comrades never left Lambu Lambu Cove as a force of cruisers and destroyers defeated the Japanese in the Battle of Empress Augusta Bay.

While the invasion operation was proceeding according to plan on Bougainville, some of the marines on Choiseul ran into trouble. It began when eighty-seven men and two native guides ventured about twenty miles northwest of the main American encampment to raid enemy positions. The group became lost in a swampy area. The Japanese discovered the intruders' presence and moved to block their escape route.

Krulak took action once it became clear the patrol was in trouble. He directed the trapped marines to fight their way to an evacuation point as he made ready to dispatch three small landing craft to extract them. Richard Keresey convinced the lieutenant colonel that more firepower was needed to support the operation and that it could be provided by PT boats. A radio message was quickly sent to Vella Lavella asking for assistance.

The call for help reached the Lambu Lambu Cove PT base late in the afternoon of November 2. Art Berndston quickly grasped the urgency of the situation. He ran from the command center down to the dock area to check on the availability of boats. At the time there were only five PT's at the base.

Two were already committed to the evening patrol and one was undergoing repairs.[478] The two remaining boats, *PT-59* and *PT-236*, were ordered to make ready for a rapid departure.

Berndston showed Kennedy the message and asked about his fuel supply. *PT-59* was at that very moment in the process of refueling, but had only about 700 gallons aboard. It amounted to little over half the capacity of the fuel tanks and not enough for a round trip to Choiseul.

There was no time to finish the slow fueling process. Berndston conferred with his two boat captains to hastily develop a plan. *PT-236* was fully fueled and could tow the 59 boat back to Vella Lavella after her fuel supply gave out. The arrangement seemed workable to both boat captains. Kennedy ordered the fueling discontinued and the engines started. "Let's go get them," the boat captain told his crew as he jumped aboard. "Wind her up!"[479] The rumbling of PT engines marked the boats rapid departure from Lambu Lambu Cove.

The boats headed across the Slot towards the main marine encampment near the village of Voza. The weather was poor with an overcast sky and occasional rain squalls. The conditions helped ensure that the Japanese did not see the PT's from the air as neither boat was attacked by floatplanes.

The boats arrived off Voza in a rain storm after a two hour voyage. The three landing craft had already departed for the run north. Richard Keresey and a marine officer came out in a small boat and climbed aboard the 59. Kennedy was surprised to see his fellow boat captain, whom he knew from previous operations. "What are you doing here," he exclaimed. "Never mind that, we have to haul ass up the coast," Keresey replied. "There's a bunch of marines trapped."[480] Kennedy was given the details of the rescue operation and provided directions of where to go as the boats disappeared into the night.

The marine patrol had retreated to the water's edge near the mouth of the Warrior River on the northwest coast of Choiseul. The Americans were under heavy fire as Japanese troops were closing fast from more than one direction. Three American soldiers had been killed and several more wounded. The Japanese were firing motors at the fleeing American as a steady rain began to fall.[481]

The landing craft had just completed loading the marines and were backing away from shore when the PT boats arrived near the evacuation point. It was difficult for the sailors to ascertain what was happening. The PT's idled at slow speed as lookouts combed the area for any sign of the landing boats.

The boats took no immediate action as the captains did not want to accidentally fire on friendly forces.

The evacuation, however, soon ran into problems when one of the landing craft hit a coral reef. It ripped open a hole in her bottom and the craft started sinking about 250 yards off shore. The marines began using their helmets to bail out water, but could not keep up. Water soon choked off the boat's engines leaving her dead in the water.[482] A second landing craft took the stricken craft under tow.

The rescue operation had turned into a perilous situation. It was unclear if the damaged boat would stay afloat long enough to make it back to Voza. Also, it was not known if the Japanese would venture out to sea to attack the small convoy as the enemy was known to have small craft in the immediate area.

Keresey was at the bow of *PT-59* when he began to hear distant gunfire. A few minutes later he heard a different noise. It was definitely not gunfire. He signaled Kennedy to turn towards the sound. Just then two of the landing craft came into view.[483]

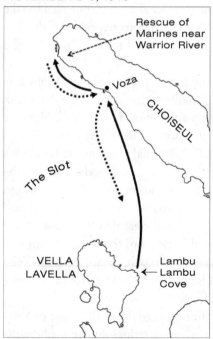

ROUTE OF *PT-59* & *PT-236*
NOVEMBER 2–3, 1943

Rescue of Marines near Warrior River

Voza

CHOISEUL

The Slot

VELLA LAVELLA

Lambu Lambu Cove

The PT boats jumped into action moving towards the landing craft. The marines were moved to the torpedo boats after the desperate situation became clear. Kennedy put *PT-59* between the damaged craft and shore while *PT-236* focused on getting the men off the other two landing boats.

Marines began to fill up any available space aboard *PT-59*. A badly wounded corporal was lifted aboard and placed below deck in Kennedy's bunk. Reports varied as to how many soldiers came aboard the 59 boat. With limited space on the gunboat due to the extra weapons, it is clear that *PT-236* took aboard more of the soldiers.[484] The small flotilla departed the area just after midnight.

The PT boats and the undamaged landing craft eventually arrived off Voza. The able-bodied soldiers were ferried ashore to the marine base camp. Three wounded men, however, were in need of medical care not available on Choiseul. They stayed abroad the 59 boat along with a marine doctor for the trip back to Vella Lavella. The fuel tanks on Kennedy's gunboat were close to empty as he set out across the Slot.

At about 1:00 a.m. the wounded marine corporal in Kennedy's bunk quietly succumbed to his wounds. *PT-59* ran out of gas two hours later. She was towed back to Lambu Lambu Cove, arriving at about 8:00 a.m.

The port stay was a short one as Kennedy's boat was ordered back to Choiseul the very next night. The diversionary operation had run its course and it was time for the entire marine force to return to Vella Lavella. *PT-59* took aboard 2,000 gallons of gasoline before departing with four other PT boats and three landing craft. The operation was completed without incident.

Kennedy remained in command of *PT-59* for the next two weeks, during which time the boat continued to make regular patrols to Choiseul. She occasionally shot at enemy barges and used her guns to pour fire onto shore positions.

Kennedy's fighting spirit remained strong even as Japanese targets were rapidly becoming scarce. At one point he concocted a dangerous plan to take his boat up the Warrior River on Choiseul. Much to the relief of the 59's crew it was squelched by Al Cluster, who happened to be visiting Lambu Lambu Cove.[485]

The area around Vella Lavella was no longer the front lines. A new forward PT base was established on Bougainville within days of the American landing at Empress Augusta Bay. Enemy activity in the Central Solomons diminished as the Japanese focused on defending islands farther north.

The night of November 16 marked *PT-59*'s final patrol under Kennedy's command. He took the boat to scout around Redman Island off the northwest coast of Choiseul, but there was no sign of the enemy during the voyage.

Although there is disagreement among biographers as to the condition of Kennedy's health during the fall of 1943, it was clear that the young officer was not well.[486] In addition to his usual back pain, the boat captain was plagued with stomach problems throughout much of his time on Vella Lavella. When the base doctor noticed Kennedy was having trouble keeping down meals, he ordered him to Tulagi for further evaluation.

On November 18 *PT-59* made a short voyage down the coast of Vella Lavella to Buloa, the location of an American airstrip. John Kennedy relinquished command of the boat and solemnly shook hands with each of his crew before catching a flight down to Tulagi. "If there is ever anything I can do for you, ask me," he said to the sailors. "You will always know where you can get in touch with me."[487] He had a particular hard time bidding farewell to his former *PT-109* comrades.

Kennedy underwent a full exam after reporting to the medical facility at Tulagi. An X-ray revealed he was suffering from a stomach ulcer. His fighting days were over. The base doctor ordered him to return to the United States, but the request became bogged down in bureaucratic red tape.[488] Kennedy spent his time at the Calvertville PT boat base with little to do but interact with fellow officers. He was often seen walking around the area with a cane. Once a forward base perilously perched on the front lines, the station was now a backwater and staging area for men and materials moving north.

Al Cluster finally broke through the red tape by issuing his own orders for Kennedy's departure. It became official on December 21 in a memo written by a base officer at Cluster's direction. ". . . you will consider yourself detached from duty in Motor Torpedo Boat Squadron Two and from other duties which may have been assigned you."[489] Kennedy was directed to proceed to the Melville training center for future assignment after taking a thirty-day leave.

As with most sailors returning to the United States from the South Pacific at the time, Kennedy's trip home was a long ocean voyage departing from Espiritu Santo. He boarded the escort carrier *Breton* in late December and arrived in San Francisco on January 7, 1944 after several intermediary stops along the way in the Pacific.[490] He traveled to the east coast after stopping to visit friends in Los Angeles and to consult with doctors at the Mayo Clinic in Minnesota.

In keeping with Cluster's orders, Kennedy proceeded to Rhode Island upon the completion of his leave. However, his stay at Melville was short and included a hospital visit for his bad back. In March he was ordered to the Subchaser Training Center in Miami, Florida. The base was also used for training new PT boat squadrons. The officer compliment included a long list of veteran PT boat captains from Guadalcanal.

While Kennedy was stationed in Miami, Secretary of the Navy James Forrestal in Washington gave the final approval for his medal. Al Cluster originally submitted a request for the Silver Star, the navy's third highest award, for the actions Kennedy took in saving some of his crew after the sinking of *PT-109*. However, as the request made its way through the chain of command, it was lowered to a Navy and Marine Corps Medal.[491] The citation summarized the boat captain's heroics: "Lieutenant Kennedy, Capt. of the boat, directed the rescue of the crew and personally rescued 3 men, one of whom was seriously injured. During the following six days, he succeeded in getting his crew ashore, and after swimming many hours attempting to secure aid and food, finally effected the rescue of the men."[492]

Kennedy was sent north to the U.S. Naval Hospital in Chelsea, MA in late May. He underwent spine surgery about a month later at the New England Baptist Hospital. The operation was unsuccessful and failed to cure his ailing back. Kennedy was diagnosed with colitis while recuperating at the hospital for eight weeks. The ailment explained his eating problems back in the South Pacific.

Kennedy's naval career had now entered its final stage as he went back to the Naval Hospital in Chelsea for treatment as an outpatient. Doctors confirmed the colitis diagnosis and recommended he be retired from the navy on account of the digestive disorder.

Months passed before Kennedy finally appeared before the Naval Retiring Board in Washington, DC. He was granted a medical discharge on December 27, 1944. A memo from the secretary of the navy made it effective on March 16, 1945.[493] The final boat captain of *PT-109* was now free to return to civilian life.

CHAPTER 19

ENDURING HISTORY

The story of *PT-109's* sinking and her crew's subsequent rescue appeared several times in newspapers and magazines in the year after the event, with much of the attention focused on John Kennedy. The initial reports came from the two war correspondents aboard the rescue boat. Their accounts appeared in major newspapers around the country with titles such as, "11 on Rammed PT Boat Saved from Jap Isle" and "Kennedy's Son is Hero in Pacific as Destroyer Splits His PT Boat."[494]

The story resurfaced in January 1944 when an article by Inga Arvad ran in the *Boston Globe*. It was based on an interview with Kennedy just after he returned to the United States. Journalist John Hersey was the next to pick up the story. He spoke with Kennedy and three other *PT-109* survivors for an essay entitled "Survival" which appeared in the June 17, 1944 issue of *The New Yorker* magazine. A condensed version of the article appeared two months later in *Reader's Digest*. The attention in the popular periodical made Kennedy a national hero.[495]

The story of *PT-109* began to slowly fade from public attention as the conflicts in Europe and the Pacific entered their final months in 1945. It likely would have become a forgotten wartime episode had it not been for Kennedy's eventual political rise. After the war in the Pacific drew to a close, life continued on for the three officers who commanded the 109 in the South Pacific.

The end of World War II did not stop Rollin Westholm from continuing to serve his country. He became a career navy man, remaining in the service for almost twenty years after Japan surrendered, with duties that took him around the globe. He was also a devoted family man, supporting his wife and kids.

Westholm's shore assignments included time at the American naval base in Yokosuka, Japan, Naval War College in Rhode Island, and Brooklyn Navy Yard, a familiar location from his PT boat days. At sea he commanded the amphibious ship *Estes*, a destroyer division, and an amphibious squadron. He also served as a staff officer of a battleship division.

The final assignment of Westholm's long navy career was to coordinate all of the arrangements for the launching of two amphibious transport ships at the Brooklyn Navy Yard in 1964. The event was a success and his commanding admiral reported the work was completed in an "outstanding manner."[496] Westholm retired from the navy on June 30, 1964 at the rank of captain with just over thirty years of service to his credit. His long list of medals included the Navy Cross, Legion of Merit, and a Presidential Unit Citation.[497]

Westholm chose to make his home in Annapolis, Maryland, where his naval career had begun decades earlier. He worked for the state of Maryland for ten years before becoming a manpower specialist for the mayor of Baltimore. The former PT boat commander retained a strong interest in small boats. He was a member of the New York Yacht Club and active in the Annapolis Yacht Club Race Committee until late in life. Rollin Westholm passed away on February 26, 1989 at the age of 77.[498] He is buried in the Naval Academy Cemetery.

Bryant Larson did not remain in the Pacific very long after the Japanese surrendered, and was on his way back to the United States within days of his last PT boat patrol off Borneo. A large flying boat arrived at the base to deliver relief personnel, including an officer who took over command of *PT-529*. "I signed off the log, flew back to Manus Island off New Guinea, caught a merchant ship that took me to Panama, transferred to a commercial airliner, landed in Chicago where my lonesome bride waited for me, and we got on with the business of raising a family," he wrote.[499] Larson, though, was not yet out of the navy.

Orders directed the officer to return to the Melville Training Center after completion of a thirty day leave. However, he never made the journey to Rhode Island. New orders came while he was still in Minnesota sending him to the Great Lakes Naval Base near Chicago to await separation. He was discharged from the navy on December 11, 1945.[500]

Larson obtained a job at First National Bank after returning home to Minneapolis and settled into civilian life. He never fully cut his navy ties, however, and was active in the U.S. Naval Reserve until receiving an honorable discharge in 1956 at the rank of lieutenant commander.[501] Larson later switched careers and worked for the Toro Corporation, eventually moving to Oregon in 1961 to start a successful power equipment distributorship.

He retired from his business in 1978 and returned to college to study history, graduating from the University of Minnesota with a doctorate degree in Russian history at the age of 65. Bryant Larson died on December 15, 2001. He was 81 years old.[502]

John Kennedy considered becoming a teacher or writer when he returned to civilian life.[503] He was soon urged by his father, however, to enter politics. The elder Kennedy's political aspirations for his first son Joe ended with the navy officer's death in a 1944 secret bombing mission in Europe. John Kennedy may not have been surprised that his father's hopes now fell on his shoulders. "I'll be back here with Dad trying to parlay a lost PT boat and a bad back into a political advantage," he told a friend shortly after the war.[504]

The young Kennedy decided to seek election to the House of Representatives from his home state of Massachusetts. His record as a war hero was a great political asset. During the campaign he spoke of a promise made to himself while in the South Pacific. "When ships were sinking and young Americans were dying ... I firmly resolved to serve my country in peace as honestly as I tried to serve it in war."[505] Kennedy easily won the contest on November 5, 1946.[506] He served six years in the House before being elected to the Senate in 1952.

In 1953 Kennedy married Jacqueline Bouvier, a reporter for the *Washington Times-Herald*. He started a family and dealt with his chronic bad back as the decade progressed. The Senator slowly grew into a powerful national political figure. After securing the Democratic Party's nomination as candidate for president, Kennedy narrowly defeated Richard Nixon in the 1960 election. His war hero status had once again been invoked in the tight campaign. John F. Kennedy (he was now known with his middle initial) was sworn into office on January 20, 1961. After the election he sent a telegram to each of his former *PT-109* crewmen inviting them to the inauguration.[507]

The election of the World War II navy veteran brought the story of *PT-109* to a new generation of Americans. A PT boat float in the inauguration day parade evoked a big smile from the new president. He happily waved at crewmen as it slowly passed his position.[508] PT veterans later visited Kennedy in the White House bearing mementos.[509] Other former navy men rushed to publically discuss their wartime associations in the South Pacific with the future president. While in office Kennedy learned the identity of Reginald Evans, the Australian coastwatcher who arranged his rescue from Blackett Strait in 1943. The name was previously unknown to him due to wartime secrecy.

Veteran journalist Robert J. Donovan set out to write a book about John F. Kennedy and *PT-109* in early 1962, and was the first person to thoroughly investigate the topic since the war. Donovan traveled 30,000 miles to conduct research, visiting the islands in Blackett Strait, and interviewing many individuals connected with the episode.[510] The manuscript focused on Kennedy's story and told little about *PT-109* under previous boat captains. The president read the page proofs shortly before publication.[511] The book was a big success, well received by critics and ordinary Americans eager to learn about the wartime experiences of their popular president. More books followed by other authors.

Donovan's book was soon adapted to the big screen. Kennedy showed great interest in the film project and was involved in selecting the lead actor, Cliff Robertson. He quipped, however, that the movie men were making the production too lengthy. "I do think, myself, that two minutes, two hours and twenty minutes for that kind of a picture is pretty long. Of course, they all get to think it's a work of art and they can't change anything."[512] The movie *PT-109* was released in the summer of 1963 with Robertson starring as Kennedy. The story of the future president and *PT-109* has since been taught to generations of American schoolchildren.

John F. Kennedy's life was cut short by an assassin's bullet on November 22, 1963. He is buried in Arlington National Cemetery along with tens of thousands of fallen heroes from World War II. Kennedy left a rich legacy of accomplishments as president, including, effectively managing the Cuban Missile Crisis, pointing America towards the moon, proposing landmark civil rights legislation, and forming the Peace Corps. He will also always be remembered as the last boat captain of *PT-109*.

———

The time aboard *PT-109* left a lasting mark on the lives of her three wartime captains. Rollin Westholm, Bryant Larson, and John Kennedy each carried the experience and memories forward into their civilian lives.

PT boat duty was only a small part of Rollin Westholm's long navy career. He wrote about his experiences in a lengthy letter in 1989: "There are very few officers who can claim they dodged bullets, shells, [torpedoes] and

Kamikazes for five consecutive years during World War II," he recorded.

It is not known if Westholm ever saw Bryant Larson after the war, although it is entirely possible the two may have been together sometime at a reunion of PT sailors. His own handwriting tells us he never had the opportunity to see Kennedy the politician. "Once while passing through Washington on my way to a new duty station, my wife and I stopped into his senate office but he was not in and not expected for two days," Westholm wrote. "As soon as he became president, he sent me an autographed picture."[513]

Westholm had a chance encounter in New York City with a former PT officer less than two weeks before President Kennedy was assassinated. Paul "Red" Fay, a boat captain in the South Pacific during the war, was serving as Undersecretary of the Navy. He told Westholm that Kennedy remembered him and suggested he make his was down to Washington for a visit. "I told Red that I couldn't without going over the heads of my navy superiors," Westholm recalled. Fay granted him permission on the spot. He vowed to make the journey on his next available day off. "I never made it," Westholm later wrote in regret.

Bryant Larson never forgot his PT boat days. "There are nights even now when I have a hard time believing my own PT duty," Larson wrote decades after the war. "The navy took a twenty-two-year-old land lubber that looked eighteen, put him in command of a fast ship and sent him in harm's way night after night after night." He survived the ordeal with a combination of skill, courage, and luck.

The original commissioning pennant of *PT-109* spent many years on display in Larson's house serving as a constant reminder "of the battles, the boats that lived and the boats that died, of the shipmates that were lost, and of the many old friends that still live to share the PT experience."[514]

A family cruise to the South Pacific in 1991 brought back his PT boat memories. The places, the boats, and the people all came rushing back into his mind. The voyage may have been the catalyst for him to create a written record of his PT boat experiences before time erased the recollections forever. "Perhaps those memories are worth saving," he wrote. "Perhaps not. But we will never know unless I leave a record of them." He wrote out his recollections in a document titled, "Memories of My Torpedo Boat (PT) Duty." It is a great asset in helping future generations know the struggles, sacrifices, and hardships endured by PT sailors in the South Pacific.

John Kennedy's comments about *PT-109's* sinking were well documented by journalists in the year after the event and later expanded in the books of the early 1960's. He never gave up while shipwrecked in Blackett Strait. Kennedy searched in vain for a way to save his men, trying anything he could think of to get help, no matter how dangerous or low the chances of success. The ordeal molded the young naval officer into the man who later became a great statesman and leader.

Kennedy considered the war experience to be a defining moment in his life. "I firmly believe that as much as I was shaped by anything, so was I shaped by the hand of fate moving in World War II," he once wrote. "Of course, the same can be said of almost any American or British or Australian man of my generation. The war made us. It was and is our greatest moment."[515]

It was a moment Kennedy never forgot and spoke of often, both in humor and seriousness. On one occasion he provided a simple straightforward response when asked how he had become a war hero. "It was involuntary. They sank my boat."[516] *Los Angeles Times* journalist Robert T. Hartmann once noted that "Kennedy's superabundant charm is never more engaging than when he leaps back to wartime reminiscence with a receptive veteran of the Solomon campaign."[517]

President Kennedy wrote a foreword to the United States Navy's official history of PT boat operations in World War II while serving in office. He connected the past role of small boats to the future: "PT boats filled an important need in World War II. . . . This need for small, fast, versatile, strongly armed vessels does not wane."[518]

———

Almost fifty-nine years after the loss of *PT-109*, noted underwater explorer Dr. Robert Ballard ventured to the South Pacific in search of the boat's wreckage. The researcher's impressive resume includes finding the ocean liner *Titanic*, battleship *Bismarck*, and sunken warships in Iron Bottom Sound near Guadalcanal. Ballard was clear as to why he wanted to find the PT boat. "Many young people these days don't even know the story of *PT-109*," he said. "[Kennedy] emerged from this experience the person who went on to become the President of the U.S."[519]

Locating the remnants of the small torpedo boat, in the deep waters of the Pacific, would be a monumental undertaking. The expedition, partially funded by National Geographic, took place in May 2002 when Ballard and his team of experts traveled to the Solomon Islands. The Australian vessel *Grayscout* served as the search platform. At their disposal was an array of sophisticated electronic imaging equipment.

The mission used techniques successfully employed by Ballard on other projects. The plan was to begin with a sonar search of a five by seven mile grid in Blackett Strait using a side-scan sonar device towed underwater by *Grayscout*. Unmanned robotic submersibles with video cameras were available to investigate possible finds. The results would then need to be reviewed against historical data.[520]

Ballard initially hoped to locate the stern of the boat thought to have sunk immediately after the collision. However, the ocean floor in the area was littered with rocks and other war wrecks. He switched focus to trying to find the bow in a more narrowly concentrated search area. It did not sink immediately like the rear portion of the boat, but stayed afloat and drifted for an undetermined length of time after the collision.

A breakthrough occurred on May 22 when sonar found a promising target some 1,200 feet down. The submersibles were dispatched for a closer look. The men controlling the undersea explorers investigated with caution, having been previously warned of the possibility that some of *PT-109's* weapons could still be explosive.

The images showed what appeared to be a broken, coral-crusted and rusted torpedo tube, with a torpedo still inside, and a cranking mechanism used to angle the tubes just before firing. However, there was more than could be seen in the pictures due to the sonar's ability to penetrate the ocean floor. The equipment indicated a larger object hidden below measuring twenty-three by forty feet.[521] One of the dimensions corresponds to the width of *PT-109*.

The shifting sand of the ocean floor may be hiding a large portion of the boat. "The strong underwater currents we encountered made *PT-109* unlike any of my past expeditions," Ballard said of the situation. "It was like conducting a search in the Sahara Desert during a blinding sandstorm."[522]

It would be up to the navy to make a final determination of the findings after the expedition ended. Ballard's films were studied by a trio of experts about a month after the find. Mark Wertheimer of the Naval Historical Center, underwater archaeologist Claire Peachey, and World War II PT boat veteran Welford West gathered at National Geographic's headquarters in Washington, DC.[523] West was a crewman aboard *PT-157*, the boat that rescued the 109's survivors. The group concluded it was the port side torpedo tube of a PT boat.

After additional research, the official word of the discovery came from the navy. "A check of Navy records indicates that no other PT-type vessels were lost in this location," an official statement read. "This information combined with the physical evidence suggests that this is likely the wreck of the *PT-109*."[524]

Ballard did not disturb the wreckage, in keeping with the wishes of the Kennedy family. He also made another important pronouncement. "We're not divulging the exact location," Ballard said of the boat's remains. The decision will hopefully ensure that one of America's most famous sunken warships, commanded by three brave officers during wartime in the South Pacific, will remain undisturbed for an eternity.

SMALL BOATS—A CONTINUING SAGA

Although *PT-109* would in time become the most famous torpedo boat in history, she was only one of hundreds of the small craft to operate during World War II. PT boats roamed the sea in nearly every theater where the United States Navy saw action—from the vast expanses of the Pacific Ocean to the confined spaces of the Mediterranean to North African and European waters. The vessels fought adversaries of all type and size, including large warships, submarines, barges, planes, and land targets. The boats are best remembered, however, for action in the Pacific.

Squadrons of torpedo boats advanced with American forces up the Solomon Islands and across the northern coast of New Guinea as the Pacific War progressed into late 1943. Their primary enemy was no longer Japanese destroyers, but land targets and the armored barges transporting troops and supplies among the tropical islands. Additional firepower was added in the form of heavier guns, small rockets, and radar. Torpedo attacks became less frequent. Often as the main American amphibious forces jumped to the next large operation, a contingent of PT's stayed behind to provide local security and help keep Japanese garrisons on bypassed islands in check.

Torpedo boats also ventured to the Aleutian Islands in the northern reaches of the Pacific. Jutting west almost 1,000 miles from the Alaskan mainland, the area was the scene of naval and land fighting when Japanese forces invaded the three westernmost islands in 1942, only to be expelled about a year later. The PT boats laid mines, transported army personnel, and conducted routine patrols, but saw little action with the Japanese. The harsh winter weather—often considered among the worst in the world—turned out to be the main enemy.

The boats joined in the triumphant American return to the Philippines in October 1944. The campaign allowed the PT's to participate in one last night battle against large warships when the Battle of Surigao Strait occurred during the night of October 24–25, 1944. It was part of a series of encounters over the course of three days collectively known as the Battle of Leyte Gulf.

The actions represented the Imperial Japanese Navy's final large-scale attempt to defeat the Americans in a sea battle and change the course of the war. The ambitious plan called for using a group of near plane-less aircraft carriers to lure the main American battle fleet away from the Philippines, while surface units moved to attack amphibious forces in Leyte Gulf on the east side of the islands. The operation required a group of Japanese battleships and cruisers to transverse the Philippines from west to east through the narrow Surigao Strait. American naval forces were waiting in ambush.

Thirty-nine PT boats under the leadership of Lieutenant Commander Robert Leeson were the first units to make contact with the enemy. Operating in thirteen groups of three boats each and spread out among various points near the western entrance of the strait, the PT's were under orders to radio contact reports and then attack with torpedoes. It was a night fight reminiscent of the actions in the Solomon Islands, but on a much larger scale.

The Japanese ships ran the deadly cauldron of torpedo attacks while exchanging fire with various groups of PT boats. No American torpedoes scored hits during the action, but the PT sailors showed great courage in battling the larger foe at close quarters. Ten PT's were hit by enemy gunfire and one boat was sunk.[525] Later in the battle a torpedo from *PT-137* struck the light cruiser *Abukuma* killing thirty-seven sailors and causing moderate damage.[526] She was later sunk by aircraft.

The Japanese faced more torpedoes after brushing past the PT boats as American destroyers closed in for attack. A group of large American warships—battleships and cruisers—delivered the smashing final blow. The Japanese force was obliterated, almost to the ship, for a resounding American victory. The battle was the last time PT boats attacked large warships in force.

Many American fleet units moved into the waters around Japan at the end of hostilities in August 1945 in preparation for the formal surrender proceedings, leaving the PT's behind at various locations in the Pacific. The boats kept busy with a variety of duties, including shuttling army personnel to remote Japanese outposts and transporting liberated Allied POW's. On

August 26, 1945 a group of six PT's delivered top Japanese commanders from Halmahera (in modern-day Indonesia) to American authorities to officially surrender a garrison of 37,000 troops.[527] It was a calm ending to almost four years of brutal fighting.

————

German U-boats were the immediate threat facing the United States in the Atlantic at the start of the war. It was not a fight, however, for the PT's as the boats were never effectively employed as anti-submarine weapons. The wooden hulls and high speeds of the torpedo boats did not provide a stable platform for sonar, the key ingredient in anti-submarine warfare.

PT boat operations in the Atlantic Theatre began in the Mediterranean. The first boats arrived in April 1943—about five months after the American invasion of North Africa—to begin operations from bases along the Algerian coast. Action eventually progressed east into Tunisia as German land forces were pushed off the continent. The PT's often worked in tandem with their British counterparts in the area.

The torpedo boats moved north as American forces invaded Sicily and mainland Italy. The numbers soon grew to a total of three squadrons. The war in the Mediterranean was dominated by small craft on both sides. The PT's often battled various types of Germans and Italian vessels, including armed barges, gunboats, and E-boats. The PT boats operated in the Mediterranean until the end of the war, claiming to have sunk twenty-eight enemy vessels while suffering the loss of four boats.[528]

The first PT boats arrived further north in British waters during the spring of 1944. There had been no need for American boats in the area previously, as British small craft were roaming the English Channel in strength since the start of the war to protect local shipping, and had been battling German ships along the European coast since 1940. The American boats initially worked with the Office of Strategic Services (forerunner of the modern CIA) in preparation for the invasion of France.

A well-known American figure was among those to arrive in Britain with the first boats. John Bulkeley remained the most famous PT boat leader for the duration of the war. After his homecoming from the Philippines as a national hero in 1942, he eventually returned to the front lines in the South Pacific before transferring to the European Theater. He was in command of all PT boats during the invasion of Normandy in June 1944. The boats provided patrol, escort, transportation, and rescue duties, but saw little action during the actual landings. "We might have had trouble with mines, with shore batteries or with E-boats," Bulkeley said of his boats' role in the large operation. "As it was, we didn't have any trouble at all."[529]

There was little need for American PT boats after Allied land forces drove inland into continental Europe during late 1944. Some were transferred to Russia, but one squadron stayed in the English Channel operating from Cherbourg, France until Germany surrendered in May 1945. Several European-based squadrons made preparations to transfer to the Pacific, but the fighting on the opposite side of the globe soon ended.

The end of World War II found thirty PT squadrons in operation, with twenty-five based in the Pacific.[530] Many large warships were mothballed—stored away for future use—as the navy began to downsize, but not PT boats. The wooden hulls were not conducive for long-term storage and the squadrons were quickly disbanded. The boats were stripped of armaments before being turned over to the War Shipping Administration for disposal. The drawdown was swift and drastic—only four boats remained in service by the end of 1946.[531]

A total of 764 PT's were constructed between 1940 and 1945, including 257 boats transferred to Britain and Russia under the lend-lease program.[532] The American sailors paid a heavy price for their courageousness in operating the PT's. Sixty-nine boats were lost from all causes, ranging from enemy surface warships and planes to accidental friendly fire, groundings, and collisions. A total of 306 PT sailors were killed in action.[533] Hundreds more were wounded.

Three squadrons received the Presidential Unit Citation, an award given to military units for bravery in combat. Two PT sailors received the Medal of Honor, the nation's highest individual award—Bulkeley for action in the Philippines in 1942 and Lieutenant Commander Arthur M. Preston for rescuing a downed navy pilot near New Guinea in 1944.[534]

The PT boats' contribution to the overall victory is difficult to quantify in hard numbers. Many reported sinkings of enemy vessels were not substantiated by an analysis of postwar records. Perhaps their greatest role was filling the void left in the Pacific after a large part of the American fleet was disabled at Pearl Harbor. The boats bought precious time—especially in the Philippines and Solomon Islands—until the American industrial machine could produce new warships to drive across the Pacific. The most famous PT boat captain of all, John F. Kennedy, may have summarized it best almost two decades after the conflict: "PT boats filled an important need in World

War II in shallow waters, complementing the achievements of greater ships in greater seas."[535]

The United States Navy accepted delivery of four experimental torpedo boats in 1951—the first PT's to enter service since World War II. The boats incorporated a number of new design features including all-metal hulls and powerful engines. The vessels operated throughout the 1950s as Motor Torpedo Squadron One and were part of the navy's Operational Development Force.[536] Although the United States used small boats in various capacities in the subsequent decades, a large-scale development of further PT boats never happened.

In Indochina, North Vietnamese torpedo boats in the Gulf of Tonkin reportedly attacked American destroyers in August 1964. No American ships were damaged, but the incident helped to escalate the Vietnam War. The United States used an assortment of small craft as coastal gunboats throughout the conflict.

A key advancement in weapons technology during the middle of the twentieth century again changed the role of small combatants—the surface-to-surface missile. The weapon greatly diminished the importance of the torpedo for use against surface ships by delivering a powerful punch faster and farther. Navies large and small were soon arming small fast vessels with missiles. The craft would see plenty of action.

Small combatants were deployed by both sides in the various Arab–Israeli Wars fought in the decades after World War II. In October 1967 a small Egyptian attack boat sank the Israeli destroyer *Elath* with a missile. Six years later Israeli and Syrian small craft fought the first missile versus missile battle in naval history.[537]

Small craft were used during a variety of conflicts in the Persian Gulf region starting with the Iran-Iraq War in the early 1980s. American naval and air units fought Iranian small boats in the Strait of Hormuz during a one-day battle in April 1988, sinking at least three vessels.[538] Comprised almost entirely of small vessels, the Iraqi Navy was virtually destroyed by Coalition forces during the Gulf War in 1991. Iran continues to use a variety of small combatants today in the ongoing tensions in the Persian Gulf.

Almost 10,000 people gathered to witness the commissioning of *Freedom* in

Milwaukee, WI on November 8, 2008.[539] The small vessel represents the newest type of warship in the U.S. Navy. She has been designed to operate both in the near-shore environment and for open-ocean missions. The navy lauds *Freedom* as an, "innovative combatant."[540] Like her PT boat predecessors, the small warship is fast, maneuverable, and able to attain speeds of over forty knots. She is designed to fulfill a variety of roles ranging from surface and anti-submarine warfare to humanitarian relief.[541]

Although the technology and weaponry will continue to evolve, the need for small combatants will always remain. As long as warships exist, there will be brave sailors willing to take small boats into action against larger adversaries, just as three young officers did with *PT-109* in the South Pacific during World War II.

NOTES

CHAPTER 1

1 Michael O'Brien. *John F. Kennedy: A Biography*. (New York: Thomas Dunne Books / St. Martin's Press, 2005), 142.

2 Associated Press. "Kennedy's Son is Hero in Pacific as Destroyer Splits His PT Boat." *New York Times*, August 20, 1943, 5.

3 Anthony J. Watts and Brian G. Gordon. *The Imperial Japanese Navy*. (New York: Doubleday & Company, Inc. 1971), 126, and Roger Chesneau, ed. *Conway's All the World's Fighting Ships: 1922–1946*. (London: Conway Maritime Press, 1980), 193.

4 Haruyoshi Kimmatsu and Joachim Heinrich Woos. "The Night We Rammed J.F.K." *Argosy*, December 1970, 18.

5 Nigel Hamilton. *JFK: Reckless Youth*. (New York: Random House, 1992), 565.

6 Curtis L. Nelson. "Did JFK's Oder Sink PT 109?" *Naval History*, February 2003, 1.

7 Intelligence Officers to CO Motor Torpedo Boat Flotilla One. "Sinking of PT 109 and Subsequent Rescue of Survivors." August 22, 1943, 1 (hereafter cited as "Sinking of PT 109 and Subsequent Rescue").

8 John Hersey. "Survival." *New Yorker*, June 17, 1944, 31.

9 Inga Arvad. "Kennedy Lauds Men, Disdains Hero Stuff." *Boston Globe*, January 11, 1944, 1.

10 John Hersey. *Men on Bataan*. (New York: Alfred A. Knopf, 1942), 36.

11 Frank D. Johnson. *United States PT-Boats of World War II in Action*. (Poole, England: Blandford Press, 1980), 19–21.

12 Ibid, 21.

13 Captain Robert J. Buckley. *At Close Quarters: PT Boats in the United States Navy*. (Washington, DC: United States Government Printing Office, 1962), 44.

14 Gary Rottman. *US Patrol Torpedo Boats*. (Oxford, UK: Osprey, 2008), 7.

15 Norman Friedman. *U.S. Small Combatants, Including PT-Boats, Subchasers, and the Brown-Water Navy: An Illustrated Design History*. (Annapolis, MD: Naval Institute Press, 1987), 115.

16 Buckley, *Close Quarters*, 1.

17 "Navy Department Communiqués and Pertinent Press Releases, December 10, 1941

to May 24, 1945." http://www.ibiblio.org/pha/comms/index.html (April 24, 2013)

18 "New Yorker Leads Daring Raid on Foe." *New York Times*, January 21, 1942, 5.

19 CO Motor Torpedo Boat Squadron Three to CinC US Fleet. "Summary of Operations Motor Torpedo Boat Squadron Three from 7 December 1941 to 10 April 1942." May 21, 1942, 2.

20 Rottman, *Patrol Torpedo Boats*, 27.

21 David Doyle. *Elco 80-Foot PT Boat On Deck*. (Carrollton, TX: Squadron Signal Publications, 2009), 50.

22 David Doyle. *PT Boats in Action*. (Carrollton, TX: Squadron Signal Publications, 2010), 12, and Buckley, *Close Quarters*, 32.

23 "PT 109" in the Naval History and Heritage Command Website. http://www.history.navy.mil accessed on various dates (hereafter cited as "PT 109").

24 Doyle, *Elco 80-Foot PT*, 2.

25 Victor Chun. *American PT Boats in World War II*. (Atglen, PA: Schiffer Publishing, 1997), 75.

26 Doyle, *Elco 80-Foot PT*, 80.

27 Rottman, *Patrol Torpedo Boats*, 30.

28 Duane Hove. "PT 109—The Early Days." *All Hands*, November 2002, 49.

CHAPTER 2

29 Rollin E. Westholm Obituary. Courtesy of Carlton County, MN Historical Society (hereafter cited as "Westholm Obituary").

30 Secretary of the Navy. *Register of the Commissioned and Warrant Officers of the Navy of the United States, Including Officers of the Marine Corps*. (Washington, DC: Government Printing Office, 1943), 88.

31 "Rollin Westholm Service Record." National Personnel Records Center, St. Louis, MO (hereafter cited as "Westholm Service Record").

32 Gary Westholm. Email to Author on February 16, 2012.

33 "Report on the Fitness of Officers," Period Ending March 22, 1937 in "Westholm Service Record."

34 Rollin Westholm. Letter Dated February 1989. Courtesy of Gary Westholm. (hereafter cited as "Westholm Letter")

35 "Mosquito Boats Speed 50 Knots in East River Demonstration." *New York Times*, November 8, 1940, 3.

36 "Report on the Fitness of Officers," Period Ending April 30, 1941 in "Westholm Service Record."

37 "Report on the Fitness of Officers," Period Ending September 16, 1941 in "Westholm Service Record."

38 Commandant, Naval Operating Base, Newport, RI to Lieutenant Rollin E. Westholm. "Admonition." August 5, 1942, in "Westholm Service Record."

39 Buckley, *Close Quarters*, 458.

40 Gary Massaro. "PT 109 Commander Before Kennedy Dies." *Rocky Mountain News*, January 12, 2002.

41 "College Transcript" in "Bryant Larson Service Record." National Personnel Records Center, St. Louis, MO (hereafter cited as "Larson Service Record").

42 Andrea Albers. "World War II Midshipmen's School a Piece of Northwestern History." http://www.northwestern.edu/newscenter/stories/2009/02/midshipmen.html. (May 17, 2001), 2.

43 Bryant Larson. "Memories of My Torpedo Boat (PT) Duty." Undated Manuscript. Courtesy of Karen Hone (hereafter cited as Larson, "PT Duty").

44 "Larson Service Record."

45 Buckley, *Close Quarters*, 60.

46 Ibid, 48.

47 Doyle, *PT Boats in Action*, 12.

48 Dick Keresey. *PT 105*. (Annapolis, MD: Naval Institute Press, 1996), 19.

49 Ibid, 23.

CHAPTER 3

50 Edwin P. Hoyt. *Deadly Craft: Fireships to PT Boats*. (Boston: Little, Brown and Company, 1968), 10.

51 Phillip Cowburn. *The Warship in History*. (New York: Macmillan, 1965), 20.

52 James L. George. *History of Warships: From Ancient Times to the Twenty-First Century*. (Annapolis, MD: Naval Institute Press, 1998), 239.

53 Ibid.

54 "Jefferson's Gunboat Navy, 1805–1812" in the Mariners' Museum website. http://www.marinersmuseum.org/sites/micro/usnavy/07.htm (April 17, 2013), 1.

55 John Batchelor, Louis S. Casey, and Anthony Preston. *Sea Power: A Modern Illustrated Military History*. (New York: Exeter Books, 1979), 16.

56 "CSS *David* (1863–1865?)" in the Naval History and Heritage Command Website. http://www.history.navy.mil (April 18, 2013), 1.

57 "H. L. Hunley, Confederate Submarine" in the Naval History and Heritage Command Website. http://www.history.navy.mil (April 18, 2013), 1.

58 Cowburn, *Warship in History*, 246.

59 Ibid.

60 Russell Thomas. "The History of the Torpedo and the Relevance to Today's U.S. Navy" in the Naval History and Heritage Command Website. http://www.history.navy.mil/museums/keyport/History_of_the_Torpedo_and_the_Relevance_to_Todays_Navy.pdf (April 17, 2013), 3.

61 Buckley, *Close Quarters*, 39.

62 George, *History of Warships*, 242.

63 Ibid, 243.

64 Hoyt, *Deadly Craft*, 77.

65 Batchelor, Casey, and Preston, *Sea Power*, 72.

66 Johnson, *PT Boats*, 11.

67 George, *History of Warships*, 246.

68 Hoyt, *Deadly Craft*, 85–86.

69 Buckley, *Close Quarters*, 43.

CHAPTER 4
70 Bureau of Yards and Docks. *Building the Navy's Bases in the Pacific: Volume II.* (Washington, DC: Government Printing Office, 1947), 40.
71 "Know Your PT Boat." http://www.hnsa.org (June 15, 2010), 89–90.
72 "PT 109."
73 Buckley, *Close Quarters*, 452.
74 Larson, "PT Duty."
75 "Westholm Service Record."
76 "PT 109's Unknown History, Chapter 1: Background." in PT King Website. http://pt-king.gdinc.com/index.html. (Accessed on various dates.)
77 Doyle, *Elco 80-Foot PT,* 80.
78 David M. Levy and Gerald A. Meehl. *Fast Boats and Fast Times: Memories of a PT Boat Skipper in the South Pacific.* (Bloomington, IN: Author House, 2008), 26.
79 "PT 109's Unknown History, Chapter 2: Off to War." in PT King Website. http://pt-king.gdinc.com/index.html. (Accessed on various dates.)
80 Larson, "PT Duty."
81 Deck Log, *PT-109*, November 25, 1942.
82 "Tulagi Harbor, Solomon Islands," in http://www.history.navy.mil. (Accessed on various dates.) and Samuel Eliot Morison. *History of United States Naval Operations in World War II Volume V: The Struggle for Guadalcanal.* (Edison, NJ: Castle Book, 2001), 187.
83 Richard B. Frank. *Guadalcanal.* (New York: Penguin Books, 1990), 497.
84 CO Motor Torpedo Boat Flotilla One to CinCPac. "Report of Motor Torpedo Boat Combat Action in the Solomon Islands, 13 October, 1942 to 2 February, 1943." March 7, 1943, 21 (hereafter cited as "Report of Motor Torpedo Boat Combat Action").
85 Ibid, 11.
86 Howard F. West. *Iron Men Wooden Boats.* (Westminster, MD: Heritage Books, 2005), 75.
87 Bureau of Yards and Docks, *Navy's Bases*, 252.
88 "Jamestown" in Dictionary of American Fighting Ships, http://www.history.navy.mil accessed on various dates.
89 John M. Searles. *Tales of Tulagi.* (New York: Vantage Press, 1992), 20.

CHAPTER 5
90 Headquarters of the Commander in Chief, United States Fleet. "Motor Torpedo Boats: Tactical Orders and Doctrine. Washington, DC: United States Government Printing Office, 1942. Retrieved from: http://www.hnsa.org/doc/pt/doctrine/index.htm (July 20, 2010), 8.
91 "Westholm Letter."
92 Larson, "PT Duty."
93 "Report on the Fitness of Officers," Period Ending December 31, 1942 in "Larson

Service Record."

94 Bureau of Yards and Docks, *Navy's Bases*, 152 and Deck Log, *PT-109*, November 26, 1942.

95 Hugh B. Cave. *Long Were the Nights*. (New York: Dodd, Mead and Company, 1943), 124.

96 Larson, "PT Duty."

97 Deck Log, *PT-109*, December 1, 1942.

98 "Guadalcanal Logs" in PT King Website. http://pt-king.gdinc.com/index.html accessed on various dates (hereafter cited as "Guadalcanal Logs").

99 Deck Log, *Pensacola*, December 1, 1942.

100 Cave, *Long Nights*, 125.

101 John W. Fitch. *Desert Sailor*. (Haverford, PA: Infinity Publishing, 2001), 150.

102 Deck Log, *PT-109*, December 1, 1942.

103 "Guadalcanal Logs."

104 Buckley, *Close Quarters*, 95.

CHAPTER 6

105 Frank, *Guadalcanal*, 501–502, and Vice Admiral Raizo Tanaka with Roger Pineau. "Japan's Losing Struggle for Guadalcanal: Part II." *Proceedings*, August 1956, 825.

106 Tanaka, 828.

107 Japanese Self Defense Force: War History Office. *Senshi Sosho (War History Series). Volume 83: Southeast Area Naval Operations, Part II.* (Tokyo: Asagumo Shibunsha, 1975), 441.

108 Frank, *Guadalcanal*, 520.

109 "IJN Nowaki: Tabular Record of Movement" in Imperial Japanese Navy Page. http://www.combinedfleet.com/bb.htm. (July 29, 2011)

110 West, *Wooden Boats*, 80.

111 Rottman, *Patrol Torpedo Boats*, 19.

112 Joan Blair and Clay Blair, Jr. *The Search for JFK*. (New York: Berkley Publishing Corporation, 1976), 211.

113 CO Motor Torpedo Boat Squadron Two to Commanding General, Cactus. "Memorandum for Commanding General, Cactus: PT Operation, Night of 7–8 December 1942." December 9, 1942, 1 (Hereafter cited as "Memorandum for Commanding General").

114 Larson, "PT Duty."

115 *Combat Narrative: Miscellaneous Actions in the South Pacific*. (Washington, DC: Office of Naval Intelligence, United States Navy, 1943), 55–56.

116 Buckley, *Close Quarters*, 96.

117 Frank, *Guadalcanal*, 521.

118 Chesneau, ed., *Conway's Ships*, 194.

119 Searles, *Tales of Tulagi*, 32.

120 Morison, *Guadalcanal*, 319.

121 Japanese Self Defense Force, *Senshi Sosho*, 445.

122 *Miscellaneous Actions in the South Pacific*, 57.
123 Frank, *Guadalcanal*, 521.
124 Morison, *Guadalcanal*, 282.
125 Deck Log, *PT-109*, December 8, 1942.
126 *Miscellaneous Actions in the South Pacific*, 57.
127 Ibid.
128 Cave, *Long Nights*, 215.
129 Japanese Self Defense Force, *Senshi Sosho*, 441–442.
130 Frank, *Guadalcanal*, 521.
131 "Report on the Fitness of Officers," Period Ending December 13, 1942 in "Westholm Service Record."
132 CO South Pacific Area and South Pacific Force to CinCPac. "Second Endorsement on Comdr. MTBRON Two Secret Memo Dates December 9, 1942." January 5, 1943, Enclosure in "Memorandum for Commanding General."

CHAPTER 7
133 Buckley, *Close Quarters*, 106.
134 Levy and Meehl, *Fast Times*, 30.
135 William Breuer. *Devil Boats: The PT War against Japan.* (New York: Jove Books, 1988), 72.
136 Buckley, *Close Quarters*, 107.
137 Tanaka, 825.
138 Frank, *Guadalcanal*, 523.
139 Johnson, *PT Boats*, 108, and Searles, *Tales*, 34.
140 Searles, *Tales*, 35, and Johnson, *PT Boats*, 108.
141 Buckley, *Close Quarters*, 96 and Watts and Gordon, *Imperial Japanese Navy*, 167.
142 Deck Log, *PT-109*, December 8–10, 1942.
143 Ibid, December 11, 1942.
144 Japanese Self Defense Force, *Senshi Sosho*, 446.
145 West, *Wooden Boats*, 84.
146 "Report of Motor Torpedo Boat Combat Action," 12.
147 Tanaka, 829.
148 Deck Log, *PT-109*, December 12, 1942, and "PT 109's Unknown History, Chapter 3: Combat." in PT King Website. http://pt-king.gdinc.com/index.html accessed on various dates (hereafter cited as "PT-109 Chapter 3: Combat").
149 "Report of Motor Torpedo Boat Combat Action," 12.
150 Doyle, *Elco 80-Foot PT*, 31, and "Know Your PT Boat," 7.
151 Johnson, *PT Boats*, 108.
152 Cave, *Long Nights*, 149.
153 Buckley, *Close Quarters*, 96.
154 Tanaka, 829.
155 "Report of Motor Torpedo Boat Combat Action," 13.
156 Frank, *Guadalcanal*, 524.

157 John Campbell. *Naval Weapons of World War II.* (Annapolis, MD: Naval Institute Press, 1985), 192.

158 Tanaka, 829.

159 Morison, *Guadalcanal*, 320.

160 Paul S. Dull. *A Battle History of the Imperial Japanese Navy.* (Annapolis, MD: Naval Institute Press, 1978), 258.

161 Cave, *Long Nights*, 151.

162 Larson, "PT Duty."

163 Morison, *Guadalcanal*, 320.

164 Robert J. Donovan. *PT 109.* (New York: McGraw-Hill Book Company, 1961), 33.

165 Tanaka, 829.

166 Bern Keating. *The Mosquito Fleet.* (New York: Scholastic Book Service, 1966), 10.

167 Chesneau, ed., *Conway's Ships*, 193–95.

168 Watts and Gordon, *Japanese Navy*, 121–24.

169 Farley, *PT Patrol*, 31.

170 Johnson, *PT Boats*, 110.

171 Morison, *Guadalcanal*, 331.

172 Buckley, *Close Quarters*, 108.

173 Deck Log, *PT-109*, December 22, 1942.

174 "PT-109 Chapter 3: Combat."

175 "Westholm Letter."

176 Doyle, *Elco 80-Foot PT*, 79, and Rottman, *Patrol Torpedo Boats*, 19.

177 Deck Log, *PT-109*, December 26, 1942.

CHAPTER 8

178 West, *Wooden Boats*, 90.

179 Tanaka, 830.

180 Deck Log, *PT-109*, January 2, 1943.

181 Campbell, *Naval Weapons*, 157.

182 Frank, *Guadalcanal*, 548.

183 Deck Log, *PT-109*, January 9, 1943.

184 Japanese Self Defense Force, *Senshi Sosho*, 512–13.

185 Ibid.

186 Johnson, *PT Boats*, 110.

187 CO Motor Torpedo Boat Flotilla & Base, Ringbolt to CinCPac. "Report of Motor Torpedo Boat Activities on the Night of 10–11 January, 1943, Local Date." January 13, 1943, 2 (hereafter cited as "Night of 10–11 January, 1943").

188 Donovan, *PT 109*, 33.

189 "Westholm Letter,"

190 Cave, *Long Nights*, 174–75.

191 Ibid, 175.

192 "Night of 10–11 January, 1943," 2.

193 Johnson, *PT Boats*, 111.

194 Larson, "PT Duty."

195 "Report of Motor Torpedo Boat Combat Action," 21.

196 Morison, *Guadalcanal*, 339.

197 Japanese Self Defense Force, *Senshi Sosho*, 513.

198 "Westholm Letter."

199 "PT 109's Unknown History, Chapter 4: Sunk at Sea." in PT King Website. http://pt-king.gdinc.com/index.html accessed on various dates (hereafter cited as "Sunk at Sea").

200 Frank, *Guadalcanal*, 549.

201 Deck Log, *PT-109*, January 18, 1943.

CHAPTER 9

202 Cave, *Long Nights*, 164–65.

203 Ibid, 131.

204 Levy and Meehl, *Fast Times*, 30.

205 Dan Van Der Vat. *The Pacific Campaign*. (New York: Simon & Schuster, 1991), 244.

206 Ronald H. Spector. *Eagle Against the Sun: The American War with Japan*. (New York: Vintage Books, 1985), 213.

207 Morison, *Guadalcanal*, 325.

208 Spector, *Eagle Against Sun*, 213.

209 Morison, *Guadalcanal*, 333.

210 Frank, *Guadalcanal*, 541.

211 West, *Wooden Boats*, 95, and Frank, *Guadalcanal*, 754.

212 Buckley, *Close Quarters*, 101.

213 Deck Log, *PT-109*, January 15, 1943, and Buckley, *Close Quarters*, 101.

214 Buckley, *Close Quarters*, 102.

215 Morison, *Guadalcanal*, 339, and "IJN Tanikaze: Tabular Record of Movement" in Imperial Japanese Navy Page. http://www.combinedfleet.com/bb.htm. (August 3, 2011)

216 Deck Log, *PT-109*, January 15, 1943.

217 Frank, *Guadalcanal*, 560–61.

218 Ibid, 541.

219 John Costello. *The Pacific War*. (New York: Rawson, Wade Publishers, Inc., 1981), 389.

220 Morison, *Guadalcanal*, 351.

221 Harry A. Gailey. *The War in the Pacific: From Pearl Harbor to Tokyo Bay*. (Novato, CA: Presidio Press, 1995), 205–06.

CHAPTER 10

222 Frank, *Guadalcanal*, 582.

223 Japanese Self Defense Force, *Senshi Sosho*, 558.

224 Morison, *Guadalcanal*, 367, and *Combat Narrative VII: Japanese Evacuation of Guadalcanal*. (Washington, DC: Office of Naval Intelligence, United States Navy, 1944), 47.

225 Japanese Self Defense Force, *Senshi Sosho*, 558.

226 "IJN Makinami: Tabular Record of Movement" in Imperial Japanese Navy Page. http://www.combinedfleet.com/bb.htm. (August 4, 2011)

227 CO Motor Torpedo Boat Flotilla One to CinCPac. "Report of Motor Torpedo Boat Actions on the Night of 1–2 February, 1943." February 2, 1943, 2 (hereafter cited as "Actions on the Night of 1–2 February, 1943").

228 West, *Wooden Boats*, 97.

229 Morison, *Guadalcanal*, 367.

230 Chesneau, ed., *Conway's Ships*, 194.

231 "Actions on the Night of 1–2 February, 1943," 3.

232 Buckley, *Close Quarters*, 103, Cave, *Long Nights*, 196, and West, *Wooden Boats*, 100.

233 "Actions on the Night of 1–2 February, 1943," 4.

234 Larson, "PT Duty."

235 Deck Log, *PT-109*, February 2, 1943.

236 Ibid, and "PT 109's Unknown History, Chapter 5: Tulagi to the Russells and back." in PT King Website. http://pt-king.gdinc.com/index.html. (Accessed on various dates.)

237 Deck Log, *PT-109*, February 2, 1943.

238 Japanese Self Defense Force, *Senshi Sosho*, 558.

239 "IJN Makigumo: Tabular Record of Movement" in Imperial Japanese Navy Page. http://www.combinedfleet.com/bb.htm. (August 12, 2011)

240 Dull, *Battle History*, 259.

241 Morison, *Guadalcanal*, 369.

242 Frank, *Guadalcanal*, 594–95.

243 Ibid, and Frank, *Guadalcanal*, 595.

244 John Miller, Jr. *Guadalcanal: The First Offensive*. (Washington, DC: Center of Military History Study, the United States Army, 1989), 348.

CHAPTER 11

245 Johnson, *PT Boats*, 112.

246 "Report of Motor Torpedo Boat Combat Action," 21.

247 Larson, "PT Duty."

248 Buckley, *Close Quarters*, 295–96.

249 "Interview with Hugh M. Robinson." Denton, TX: Admiral Nimitz Museum and University of North Texas Oral History Collection, 1997, 30.

250 "Westholm Letter."

251 Morison, *Guadalcanal*, 369.

252 "Westholm Service Record."

253 Levy and Meehl, *Fast Times*, 48.

254 "Report on the Fitness of Officers," Period Ending January 31, 1943 in "Westholm Service Record."

255 Deck Log, *PT-109*, February 1–15, 1943.

256 Deck Log, *PT-109*, February 13, 1943.

257 "Report on the Fitness of Officers," Period Ending February 1, 1943 in "Larson Serv-

ice Record."

258 Miller, *Guadalcanal*, 353.

259 Deck Log, *PT-109*, February 18–19, 1943.

260 Buckley, *Close Quarters*, 108.

261 Samuel Eliot Morison. *History of United States Naval Operations in World War II Volume VI: Breaking the Bismarcks Barrier.* (Edison, NJ: Castle Book, 2001), 100.

262 Miller, *Guadalcanal*, 356.

263 Buckley, *Close Quarters*, 108.

264 Michael Bell. "The Story of Leonard Jay Thom." http://www.petertare.org/nav.htm (July 1, 2010), 1.

265 William Alcorn. "Of Friendship and War." http://www.vindy.com/news/2008/may/25/of-friendship-and-war/ (September 26, 2011), 2.

266 Levy and Meehl, *Fast Times*, 70.

267 Buckley, *Close Quarters*, 108.

268 "Niagara" in Dictionary of American Fighting Ships. http://www.history.navy.mil/danfs (September 28, 2011)

269 John Miller. *Cartwheel: The Reduction of Rabaul.* (Washington, DC: Center of Military History Study, the United States Army, 1990), 70.

270 Morison, *Bismarcks Barrier*, 90.

271 Blair and Blair, *Search for JFK*, 166.

CHAPTER 12

272 "Life of John F. Kennedy," in John F. Kennedy Presidential Library Website. http://www.jfklibrary.org, accessed on various dates (hereafter cited as "Life of John F. Kennedy," in "JFK Library").

273 "Academic Records, 1937–1940," in "JFK Library."

274 Robert Ballard and Michael Hamilton Morgan. *Collision with History: The Search for John F. Kennedy's PT-109.* (Washington, DC: National Geographic, 2002), 34.

275 Robert Dallek. *An Unfinished Life: John F. Kennedy 1917–1963.* (New York: Little, Brown and Company, 2003), 82.

276 Geoffrey Perret. *Jack: A Life Like No Other.* (New York: Random House, 2001), 93–94.

277 "Officer Service Record," in "JFK Library."

278 "Lieutenant John Fitzgerald Kennedy, U.S. Naval Reserve," in Naval History and Heritage Command Website. http://www.history.navy.mil accessed on various dates (hereafter cited as "Lieutenant John Fitzgerald Kennedy").

279 Dallek, *Unfinished Life*, 83–84.

280 "Hero to Pick 50 with Guts for Mosquito Fleet." *Chicago Tribune*, September 3, 1942, 6.

281 "Mosquito Boat Skipper to be Pine for Action." *Chicago Tribune*, September 4, 1942, 10.

282 William B. Breuer. *Sea Wolf: The Daring Exploits of Navy Legend John D. Bulkeley.* (Novato, CA: Presidio Press, 1998), 108.

283 Blair and Blair, *Search for JFK*, 158.

284 "Lieutenant John Fitzgerald Kennedy."

285 Blair and Blair, *Search for JFK*, 168–169.

286 Lt. (jg) John F. Kennedy to Chief of Bureau of Personnel. "Change of Assignment-Request For." February 20, 1943, in "JFK Library."

287 Hamilton, *Reckless Youth*, 519.

288 Samuel Eliot Morison. *History of United States Naval Operations in World War II Volume III: The Rising Sun in the Pacific.* (Edison, NJ: Castle Book, 2001), 94.

289 Deck Log, *PT-109*, April 7, 1943.

290 Chesneau, ed., *Conway's Ships*, 162.

291 CO *LST-449* to CinCPac. "Attacked by Enemy Aircraft, Report of." April 14, 1943, 1.

292 Lawrence O. Ealy. *I Joined the Navy and Saw World War II.* (New York: Vantage Press, 1998), 131.

293 Blair and Blair, *Search for JFK*, 177.

294 Deck Log, *PT-109*, April 20, 1943.

295 Donovan, *PT-109*, 50.

296 Blair and Blair, *Search for JFK*, 179.

297 Larson, "PT Duty."

298 Deck Log, *PT-109*, April 25, 1943.

299 "Letter to Parents dated May 14, 1943, John F. Kennedy Personal Papers" in "JFK Library" (hereafter cited at "May 14, 1943 Letter").

300 Donovan, *PT-109*, 54, and Ballard, *Collision with History*, 48.

301 Patrick Munroe. "Luck of the Toss." *American Heritage* Oct. 1992: 32+. General Reference Center Gold. Web. http://find.galegroup.com (July 13, 2010)

302 Hamilton, *Reckless Youth*, 542.

303 "May 14, 1943 Letter."

304 "Westholm Letter."

305 Searles, *Tales of Tulagi*, 46.

306 Levy and Meehl, *Fast Times*, 42.

307 Donovan, *PT-109*, 71.

308 Ibid, 75.

309 Deck Log, *PT-109*, June 13–16, 1943.

310 Duane T. Hove *American Warriors: Five Presidents in the Pacific Theater of World War II.* (Shippensburg, PA: Burd Street Press, 2003), 48.

CHAPTER 13

311 West, *Wooden Boats*, 140.

312 Keresey, *PT 105*, 56.

313 Buckley, *Close Quarters*, 115.

314 Ibid.

315 "McCawley" in Dictionary of American Fighting Ships, http://www.history.navy.mil. (Accessed on various dates.)

316 Morison, *Bismarcks Barrier*, 155.

317 Donovan, *PT-109*, 78.

318 Hamilton, *Reckless Youth*, 548.

319 "May 14, 1943 Letter."

320 West, *Wooden Boats*, 140.

321 Hove, *American Warriors*, 49.

322 Hank Brantingham. *Fire and Ice.* (San Diego, CA: ProMotion Publishing, 1995), 41.

323 West, *Wooden Boats*, 141.

324 Blair and Blair, *Search for JFK*, 201.

325 Dull, *Battle History*, 275–76.

326 Morison, *Bismarcks Barrier*, 209.

327 Farley, *PT Patrol*, 42, and Morison, *Bismarcks Barrier*, 208.

328 Johnson, *PT Boats*, 124.

329 Staff Intelligence Office, CO Motor Torpedo Boat Squadrons South Pacific Force. "Out of the Night: South Pacific MTB's vs. Jap Float Planes." February 20, 1944, 13 (hereafter cited as "Out of the Night").

330 Blair and Blair, *Search for JFK*, 201.

331 CO Motor Torpedo Boats, Rendova to CinC US Fleet. "PT Operations Night 27–28 July 1943." July 30, 1943, 1 (hereafter cited as "PT Operations Night 27–28 July").

332 West, *Wooden Boats*, 130.

333 CO Motor Torpedo Boats, Rendova to CinC US Fleet. "PT Operations Night 17–18 July 1943." July 18, 1943, 2.

334 Joint Army-Navy Assessment Committee. *Japanese Naval and Merchant Shipping Losses during World War II by All Causes.* (Washington, DC: U.S. Government Printing Office, 1947), 210.

335 Buckley, *Close Quarters*, 119.

336 West, *Wooden Boats*, 133.

337 Donovan, *PT-109*, 91–92.

338 Ibid, 98.

339 Chandler Whipple. *Lt. John F. Kennedy—Expendable.* (New York: Universal Publishing. 1964), 91.

340 "Out of the Night," 19.

341 Ibid and Whipple, *Expendable*, 92–93.

CHAPTER 14

342 Morison, *Bismarcks Barrier*, 203.

343 "PT Operations Night 27–28 July," 2.

344 CO Motor Torpedo Boats, Rendova to CinC US Fleet. "PT Operations Night 26–27 July 1943." July 27, 1943, 1–2.

345 "PT Operations Night 27–28 July," 1.

346 CO Motor Torpedo Boats, Rendova to CinC US Fleet. "PT Operations Night 28–29 July 1943." July 29, 1943, 1.

347 CO Motor Torpedo Boats, Rendova to CinC US Fleet. "PT Operations Night 29–30 July 1943." July 30, 1943, 1–2.

348 CO Motor Torpedo Boats, Rendova to CinC US Fleet. "PT Operations Night 30–31 July 1943." July 31, 1943, 1.

349 Donovan, *PT-109*, 106.

350 Ibid, 111.

351 West, *Wooden Boats*, 148.

352 Hamilton, *Reckless Youth*, 555.

353 Buckley, *Close Quarters*, 120–21 and 486–87.

354 Blair and Blair, *Search for JFK*, 210.

355 Hove, *American Warriors*, 49.

356 Blair and Blair, *Search for JFK*, 211.

357 O'Brien, *John F. Kennedy*, 141.

358 "PT Operations Night 27–28 July," 2.

359 Brantingham, *Fire and Ice*, 20–23.

360 West, *Wooden Boats*, 145.

361 Tameichi Hara, with Fred Saito and Roger Pineau. *Japanese Destroyer Captain.* (New York: Ballantine Books 1961), 181.

362 Rich Pedroncelli. "JFK: A PT Skipper Remembers." *Naval History*, December 1999, 4.

363 Hove, *American Warriors*, 49.

364 Hamilton, *Reckless Youth*, 556.

365 West, *Wooden Boats*, 150.

366 Donovan, *PT-109*, 52.

367 "PT-109 Final Crew List." http://www.maritimequest.com. (March 29, 2010)

368 "Patrick H. McMahon Dead at 84; Burned Sailor Saved by Kennedy." *New York Times*, February 22, 1990, B10.

369 "PT-109 Final Crew List."

370 West, *Wooden Boats*, 151.

371 "Letter to Parents dated September 12, 1943, John F. Kennedy Personal Papers" in "JFK Library" (hereafter cited at "September 12, 1943 Letter").

372 Hamilton, *Reckless Youth*, 553 & 607.

373 Donovan, *PT-109*, 128.

374 Chandler Whipple. *Code Word Ferdinand: Adventures of the Coast Watchers.* (New York: George Putnam and Son's. 1971), 104.

375 Eric A. Feldt. *The Coast Watchers.* (New York: Nelson Doubleday, 1946), 146.

CHAPTER 15

376 Donovan, *PT-109*, 126.

377 Keresey, *PT 105*, 76.

378 CO Motor Torpedo Boats, Rendova to CinC US Fleet. "PT Operations Night 1–2 August 1943." August 5, 1943, 1 (hereafter cited as "PT Operations August 1–2").

379 West, *Wooden Boats*, 151.

380 "Sinking of PT 109 and Subsequent Rescue," 1, and Blair and Blair, *Search for JFK*, 223.

381 O'Brien, *John F. Kennedy*, 142.
382 "PT Operations August 1–2," 2.
383 Hamilton, *Reckless Youth*, 558.
384 "PT Operations August 1–2," 2.
385 West, *Wooden Boats*, 153–54.
386 O'Brien, *John F. Kennedy*, 142.
387 Hara, Saito and Pineau. *Destroyer Captain*, 181.
388 Blair and Blair, *Search for JFK*, 223–24.
389 Ballard and Morgan, *Collision with History*, 87.
390 Hamilton, *Reckless Youth*, 563, and Blair and Blair, *Search for JFK*, 230.
391 West, *Wooden Boats*, 154, and "Sinking of PT 109 and Subsequent Rescue," 1.
392 Stephen Plotkin. "Sixty Years Later, the Story of PT-109 Still Captivates." http://www.archives.gov/publications/prologue/2003/summer/pt109.html. (July 1, 2009), 2.
393 Hara, Saito and Pineau. *Destroyer Captain*, 181.
394 "PT Operations August 1–2," 4.
395 Hove, *American Warriors*, 56.
396 Dick Keresey. "Farthest Forward." http://www.americanheritage.com/articles. (October 3, 2009), 7.
397 Hove, *American Warriors*, 58.
398 Ballard and Morgan, *Collision with History*, 84–85, and Donovan, *PT-109*, 126.
399 Blair and Blair, *Search for JFK*, 241.
400 Hamilton, *Reckless Youth*, 558, and Blair and Blair, *Search for JFK*, 233.
401 "PT Operations August 1–2," 4.
402 West, *Wooden Boats*, 157–58.

CHAPTER 16
403 Blair and Blair, *Search for JFK*, 241.
404 Hersey, 32.
405 Donovan, *PT-109*, 153.
406 Associated Press, "Kennedy's Son," 5.
407 Richard Tregaskis. *John F. Kennedy and PT-109*. (New York: Random House, 1962), 114.
408 Ibid, 115.
409 Associated Press, "Kennedy's Son," 5.
410 Ballard and Morgan, *Collision with History*, 83.
411 Hove, *American Warriors*, 62.
412 Arvad, 6.
413 Blair and Blair, *Search for JFK*, 249.
414 CO Motor Torpedo Boats, Rendova to CinC US Fleet. "PT Operations Night 2–3 August 1943." August 4, 1943, 1.
415 O'Brien, *John F. Kennedy*, 153–54.
416 Keresey, *PT 105*, 92–93.
417 "Interview with Richard E. Keresey." Denton, TX: Admiral Nimitz Museum and

University of North Texas Oral History Collection, 1997, 66.

418 Theodore M. Robinson. *Water in My Veins: The Pauper Who Helped Save a President.* (Bennington, VT: Merriam Press, 2008), 237.

419 Walter Lord. *Lonely Vigil: Coastwatchers of the Solomons.* (New York: Viking Press, 1977), 222–23.

420 Plotkin, 3.

421 Arvad, 6.

422 Edward Oxford. "Ten Lives for Kennedy." *Argosy*, July 1960, 81.

423 CO Motor Torpedo Boats, Rendova to CinC US Fleet. "PT Operations Night 4–5 August 1943." August 8, 1943, 1.

424 "Sinking of PT 109 and Subsequent Rescue," 2.

425 Ballard and Morgan, *Collision with History*, 101.

426 Donovan, *PT-109*, 188–89.

427 Chamberlain, Ted. "JFK's Island Rescuers Honored at Emotional Reunion." http://news.nationalgeographic.com/news (June 4, 2010), 2.

428 Bengt Danielson and Marie-Therese Danielson. "New Light on JFK and PT 109." *Pacific Islands Monthly*, January 1986, 26.

429 "The President's Desk," in "JFK Library."

430 "Kennedy Learns Name of Aussie Who Saved Him." *Chicago Tribune*, February 26, 1961, 2.

431 Lord, *Lonely Vigil*, 228.

432 Hove, *American Warriors*, 62.

433 CO Motor Torpedo Boats, Rendova to CinCPac. "PT Operations Night 7–8 August 1943." August 5, 1943, 1.

434 Donovan, *PT-109*, 211.

435 William Liebenow. "The Incident: August 1–2, 1943," in PT Boats, Inc. *Knights of the Sea*. (Dallas, TX: Taylor Publishing Co., 1982), 102.

436 Hamilton, *Reckless Youth*, 601.

437 "September 12, 1943 Letter."

CHAPTER 17

438 "Report on the Fitness of Officers," Period Ending November 22, 1943 in "Westholm Service Record."

439 Buckley, *Close Quarters*, 116–17.

440 "Report on the Fitness of Officers," Period Ending February 29, 1944 in "Westholm Service Record."

441 "Bush" in Dictionary of American Fighting Ships, http://www.history.navy.mil. (Accessed on various dates) (hereafter cited as "Bush").

442 "Excerpts from deck Logs," in U.S.S. Bush (DD 529) Website. http://www.ussbush.com. (Accessed on February 2, 2012)

443 Dave McComb. *U.S. Destroyers 1942–45.* (Oxford, UK: Osprey Publishing, 2010), 8.

444 "Bush."

445 "Legion of Merit Citation" in "Westholm Service Record."

446 Robert Gandt. *The Twilight Warriors*. (New York: Broadway Books, 2010), 145 & 212.

447 CO U.S.S. *Bush* to CinC US Fleet. "Action Report – Okinawa Operation, 15 March to 6 April 1945." April 24, 1945, 4.

448 Samuel Eliot Morison. *History of United States Naval Operations in World War II Volume XIV: Victory in the Pacific*. (Edison, NJ: Castle Book, 2001), 188–90.

449 "Navy Cross Citation," in "Westholm Service Record."

450 "Report on the Fitness of Officers," Period Ending August 31, 1945 in "Westholm Service Record."

451 CO South Pacific to Lieutenant (jg) Bryant Leroy Larson. "Change of Duty." June 25 1943 in "Larson Service Record."

452 "Acknowledgement of Notice of Temporary Appointment" dated May 7, 1943 in "Larson Service Record."

453 Larson, "PT Duty."

454 Massaro.

455 "Telegram Dated June 1943" in "Larson Service Record."

456 "Report on the Fitness of Officers," Period Ending July 4, 1943 in "Larson Service Record."

457 Buckley, *Close Quarters*, 478.

458 "Statement of Temporary Assignment" dated July 1, 1944 in "Larson Service Record."

459 Buckley, *Close Quarters*, 420.

460 Samuel Eliot Morison. *History of United States Naval Operations in World War II Volume XIII: The Liberation of the Philippines*. (Edison, NJ: Castle Book, 2001), 259–60.

461 Buckley, *Close Quarters*, 432.

462 "Report on the Fitness of Officers," Period Ending August 15, 1945 in "Larson Service Record."

463 Morison, *Victory in the Pacific*, 359.

CHAPTER 18

464 Tregaskis, *PT–109*, 151.

465 "Letter to Parents dated October 30, 1943, John F. Kennedy Personal Papers" in "JFK Library" (hereafter cited at "October 30, 1943 Letter").

466 Ibid.

467 "September 12, 1943 Letter."

468 Blair and Blair, *Search for JFK*, 288.

469 "Lieutenant John Fitzgerald Kennedy."

470 "Letter to Parents dated November 1, 1943, John F. Kennedy Personal Papers" in "JFK Library."

471 "October 30, 1943 Letter."

472 Buckley, *Close Quarters*, 135.

473 Donovan, *PT-109*, 219.

474 Tregaskis, *PT-109*, 160–61.

475 Bradsher, Greg. "Operation Blissful: How the Marines Lured the Japanese Away from a Key Target—and How 'the Brute' Got Some Help from JFK." http://www.

archives.gov/publications/prologue/2010/fall (December 20, 2011), 2.

476 Morison, *Bismarcks Barrier*, 296.

477 Bradsher, 2.

478 Donovan, *PT-109*, 226.

479 O'Brien, *John F. Kennedy*, 164.

480 Keresey, *PT-105*, 153.

481 Bradsher, 7.

482 Hove, *American Warriors*, 93.

483 Keresey, *PT-105*, 153.

484 Hove, *American Warriors*, 94.

485 Hamilton, *Reckless Youth*, 622.

486 Blair and Blair, *Search for JFK*, 302.

487 O'Brien, *John F. Kennedy*, 165.

488 Hamilton, *Reckless Youth*, 631.

489 CO MTB Two to Lieutenant John Fitzgerald Kennedy. "Orders." December 21, 1943 in "JFK Library."

490 Hamilton, *Reckless Youth*, 631.

491 Blair and Blair, *Search for JFK*, 273.

492 "Lieutenant John Fitzgerald Kennedy."

493 Secretary of the Navy to Lieutenant John Fitzgerald Kennedy. "Action of Retiring Board." March 16, 1945 in "JFK Library."

CHAPTER 19

494 Leif Erickson. "11 on Rammed PT Boat Saved from Jap Isle." *Chicago Tribune*, August 18, 1943, and Associated Press, "Kennedy's Son," 1.

495 Hamilton, *Reckless Youth*, 644–45 and 652–53.

496 "Report on the Fitness of Officers," Period Ending June 30, 1964 in "Westholm Service Record."

497 "Report of Transfer or Discharge," in "Westholm Service Record."

498 "Westholm Obituary."

499 Larson, "PT Duty."

500 "Notice of Separation from the U.S. Naval Service," in "Larson Service Record."

501 "Honorable Discharge from the U.S. Naval Reserve," in "Larson Service Record."

502 Massaro.

503 "Life of John F. Kennedy," 2.

504 Thomas C. Reeves. *A Question of Character: A Life of John F. Kennedy*. (New York: The Free Press, 1991), 73.

505 "National Affairs: Promise Kept." http://www.time.com/time/magazine/article/0,9171,803735,00.html#ixzz2TK17ZoQH (May 14, 2013), 1.

506 O'Brien, *John F. Kennedy*, 201–205.

507 Will Haygood. "Of Love and War." *Boston Globe*, June 23, 1989, 40.

508 Russell Baker. "Capitol Paraders Don Overcoats to Pass in White House Review."

New York Times, January 21, 1961, 9.

509 Paul B. Fay, Jr. *The Pleasure of His Company.* (New York: Harper & Row, 1966), 214.

510 Anthony Ramirez. "Robert J. Donovan, 90, Author of PT-109." *New York Times,* August 10, 2003, N24.

511 Robert J. Donovan. *Boxing the Kangaroo: A Reporter's Memoir.* (Columbia, MO: University of Missouri Press, 2000), 105.

512 Ted Widmer, ed. *Listening In: The Secret White House Recordings of John F. Kennedy.* (New York: Hyperion, 2012), 280.

513 "Westholm letter."

514 Bryant Larson. "Bryant L. Larson—Ron 2, 5, 36." Manuscript Courtesy of WW II PT Boats Museum and Archives, Germantown Tennessee, 1.

515 Edward J. Reneham, Jr. *The Kennedy's at War 1937–45.* (New York: Doubleday, 2002), 2.

516 "John F. Kennedy and PT-109" in "JFK Library."

517 Reneham, *The Kennedy's at War,* 1.

518 Buckley, *Close Quarters,* viii.

519 Ted Chamberlain. "JFK's PT-109 Found, U.S. Navy Confirms." http://news.nationalgeographic.com/news (June 4, 2010), 2.

520 Ken Harder. "Has Ballard Found JFK's PT-109?" http://news.nationalgeographic.com/news (June 4, 2010), 1.

521 Ballard and Morgan, *Collision with History,* 180.

522 William Broad. "Sea Explorer Uncovers Kennedy's PT 109." *New York Times,* July 11, 2002, A18.

523 Ballard and Morgan, *Collision with History,* 181 & 186.

524 Michael Kilian. "Navy Says Wreck Must Be PT-109." *Chicago Tribune,* July 11, 2002, 18.

EPILOGUE

525 Samuel Eliot Morison. *History of United States Naval Operations in World War II, Volume XII: Leyte.* (Edison, NJ: Castle Books, 2001), 211.

526 Anthony Tully. *Battle of Surigao Strait.* (Bloomington, IN: Indiana University Press, 2009), 166–67.

527 Buckley, *Close Quarters,* 442.

528 Rottman, *Patrol Torpedo Boats,* 44.

529 Buckley, *Close Quarters,* 352.

530 Ibid, 445.

531 Johnson, *PT Boats,* 154.

532 Rottman, *Patrol Torpedo Boats,* 8.

533 Buckley, *Close Quarters,* 510–13.

534 Ibid, 491–92.

535 Ibid, Preface.

536 Ibid, 348.

537 George, *History of Warships,* 252–54.

538 Comerford, Tim. "Operation Praying Mantis Demonstrates Same Priorities Navy Values Today."http://www.navy.mil/submit/display.asp?story_id=73436 (May 3, 2013), 1.

539 Burke, Rhonda. "USS Freedom Commissioned in Milwaukee." http://www.navy.mil/submit/display.asp?story_id=40822 (May 8, 2013), 1.

540 "Littoral Combat Ship Class—LCS." http://www.navy.mil/navydata/fact_display.asp?cid=4200&tid=1650&ct=4 (May 8, 2013), 1.

541 "USS Freedom to Conduct Maiden Deployment to the Asia-Pacific." http://www.public.navy.mil/surfor/lcs1/Pages/USSFreedomtoConductMaidenDeploymenttotheAsia-Pacific.aspx#.UYP_oMco6AU (May 3, 2013)

MAP NOTES

Movements on all maps are approximate. Maps are not
drawn to scale and are adapted from the following sources:

MAP 1 — *Combat Narrative X: Operations in the New Georgia Area.* Washington, DC: Office of Naval Intelligence, United States Navy, 1944.

MAP 2 — *Combat Narrative: The landing in the Solomons.* Washington, DC: Office of Naval Intelligence, United States Navy, 1943.

MAP 3 — Bureau of Yards and Docks. *Building the Navy's Bases in the Pacific (Volume II).* Washington, DC: Government Printing Office, 1947.

MAP 4 — *Combat Narrative: Miscellaneous Actions in the South Pacific.* Washington, DC: Office of Naval Intelligence, United States Navy, 1943.

MAP 5 — Ibid

MAP 6 — *Combat Narrative: Miscellaneous Actions in the South Pacific.* Washington, DC: Office of Naval Intelligence, United States Navy, 1943, and CO Motor Torpedo Boat Flotilla One to CinCPac. "Report of Motor Torpedo Boat Actions on the Night of 1–2 February, 1943." February 2, 1943.

MAP 7 — *Combat Narrative XI: Kolombangara and Vella Lavella.* Washington, DC: Office of Naval Intelligence, United States Navy, 1944.

MAP 8 — Ibid

MAP 9 — Ibid

MAP 10 — Author's map.

MAP 11 — Ibid

BIBLIOGRAPHY

BOOKS

Ballard, Robert and Michael Hamilton Morgan. *Collision with History: The Search for John F. Kennedy's PT-109*. Washington, DC: National Geographic, 2002.

Batchelor, John, Louis S. Casey, and Anthony Preston. *Sea Power: A Modern Illustrated Military History*. New York: Exeter Books, 1979.

Blair, Joan and Clay Blair, Jr. *The Search for JFK*. New York: Berkley Publishing Corporation, 1976.

Brantingham, Hank. *Fire and Ice*. San Diego, CA: ProMotion Publishing, 1995.

Breuer, William. *Devil Boats: The PT War against Japan*. New York: Jove Books, 1988.

Breuer, William. *Sea Wolf: The Daring Exploits of Navy Legend John D. Bulkeley*. Novato, CA: Presidio Press, 1998.

Buckley, Captain Robert J. *At Close Quarters: PT Boats in the United States Navy*. Washington, DC: United States Government Printing Office, 1962.

Campbell, John. *Naval Weapons of World War II*. : Naval Institute Press, 1985.

Cave, Hugh B. *Long Were the Nights*. New York: Dodd, Mead and Company, 1943.

Chesneau, Roger, ed. *Conway's All the World's Fighting Ships: 1922–1946*. London: Conway Maritime Press, 1980.

Chun, Victor. *American PT Boats in World War II*. Atglen, PA: Schiffer Publishing, 1997.

Costello, John. *The Pacific War*. Rawson, Wade Publishers, Inc., 1981.

Cowburn, Philip. *The Warship in History*. New York: Macmillan, 1965.

Dallek, Robert. *An Unfinished Life: John F. Kennedy 1917–1963*. New York: Little, Brown and Company, 2003.

Donovan, Robert J. *Boxing the Kangaroo: A Reporter's Memoir*. Columbia, MO: University of Missouri Press, 2000.

Donovan, Robert J. *PT 109*. New York: McGraw-Hill Book Company, 1961.

Doyle, David. *Elco 80-Foot PT Boat On Deck*. Carrollton, TX: Squadron Signal Publications, 2009.

Doyle, David. *PT Boats in Action*. Carrollton, TX: Squadron Signal Publications, 2010.

Dull, Paul S. *A Battle History of the Imperial Japanese Navy*. Annapolis, MD: Naval Institute Press, 1978.

Ealy, Lawrence O. *I Joined the Navy and Saw World War II*. New York: Vantage Press, 1998.

Farley, Edward J. *PT Patrol*. New York: Exposition Press, 1957.

Fay, Paul B., Jr. *The Pleasure of His Company*. New York: Harper & Row, 1966.

Fitch, John W. *Desert Sailor*. Haverford, PA: Infinity Publishing, 2001.

Frank, Richard B. *Guadalcanal*. New York: Penguin Books, 1990.

Friedman, Norman. *U.S. Small Combatants, Including PT-Boats, Subchasers, and the Brown-Water Navy: An Illustrated Design History*. Annapolis, MD: Naval Institute Press, 1987.

Gailey, Harry A. *The War in the Pacific: From Pearl Harbor to Tokyo Bay*. Novato, CA: Presidio Press, 1995.

Gandt, Robert. *The Twilight Warriors*. New York: Broadway Books, 2010.

George, James L. *History of Warships: From Ancient Times to the Twenty-First Century*. Annapolis, MD: Naval Institute Press, 1998.

Hamilton, Nigel. *JFK: Reckless Youth*. New York: Random House, 1992.

Hara, Tameichi, with Fred Saito and Roger Pineau. *Japanese Destroyer Captain*. New York: Ballantine Books, 1961.

Hersey, John. *Men on Bataan*. New York: Alfred A. Knopf, 1942.

Hove, Duane T. *American Warriors: Five Presidents in the Pacific Theater of World War II*. Shippensburg, PA: Burd Street Press, 2003.

Hoyt, Edwin P. *Deadly Craft: Fireships to PT Boats*. Boston: Little, Brown and Company, 1968.

Japanese Self Defense Force: War History Office. *Senshi Sosho (War History Series). Volume 83: Southeast Area Naval Operations, Part II*. Asagumo Shibunsha, 1975.

Johnson, Frank D. *United States PT-Boats of World War II in Action*. Poole, England: Blandford Press, 1980.

Keating, Bern. *The Mosquito Fleet*. New York: Scholastic Book Service, 1966.

Keresey, Dick. *PT 105*. Annapolis, MD: Naval Institute Press, 1996.

Levy, David M. and Gerald A. Meehl. *Fast Boats and Fast Times: Memories of a PT Boat Skipper in the South Pacific*. Bloomington, IN: Author House, 2008.

Lord, Walter. *Lonely Vigil: Coastwatchers of the Solomons*. : Viking Press, 1977.

McComb, Dave. *U.S. Destroyers 1942–45*. Oxford, UK: Osprey Publishing, 2010.

Miller, Jr., John. *Cartwheel: The Reduction of Rabaul*. Washington, DC: Center of Military History Study, the United States Army, 1990.

Miller, Jr., John. *Guadalcanal: The First Offensive*. Washington, DC: Center of Military History Study, the United States Army, 1989.

Morison, Samuel Eliot. *History of United States Naval Operations in World War II Volume III: The Rising Sun in the Pacific*. Edison, NJ: Castle Books, 2001.

Morison, Samuel Eliot. *History of United States Naval Operations in World War II Volume V: The Struggle for Guadalcanal*. Edison, NJ: Castle Books, 2001.

Morison, Samuel Eliot. *History of United States Naval Operations in World War II Volume VI: Breaking the Bismarcks Barrier*. Edison, NJ: Castle Books, 2001.

Morison, Samuel Eliot. *History of United States Naval Operations in World War II Volume XII: Leyte*. Edison, NJ: Castle Books, 2001.

Morison, Samuel Eliot. *History of United States Naval Operations in World War II Volume XIII: The Liberation of the Philippines*. Edison, NJ: Castle Books, 2001.

Morison, Samuel Eliot. *History of United States Naval Operations in World War II Volume XIV: Victory in the Pacific*. Edison, NJ: Castle Books, 2001.

O'Brien, Michael. *John F. Kennedy: A Biography*. New York: Thomas Dunne Books / St. Martin's Press, 2005.

Perret, Geoffrey. *Jack: A Life Like No Other*. New York: Random House, 2001.

PT Boats, Inc. *Knights of the Sea*. Dallas, TX: Taylor Publishing Co., 1982.

Reneham, Jr. Edward J. *The Kennedy's at War 1937–45*. New York: Doubleday, 2002.

Reeves, Thomas C. *A Question of Character: A Life of John F. Kennedy*. New York: The Free Press, 1991.

Robinson, Theodore M. *Water in My Veins: The Pauper Who Helped Save a President*. Bennington, VT: Merriam Press, 2008.

Rottman, Gary. *US Patrol Torpedo Boats*. Oxford, UK: Osprey, 2008.

Searles, John M. *Tales of Tulagi*. New York: Vantage Press, 1992.

Spector, Ronald H. *Eagle Against the Sun: The American War with Japan*. New York: Vintage Books, 1985.

Tregaskis, Richard. *John F. Kennedy and PT-109*. New York: Random House, 1962.

Tully, Anthony. *Battle of Surigao Strait*. Bloomington, IN: Indiana University Press, 2009.

Van Der Vat, Dan. *The Pacific Campaign*. New York: Simon & Schuster, 1991.

Watts, Anthony J. and Brian G. Gordon. *The Imperial Japanese Navy*. New York: Doubleday & Company, Inc. 1971.

West, Howard F. *Iron Men Wooden Boats*. Westminster, MD: Heritage Books, 2005.

Widmer, Ted. ed. *Listening In: The Secret White House Recordings of John F. Kennedy*. New York: Hyperion, 2012.

Whipple, Chandler. *Code Word Ferdinand: Adventures of the Coast Watchers*. New York: George Putnam and Son's. 1971.

Whipple, Chandler. *Lt. John F. Kennedy—Expendable.* New York: Universal Publishing. 1964.

ACTION REPORTS AND OFFICIAL DOCUMENTS

"Bryant Larson Service Record." National Personnel Records Center, St. Louis, MO.

Bureau of Yards and Docks. *Building the Navy's Bases in the Pacific (Volume II).* Washington, DC: Government Printing Office, 1947.

CO *LST-449* to CinCPac. "Attacked by Enemy Aircraft, Report of." April 14, 1943.

CO Motor Torpedo Boat Flotilla & Base, Ringbolt to CinCPac. "Report of Motor Torpedo Boat Activities on the Night of 10–11 January, 1943, Local Date." January 13, 1943.

CO Motor Torpedo Boat Flotilla One to CinCPac. "Report of Motor Torpedo Boat Actions on the Night of 1–2 February, 1943." February 2, 1943.

CO Motor Torpedo Boat Flotilla One to CinCPac. "Report of Motor Torpedo Boat Combat Action in the Solomon Islands, 13 October, 1942 to 2 February, 1943." March 7, 1943.

CO Motor Torpedo Boats, Rendova to CinCPac. "PT Operations Night 7–8 August 1943." August 8, 1943.

CO Motor Torpedo Boats, Rendova to CinC US Fleet. "PT Operations Night 1–2 August 1943." August 5, 1943.

CO Motor Torpedo Boats, Rendova to CinC US Fleet. "PT Operations Night 2–3 August 1943." August 5, 1943.

CO Motor Torpedo Boats, Rendova to CinC US Fleet. "PT Operations Night 4–5 August 1943." August 5, 1943.

CO Motor Torpedo Boats, Rendova to CinC US Fleet. "PT Operations Night 17–18 July 1943." July 18, 1943.

CO Motor Torpedo Boats, Rendova to CinC US Fleet. "PT Operations Night 26–27 July 1943." July 27, 1943.

CO Motor Torpedo Boats, Rendova to CinC US Fleet. "PT Operations Night 27–28 July 1943." July 30, 1943.

CO Motor Torpedo Boats, Rendova to CinC US Fleet. "PT Operations Night 28–29 July 1943." July 29, 1943.

CO Motor Torpedo Boats, Rendova to CinC US Fleet. "PT Operations Night 29–30 July 1943." July 30, 1943.

CO Motor Torpedo Boats, Rendova to CinC US Fleet. "PT Operations Night 30–31 July 1943." July 31, 1943.

CO Motor Torpedo Boat Squadrons, South Pacific Force to CinCPac. "Loss of PT 109—Information Concerning." January 13, 1944.

CO Motor Torpedo Boat Squadron Three to CinC US Fleet. "Summary of Operations Motor Torpedo Boat Squadron Three from 7 December 1941 to 10 April 1942." May 21, 1942.

CO Motor Torpedo Boat Squadron Two to Commanding General, Cactus. "Memorandum for Commanding General, Cactus: PT Operation, Night of 7–8 December 1942." December 9, 1942.

CO U.S.S. *Bush* to CinC US Fleet. "Action Report—Okinawa Operation, 15 March to 6 April 1945." April 24, 1945.

Combat Narrative: Miscellaneous Actions in the South Pacific. Washington, DC: Office of Naval Intelligence, United States Navy, 1943.

Combat Narrative VII: Japanese Evacuation of Guadalcanal. Washington, DC: Office of Naval Intelligence, United States Navy, 1944.

Deck Logs: *Pensacola, PT-109, PT-157, PT-162 & PT-169.*

Headquarters of the Commander in Chief, United States Fleet. "Motor Torpedo Boats: Tactical Orders and Doctrine. Washington, DC: United States Government Printing Office, 1942. Retrieved from: http://www.hnsa.org/doc/pt/doctrine/index.htm (July 20, 2010)

Intelligence Officers to CO Motor Torpedo Boat Flotilla One. "Sinking of PT 109 and Subsequent Rescue of Survivors." August 22, 1943.

Joint Army-Navy Assessment Committee. *Japanese Naval and Merchant Shipping Losses during World War II by All Causes.* Washington, DC: U.S. Government Printing Office, 1947

"Rollin Westholm Service Record." National Personnel Records Center, St. Louis, MO.

Secretary of the Navy. *Register of the Commissioned and Warrant Officers of the Navy of the United States, Including Officers of the Marine Corps.* Washington, DC: Government Printing Office, 1943.

Staff Intelligence Office, CO Motor Torpedo Boat Squadrons South Pacific Force. "Out of the Night: South Pacific MTB's vs. Jap Float Planes." February 20, 1944.

ARTICLES

Albers, Andrea. "World War II Midshipmen's School a Piece of Northwestern History." http://www.northwestern.edu/newscenter/stories/2009/02/midshipmen.html (May 17, 2001)

Alcorn, William. "Of Friendship and War." http://www.vindy.com/news/2008/may/25/of-friendship-and-war/ (September 26, 2011)

Arvad, Inga. "Kennedy Lauds Men, Disdains Hero Stuff." *Boston Globe,* January 11, 1944.

Associated Press. "Kennedy's Son is Hero in Pacific as Destroyer Splits His PT Boat." *New York Times*, August 20, 1943.

Baker, Russell. "Capitol Paraders Don Overcoats to Pass in White House Review." *New York Times*, January 21, 1961.

Baker, Russell. "Kennedy, After 17 years, Solves Mystery of His Pacific Rescuer." *New York Times*, February 26, 1961.

Bell, Michael. "The Story of Leonard Jay Thom." http://www.petertare.org/nav.htm (July 1, 2010)

Bradsher, Greg. "Operation Blissful: How the Marines Lured the Japanese Away from a Key Target—and How 'The Brute' Got Some Help from JFK." www.archives.gov/publications/prologue/2010/fall (December 20, 2011)

Broad, William. "Sea Explorer Uncovers Kennedy's PT 109." *New York Times*, July 11, 2002.

Burke, Rhonda. "USS Freedom Commissioned in Milwaukee." http://www.navy.mil/submit/display.asp?story_id=40822 (May 8, 2013)

Chamberlain, Ted. "JFK's Island Rescuers Honored at Emotional Reunion." http://news.nationalgeographic.com/news (June 4, 2010)

Chamberlain, Ted. "JFK's PT-109 Found, U.S. Navy Confirms." http://news.nationalgeographic.com/news (June 4, 2010)

Comerford, Tim. "Operation Praying Mantis Demonstrates Same Priorities Navy Values Today." http://www.navy.mil/submit/display.asp?story_id=73436 (May 3, 2013)

Danielson, Bengt and Marie-Therese Danielson. "New Light on JFK and PT 109." *Pacific Islands Monthly*, January 1986.

Erickson, Leif. "11 on Rammed PT Boat Saved from Jap Isle." *Chicago Tribune*, August 18, 1943.

Harder, Ken. "Has Ballard Found JFK's Pt-109?" http://news.nationalgeographic.com/news (June 4, 2010)

Haygood, Will. "Of Love and War." *Boston Globe*, June 23, 1989.

"Hero to Pick 50 with Guts for Mosquito Fleet." *Chicago Tribune*, September 3, 1942.

Hersey, John. "Survival." *New Yorker*, June 17, 1944.

Hove, Duane. "PT 109—The Early Days." *All Hands*, November 2002.

"Jefferson's Gunboat Navy, 1805–1812" in the Mariners' Museum website. http://www.marinersmuseum.org/sites/micro/usnavy/07.htm (April 17, 2013)

"Kennedy Erred on Island's Name." *New York Times*, June 4, 1961.

"Kennedy Learns Name of Aussie Who Saved Him." *Chicago Tribune*, February 26, 1961.

Keresey, Dick. "Farthest Forward." http://www.americanheritage.com/articles. (October 3, 2009)

Kilian, Michael. "Navy Says Wreck Must be PT-109." *Chicago Tribune*, July 11, 2002.

Kimmatsu, Haruyoshi and Joachim Heinrich Woos. "The Night We Rammed J.F.K." *Argosy*, December 1970.

Massaro, Gary. "PT 109 Commander Before Kennedy Dies." *Rocky Mountain News*, January 12, 2002.

"Mosquito Boat Skipper to be Pine for Action." *Chicago Tribune*, September 4, 1942.

"Mosquito Boats Speed 50 Knots in East River Demonstration." *New York Times*, November 8, 1940.

Munroe, Patrick. "Luck of the Toss." *American Heritage* Oct. 1992: 32+. General Reference Center Gold. Web. http://find.galegroup.com (July 13, 2010)

"National Affairs: Promise Kept." http://www.time.com/time/magazine/article/0,9171,803735,00.html#ixzz2TK17ZoQH (May 14, 2013)

Nelson, Curtis L. "Did JFK's Oder Sink PT 109?" *Naval History*, February 2003.

"New Yorker Leads Daring Raid on Foe." *New York Times*, January 21, 1942.

Oxford, Edward. "Ten Lives for Kennedy." *Argosy*, July 1960.

"Patrick H. McMahon Dead at 84; Burned Sailor Saved by Kennedy." *New York Times*, February 22, 1990.

Pedroncelli, Rich. "JFK: A PT Skipper Remembers." *Naval History*, December 1999.

Plotkin, Stephen. "Sixty Years Later, the Story of PT-109 Still Captivates." http://www.archives.gov/publications/prologue/2003/summer/pt109.html. (July 1, 2009)

Ramirez, Anthony. "Robert J. Donovan, 90, Author of PT-109." *New York Times*, August 10, 2003.

Tanaka, Vice Admiral Razio with Roger Pineau. "Japan's Losing Struggle for Guadalcanal: Part II." *Proceedings*, August 1956.

"USS Freedom to Conduct Maiden Deployment to the Asia-Pacific." http://www.public.navy.mil/surfor/lcs1/Pages/USSFreedomtoConductMaidenDeploymenttotheAsia-Pacific.aspx#.UYP_oMco6AU (May 3, 2013)

OTHER

Imperial Japanese Navy Page. http://www.combinedfleet.com/bb.htm. (Accessed on various dates)

"Interview with Hugh M. Robinson." Denton, TX: Admiral Nimitz Museum and University of North Texas Oral History Collection, 1997.

"Interview with Richard E. Kersey." Denton, TX: Admiral Nimitz Museum and University of North Texas Oral History Collection, 1997.

John F. Kennedy Presidential Library Website. http://www.jfklibrary.org. (Accessed on various dates)

"Know Your PT Boat." http://www.hnsa.org (June 15, 2010)

Larson, Bryant. "Bryant L. Larson—Ron 2, 5, 36." Manuscript Courtesy of WW II PT Boats Museum and Archives, Germantown Tennessee, USA.

Larson, Bryant. "Memories of My Torpedo Boat (PT) Duty." Undated Manuscript. Courtesy of Karen Hone.

"Littoral Combat Ship Class – LCS." http://www.navy.mil/navydata/fact_display.asp?cid=4200&tid=1650&ct=4 (May 8, 2013)

Miscellaneous Documents. Courtesy of Karen Hone.

"Navy Department Communiqués and Pertinent Press Releases, December 10, 1941 to May 24, 1945." http://www.ibiblio.org/pha/comms/index.html (April 24, 2013)

Naval History and Heritage Command Website. http://www.history.navy.mil. (Accessed on various dates.)

"PT-109 Final Crew List." http://www.maritimequest.com. (March 29, 2010)

PT-109 Obituaries. http://infoweb.newsbank.com. (November 5, 2010)

PT King Website. http://pt-king.gdinc.com/index.html. (Accessed on various dates.)

Rollin E. Westholm Obituary. Courtesy of Carlton County, MN Historical Society.

U.S.S. Bush (DD 529) Website. http://www.ussbush.com. (Accessed on February 2, 2012)

Westholm, Rollin. Letter Dated February 1989. Courtesy of Gary Westholm.

INDEX